Macromedia® Flash
Super Samurai

Eric E. Dolecki

Michael Grundvig

Klaus L. Hougesen

Allan Kennedy

Jobe Makar

Til Mauder

Torben Nielsen

Max Oshman

Robert(son) Ramirez

Oliver Shaw

Geoff Stearns

Michael Brandon Williams

macromedia®
PRESS

MW00681520

Macromedia Flash: Super Samurai

Eric E. Dolecki, Michael Grundvig, Klaus L. Hougesen, Allan Kennedy, Jobe Makar, Til Mauder, Torben Nielsen, Max Oshman, Robert(son) Ramirez, Oliver Shaw, Geoff Stearns, and Michael Brandon Williams

Peachpit Press
1249 Eighth Street
Berkeley, CA 94710
510/524-2178
510/524-2221 (fax)

Find us on the World Wide Web at: **www.peachpit.com**

To report errors, please send a note to errata@peachpit.com

Peachpit Press is a division of Addison Wesley Longman.

Project Editor: Rebecca Gulick
Editor: Missy Roback
Additional Editing: Kari Brooks and Wendy Katz
Production Coordinator: Connie Jeung-Mills
Technical Editors: Erika Burback, of Macromedia Inc.; the Super Samurai book team
Compositors: Rick Gordon, Debbie Roberti, David Van Ness, and Melanie Haage
Indexer: Karin Arrigoni
Cover Design: Mimi Heft, with Eric E. Dolecki
Interior Design: Mimi Heft

ISBN 0-201-77144-6

9 8 7 6 5 4 3 2 1

Printed and bound in the United States of America

Words of Thanks

Eric E. Dolecki (Component System Architecture): I would like to thank Eugene and Suzanne Dolecki for being the best parents ever; the Taylors (a big shout out to Summer); the entire Duda clan (you all rock!); my love, Deanna Charpentier; Bob and Eileen; and the entire Carew and Charpentier families. I would also like to thank Macromedia, Branden Hall and all the Flashcoders, Andries Odendaal of Wireframe, and Eric Jordan of 2Advanced for serving as great inspiration. Finally, I would like to thank the entire book team, everyone at Peachpit and Bumblebee, The Men of Rohan, pre-MS Bungie, and Steve Wozniak.

Allan Kennedy (Programming Sound in Flash): I would like to thank Jason Krogh (aka zincroe) for his support while I was writing the chapter. He has also greatly influenced my approach to Flash programming and drinking dark German beers. Thanks to Nancy and Anne Sophie for tolerating me during my extended spaced-out periods after gluing myself to a computer for days on end. I also have to thank Branden Hall, Helen Triolo, and Dave Yang for making me think about the Sound object with a more OOP perspective.

Michael Grundvig (XML and Flash): This chapter is the work of many people, and while I can't thank them all, I hope to try! My most humble and appreciative thanks goes to my wife Jamie. Without her understanding and support, I would never have finished the first page. Wendy Katz, my editor, for taking my chapter and turning it into something that I can be proud of. Rebecca Gulick and Peachpit for giving me an opportunity that I never thought I would have. Jobe and Robert, my business partners, for putting up with me while I neglected them. Lastly, I thank my parents. No matter how hair-brained the idea, they have stuck with me to the very end.

Klaus L. Hougesen (JavaScript-Flash Interactions): Thanks go out to my entire family for being just that and giving support and understanding when it mattered. Special thanks go to the insane posse that constitutes my friends for unrelenting support and the occasional burst of pure insanity that makes life that much more interesting. I would also like to thank Kojle for always being there, my brother for being a kindred spirit, and last but certainly not least Peachpit and everyone associated for believing.

Jobe Makar (Flash Physics): Thank you Kelly for turning the music down; without your support I'd have no direction. (If you say "I do," we'll be married by the time you read this!) Missy Roback, your ability to spin straw into gold is truly amazing; thank you for your editorial work. I would also like to thank Rebecca Gulick and everyone else at Peachpit who helped create this book! The support and suggestions from the entire Samurai team are much appreciated—thanks guys! Thank you Allen Interactions for giving me room to grow as a Flash programmer. I'd also like to thank Rhett for helping me solve a conceptual problem. Thanks to my family for encouragement during my learning of physics and my early career. And of course I cannot forget my biggest supporter, my dog Free—thank you for being the best of friends and a good footrest.

Max Oshman (Creating Dynamic Flash Pages): I would like to thank my parents, Anne and Ted, for being the best parents in the world. I would also like to thank my brother Charlie, sister Sophie, and the rest of the Oshman crew for all of your support. Special thanks to Dennis Baldwin of Flashcfm.com for all of your invaluable help. Thank you to everyone at Xypno Interactive (www.xypno.com), especially Eddie Park and Angel Espirutu. Thanks to all the special people in my life: Alexandra, Doades, Danny, and Twersk for your ongoing friendship. Finally, I would like to thank the other members of the book team. It has been a long and tedious journey, but the outcome was sensational—thanks to you all.

Oliver Shaw (Flash Interface Design): First off, I'd like to thank Til (who's time difference meant one of us was always working on the chapter); Robert(son) for getting us organized; and all the super samurai, especially Eric for having enough motivation and energy for all of us. I want to thank Peachpit for everything, from start to finish; it has been a good experience, and we have one of the best books around. Props go to Branden Hall and the Flashcoders people, without whom the samurai team might never have met. Thanks to Nigel "theBiscuit" Aono-Billson for collaborating on the chewy interface, and to Andy R. for letting me test the interfaces on him throughout the development of the chapter. This has been one of the most unusual experiences of my life, and one of the best.

Geoff Stearns (Breathing Life into Flash): I would like to thank Robert(son) for pushing this project until the end, Missy Roback for her great editing, and all the people at Peachpit who made this book possible. I would also like to thank Branden Hall (and the whole Flashcoders list), Neuralust and #dreamless, and my parents for always telling me I can do and be whatever I want. And thanks to Nathan Hendler for my picture.

Til Mauder (Flash Interface Design): Kat deserves my deepest gratitude for being in this world and being herself (purr!). Thanks to Randy for being a great friend and always inspiring me during our discussions of half-baked ideas like writing a chapter for a technical book. Professionally, I would not be here without the passion and keen tutoring of Octavian Dibrov, who taught me Lingo and Photoshop at Art Center in La-Tour-de-Peilz. Thanks to Tarik Thami and Chris Marler at MSP for their unbridled support, and to Andrew Sirotnik for invaluable, albeit brief, mentorship in consulting. Certainly I owe thanks to Robert(son) for starting the project, Eric for being a continuously driving force in our group process, Oliver (I don't even know what you look like!) for creating the FLA files, and Rebecca Gulick for helping with the wordsmithing.

Torben Nielsen (3D and Flash): I would like to thank Marzia Nielsen for supporting me and being a very patient wife during the writing process; Brith and Kaj Nielsen, my parents, who always backed me up in all my crazy creative ideas; my dog Donatello, who kept on bringing his leash hoping that it was time for a break with a trip to the park; and to the whole book team that has giving wonderful technical and moral support. Also, thanks to all the folks at Peachpit and to Dave Klein from Electric Rain who put up with all my strange inquiries about Swift 3D. Finally, a special thank you to Robert(son) Ramirez, who put this team together and made it all happen.

Robert(son) Ramirez (team manager): My gratitude and appreciation goes to my Super Samurai team for a job well done. I could not have picked a better team to write this book. Thanks to all of you, I can say that I made my mark in this world. I would also like to thank my family, especially my mother for her support and understanding. A lot of sleepless nights went into this project, but I am just glad that my kids, Robert and Jolie, will have something to remember me by.

Michael Brandon Williams (3D and Flash): I thank God. My life is devoid of absolutely nothing because of Him, and I am thankful beyond anything my words can describe. A warm thank you goes to my mother for her love and support. My affectionate thanks goes to my supportive friends Jong Yoo, Lester Vega, and Sindy Sagastume. Thanks and kudos to Missy Roback for her incredible editing, as well as to the whole Peachpit team. The Samurai team also gets my deepest gratitude for producing an incredible book from which even I can learn something. Lastly, Robert(son) in particular receives my praise for keeping the team together and organized.

Table of Contents

Chapter 7: Flash Interface Design   262

Chapter 8: XML and Flash   290

Introduction

Welcome to *Macromedia Flash: Super Samurai*.

Unlike many Flash books, this one doesn't rehash the same old concepts and topics you already know. Instead, our goal is to present new Flash programming and implementation concepts, as well as to help expand your knowledge of those concepts you're familiar with. By covering topics such as advanced interfaces, XML, and physics, we hope to not only offer you new ways to approach your projects, but inspire you to develop your own techniques.

How This Book Began

The seeds for this book were sown on an advanced Flash mailing list called Flashcoders (http://chattyfig.figleaf.com), hosted by Figleaf Software. (The man behind the curtains, Branden Hall, does this out the goodness of his heart because he enjoys coding in ActionScript.) The list is a popular place for advanced Flash developers to exchange information about Flash development and, more importantly, ActionScript.

After several months on the list, I realized that the wealth of information discussed there needed to be collected and stored as a reference source. At first, I thought a database would work, but I decided that a search-and-retrieve interface wouldn't do the information justice. Instead, why not gather a group of Flashcoders to create a central source of information—specifically, a book?

As soon as I put the word out, the responses came pouring in. And when I saw the expertise of these individuals, I was blown away. How amazing to have such a handful of talent to choose from!

Once the team was set, we spent months developing the table of contents. We collaborated through an online message board system (created by original team member Bob Clagget) called Super Samurai. We liked the name, and it stuck.

Who's This Book For?

This book is for advanced Flash developers who are looking to learn new, advanced techniques and expand on old ones. You should be well versed in ActionScript. You should also have some familiarity with other technologies discussed in various chapters, such as XML and SQL.

How to Use This Book

This book is divided into nine chapters, each covering an advanced Flash 5 topic. The chapters are meant to stand alone, so you may read them in any order you like. Each chapter is written by a different author, except for chapters 2 and 7, which were each co-written by a pair of authors.

At the heart of each chapter is a developer showcase, an original Flash project created to demonstrate the chapter's topic. Each author will give you a guided tour of his showcase, pointing out the key concepts and techniques behind it. Some of our more enterprising authors created more than one showcase; others created many smaller demos that lead up to the showcase.

As a bonus, all of the source files are included on an accompanying CD-ROM, which you can find at the back of this book. I encourage you to experiment with the files, play around with the code, and see what you come up with. The CD also includes a demo version of Flash as well as some extra sample files that were not discussed in the chapters.

What the Icons Mean

This book uses several icons to alert you to special information.

 CD-ROM. You'll see this icon whenever the author refers to a file on the CD-ROM.

 Key concept. This icon appears whenever a concept crucial to the chapter's topic is introduced.

 Tip. Wherever you see this icon, you'll find advice on how to make your Flash life a little easier.

 Warning. This icon alerts you to a potential problem.

What's in the Chapters

Here's a rundown of each chapter:

Chapter 1: Breathing Life into Flash

This chapter looks at ways to script lifelike movement into your Flash projects. Discover new coding and design techniques to make creatures move and crawl.

Chapter 2: 3D and Flash

More and more Flash developers are catching on to the power of 3D. This two-part chapter looks at two very different methods of creating the illusion of 3D shape and motion: ActionScript 3D and Rendered 3D.

Chapter 3: Flash Physics

This chapter shows you how to use ActionScript to apply Flash physics to create realistic movement, including motion in a straight line, motion under gravity, collisions, and collision reactions of simple objects.

Chapter 4: Programming Sound in Flash

The effective use of sound can add richness and excitement to animation sequences, interactive games, and other Flash projects. This chapter focuses on innovative programming techniques using Flash's Sound object.

Chapter 5: Component System Architecture

Component system architecture means easier updates for you and faster load times for your site's viewers. Learn how to plan and build a fast-loading component-based system, and how to prevent usability problems from hampering your project.

Chapter 6: Creating Dynamic Flash Pages

Learn how to create dynamic Flash sites through a combination of server-side scripting languages and ActionScript. This chapter explains the coding techniques you need and shows them in action in three real-world applications that you can adapt to any Web site.

Chapter 7: Flash Interface Design

Using widgets for often-used interface elements such as pull-down menus and hyperlinks makes Flash Web sites more consistent and efficient. This chapter shows you how to make and use widgets for subtle interface effects that create a memorable experience for your viewers.

Chapter 8: XML and Flash

The combination of XML and Flash lets you design interactive, adaptable front-end applications that you might not have thought were within your grasp. This chapter offers ideas for using XML to create reusable, understandable code that can simplify and speed processing, and even minimize errors.

Chapter 9: JavaScript-Flash Interactions

With basic knowledge of JavaScript, you can greatly extend Flash tools, plug-ins, and functionality. This chapter provides real-world examples and expert advice on influencing browsers via Flash and JavaScript integrations.

I hope these descriptions inspire you to read on. One thing's for sure: If you retain even one-third of the information in this book, you'll be able to produce amazing Flash sites.

What's Next

By the time this book is on the shelves, we'll have our own Web site (www.supersamuraiflash.com) in place. There, you'll find more experimental Flash movies, updates to the books, corrections to any mistakes we may have found (not that there will be any), and a place where you can voice your opinion.

I hope you enjoy this book.

Robert(son) Ramirez
Flash user and database consultant
Queens, New York

1: Breathing Life into Flash

Geoff Stearns is a freelance Flash developer and trainer based in Tucson, Arizona. In his spare time he maintains www.deconcept.com, an online playground he uses to explore the limits of Flash and emerging Web technologies.

In this chapter, we'll look at different ways to code lifelike movement into your Flash projects. We'll also explore some basic concepts of programmatic movement, which will let you dynamically move objects around your movies whenever and wherever you want.

To illustrate the concepts in this chapter, I'll walk you through two experiments from my Web site, www.deconcept.com. I'll explain how I designed and coded them, and more importantly, why I chose to build them the way I did.

When you're mastering a new programming language, coding technique can be one of the hardest things to learn. Flash, being such a broad program, only adds to the challenge—there are many ways to accomplish most goals. By explaining my code placement and discussing why I chose certain techniques, I hope to teach you how to use ActionScript more effectively.

Creating an Interactive Spider

My first project is an interactive spider. By examining the source file, you'll get an overview of how to use ActionScript to create lifelike behavior and movement, as well as how to use clip events effectively.

 Open spider.swf from the CD-ROM.

A transparent button on the spider's body lets you drag it around the screen. Try it out so you can see how it works (**Figure 1.1**).

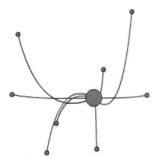

Figure 1.1 Grab the spider's body and drag it.

Setting Up the Spider Source File

 Open spider.fla from the CD-ROM.

I created this file at 500 x 300 pixels and with a frame rate of 20 fps. (If you set the frame rate higher, the spider's legs will move too fast, which might look a little strange.)

To keep things fairly modular, I placed all the contents of the spider inside another movie clip. This lets the spider work on its own, no matter where I drag it on the Stage. Also, because there aren't any tweens in this movie, the main (_root) timeline contains only one frame and two layers—one for the spider and one for the actions. Keeping all my actions on one layer makes it easier to find and edit them.

On the first frame of the Actions layer, I placed this code:

```
fscommand("allowscale", false);
stop();
```

The first line of code keeps the movie from scaling and stretching during testing; I use this code in most of my movies. The stop() action prevents the movie from looping.

 I always program in Expert mode because it's faster and easier for typing code. I encourage you to use it, even if you're uncomfortable using it in the ActionScript window or you don't have all the syntax memorized. If you forget a command or syntax, switch to Normal mode and use the ActionScript menu to place the command in the window, and then change back to Expert mode and fill in the variables. Also, keep your Flash 5 ActionScript Reference Guide close by so you can look up commands you don't use often.

Creating the Spider Parts

The spider's parts are quite simple: a round body surrounded by eight legs, each ending with a toe. While the figure itself is created of basic shapes— circles and lines—there's more going on behind the scenes. In this section, I'll briefly discuss each part, pointing out what was interesting about creating it.

The Body

To make the spider's body, I created a movie clip called m-body. This movie clip has two layers: a graphic of the body, and a transparent button that makes the spider interactive.

 Look in the library. Notice that the graphic of the spider's body is called g-body and the button is called b-body. Flash doesn't allow duplicate names in the library, so putting a letter in front of the word "body" lets me use the word multiple times. This method also gives me a quick visual way to indicate a symbol's behavior.

The Toes

I used clip events to make the toes move. Flash 5 can attach clip events only to a movie clip that's on a Stage. Therefore, I created a container movie clip, placed the m-toe movie clip inside it, and put the clip events on the m-toe movie clip. I created one toe, and then used the `attachMovie()` method to pull the toe out of the library eight times.

The Legs

I needed to create eight legs, so it was easier to use the `attachMovie()` method: I could just grab the legs from the library and attach them onto the Stage wherever I wanted. If I had used the `duplicateMovieClip()` method, I would have had to position a leg on the Stage where I planned to create it.

Because `attachMovie()` can only attach movie clips from the library, the spider leg needed to be a movie clip. It's good practice, however, to make all your raw graphics actual graphic symbols, as opposed to just drawing directly inside a movie clip.

To draw the lines for the spider legs, I created a line at a 45-degree angle, made it 100 x 100 pixels, and stretched it between two points. (The top left corner of the line should be aligned to the 0,0 coordinates of the movie clip in which it resides.) I put a slight curve in the line to give the legs a nice rounded look.

Making the Spider Move

Now that we've gone over the spider's body parts, let's review the code that makes the spider work.

Making the Toes Move

Whenever a user drags the spider's body to a new position on the screen, the legs and toes must follow. Making the toes move was fairly straightforward. I used clip events and some movement code to slide the toes to their new position. I also added code to maintain the amount of offset each toe has from the body. This keeps each toe in the same area relative to its initial position: Toes under the body will stay roughly under the body, and toes above the body or to the left of it will stay above or to the left of it, respectively.

 It's good practice to place code locally, instead of all in one place. This way, if something isn't working, it's much easier to track down the broken part.

Here's the code on the m-toe movie clip:

```
onClipEvent (load) {
    // -- set up variables
    // -- "a" controls how fast the toes move, a lower number
    → will make them slide faster
    var a = 2;
    var newX = _parent._x;
    var newY = _parent._y;
    var xSpeed = 0;
    var ySpeed = 0;
    // -- offset is the distance of this movie clip to
    → the body
    var xOffset = _parent._x -_parent._parent.body._x;
    var yOffset = _parent._y-_parent._parent.body._y;
}
onClipEvent (enterFrame) {
    // -- Calculate the speed each frame
    xSpeed = (_parent._x-(newX+xOffset))/a;
    ySpeed = (_parent._y-(newY+yOffset))/a;
    // -- adjust parent movie clip position
    _parent._x -= xSpeed;
    _parent._y -= ySpeed;
}
```

Now let's review the code that tells the toes when and to where they should move.

Controlling the Toes

The spider is motionless until the user drags its body; when this happens, the toes should stay close to the body. To do this, I set up a clip event on the body that checks the distance of each toe from the body. If it's past a distance that's randomly generated and based from the variable walkDist, the toe moves to a new random position near the body.

I also wanted the toes to stay in the same area relative to the body. In other words, the toes below the body should stay below the body (or at least close enough) and the toes positioned at the top of the body should stay near the top. This keeps the spider fairly balanced so all of its toes won't end up on one side.

The code on the m-body movie clip looks like this:

```
onClipEvent (load) {
  // -- first swap the depths of the body to place it above
  → the leg lines (This is only a cosmetic change)
  this.swapDepths(1000);
  // -- set up the variables
  // -- walkDist is used as a base number to keep the toes
  → close to the body
  // -- the higher this number is, the further the legs will
  → be allowed to travel
  // -- from the body
  var walkDist = 60;
  var maxDist = 0;
  // -- this tells the body how many legs we have
  var toes = 8;
  // -- attach the leg lines from the library and name them
  for (i=1; i<=toes; i++) {
    _parent.attachMovie("leg", "leg"+i, i+100);
  }
}
onClipEvent (enterFrame) {
  // -- loop through each toe and check its distance from
  → the body
  for (i=1; i<=toes; i++) {
    myToe = _parent["toe"+i];
    xDist = Math.abs(myToe.toe.newX-this._x);
    yDist = Math.abs(myToe.toe.newY-this._y);
    maxDist = Math.floor(Math.random()*walkDist)+walkDist;
```

```
// -- if the distance is farther than a certain amount,
 → tell that toe to move
if (xDist>maxDist || yDist>maxDist) {
  myToe.toe.newX =
   → this._x+Math.floor(Math.random()*walkDist)-walkDist/2;
  myToe.toe.newY =
   → this._y+Math.floor(Math.random()*walkDist)-walkDist/2;
  }
// -- adjust the "legs" each cycle (the lines)
myLeg = _parent["leg"+i];
myLeg._x = this._x;
myLeg._y = this._y;
myLeg._xscale = myToe._x-this._x;
myLeg._yscale = myToe._y-this._y;
 }
}
```

Here's how this code works:

When the movie starts, the code in the body grabs the leg movie clip from the library eight times. Whenever the playhead enters a frame, the Spider does these actions: A loop checks the distance of each toe from the body. If the distance is further than the variable maxDist, the code chooses a random _x and _y position for that toe. Once this is done, the code updates the position of each leg.

Making the Spider Interactive

To makes the spider draggable, I added actions to the button in the body. Here's the button code inside the m-body movie clip:

```
on (press) {
  this.startDrag();
}
on (release) {
  stopDrag();
}
```

That does it for the code on the spider. Now let's look at the Walking Insect.

Creating a Walking Insect

My second project is a walking insect. Examining the source file will give you a more advanced look at programmatic movement, controlling multiple objects using ActionScript, and writing generic code.

 Open walking_insect.swf from the CD-ROM to see how the animation works (**Figure 1.2**). Although there are three insects in the movie, I'll only discuss how I created one of them.

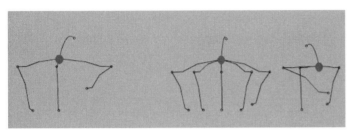

Figure 1.2 *The walking insects in action.*

When the insect is first attached to the Stage, it picks a random number to determine its number of legs. Then it generates the legs and begins walking around. The insect has three states: walking forward, walking backwards, and standing still.

Creating the Insect Parts

 Open walking_insect.fla from the CD-ROM.

I created this file at 750 x 285 pixels and with a frame rate of 20 fps.

Attached to the insect's head is an antenna with a small dot atop it. The insect's legs are lines that extend down from its head to its knees, and then from its knees to its toes. Both the knees and toes are indicated with a small dot.

As with the spider project, I placed the code for the walking insect on its associated body parts. This way, if something doesn't work right, I'll know exactly where to locate the code.

The Toes

In the library, find the m-toe holder movie clip (it's in the folder named toes – knees – head dot). Inside it is a small dot graphic named m-small dot, which, itself, is a movie clip with the graphic g-small dot inside it. I used the m-small dot movie clip to control the insect's knees, toes, and antenna. Each time, I placed it inside a container movie clip and put different code on it, depending on what I wanted it to do.

Here's the code for the m-toe holder movie clip:

```
onClipEvent (load) {
  var a = 3;
  var ay = 2;
  oYpos = _parent._y;
  newX = _parent._x;
  newY = _parent._y;
}
onClipEvent (enterFrame) {
  _parent._x -= (_parent._x-newX)/a;
  _parent._y -= (_parent._y-newY)/ay;
}
```

The variables a and ay are acceleration variables. The first variable controls the speed of the toe's x movement; the second controls the speed of the y movement. I gave the x and y speeds different variables because I wanted the insect to lift its toes faster than they moved left to right. The oYpos variable grabs the _y position of the parent movie clip when it loads for later use. The newX and newY variables tell the toe where it should be located. The two lines of code inside the enterFrame clip event move the clip around on the Stage.

Here's how this basic movement script works:

The toe looks at its current position, subtracts the new variable from its current position, then divides that by a number (a) and updates its position. Because this is executed every frame, if I want to move the toe to a new position, all I have to do is change the newX or newY variables and the toe will slide to its new position.

The Knees

Here's the code for the m-knee holder movie clip:

```
onClipEvent (load) {
  a = 1.5;
  d = 1.7;
  newX = _parent._x;
}
onClipEvent (enterFrame) {
  newX = (_parent._parent["toe"+_parent.num]._x-
    → _parent._parent.head._x)*1.5+_parent._parent.head._x;
```

```
    xSpeed = ((_parent._x - newX)/a+xSpeed)/d;
    _parent._x -= xSpeed;
}
```

You can see that I'm using the same movement code with slight variations to achieve different behaviors. To add a bit of lifelike springiness to the knee movement, I added the variable d to the code. Also, note that I'm updating only the knee's *x* positions. When the knees are attached to the insect, the code in the head sets their *y* position. Because the *y* position will always be the same, there's no need to update it with code.

The first line in the enterFrame clip event keeps each knee offset from its associated toe. Each toe and knee is assigned a number num when it's attached (toe1, toe2, knee1, knee2, and so on) to the head. Therefore, in every frame, each knee will check the *x* position of the toe with the same num as it, and update itself depending on the position of that toe.

The Antenna

Now let's look at the m-head dot holder movie clip, the last movie clip that uses the m-small dot movie clip. Here's the code:

```
onClipEvent (load) {
  a = 6;
  d = 1.04;
  _parent._parent.attachMovie("headline", "headline", 5);
}
onClipEvent (enterFrame) {
  newX = _parent._parent.head._x;
  newY = _parent._parent.head._y-30;
  myXSpeed = ((_parent._x-newX)/a+myXSpeed)/d;
  myYSpeed = ((_parent._y-newY)/a+myYSpeed)/d;
  _parent._x -= myXSpeed;
  _parent._y -= myYSpeed;
}
```

Again, I'm using the same movement code as in the previous examples, but with slight variations. By changing the value of the d variable, I made the antenna dot swing around a specific point: The newX and newY variables line up the *x* position of the dot with the insect's head, and the *y* position 30 pixels above its head. The movement code takes care of the rest—we never have to worry about updating the dot's position, because it does so by itself every frame.

BREATHING LIFE INTO FLASH : CREATING A WALKING INSECT

The Legs

Look inside the Lines folder in the library. Note that there are two different line movie clips: one for the head dot (g-headline), and one for the legs (g-line). I exported both lines so I could use the `attachMovie()` method whenever I want to use the lines in my movie.

Making the Insect Walk

Locate the m-walker movie clip in the library, and look at the actions on the head movie clip. There's quite a bit of code in here, so I'll go through it in segments.

Here's the basic idea behind the code: When the movie loads, the actions on the first frame of the main timeline attach the m-walker movie clip to the Stage. When this clip loads, it triggers the actions in the clip events. The code chooses a random number between three and five; this determines the number of legs the insect will have. Then, the code attaches the toes, knees, and head dot, as well as the legs. It evenly spaces the toes underneath the insect, and does the same for the knees and head dots.

 This is an example of generic code. The insect doesn't have a preset number of legs: The number is randomly determined when the insect loads for the first time. This technique can be useful in just about any project. If I built this insect without generic code—let's say I gave it five legs—and my client decided it wanted three legs, I would have to manually remove two legs from the file, and then re-export it. With generic code, all I have to do is change a variable and the insect updates itself.

Once the clips are attached, the enterFrame clip events take over. If the insect is standing still, it does nothing; if it's walking forward, it will figure out which leg is behind it, and tell that leg to move to the front. If it's walking backwards, it does the reverse.

Building the Legs

Let's look at the code that builds the insect's legs:

```
onClipEvent (load) {
  this.swapDepths(_root.level);
  _root.level++;
  // -- vars
  counter = random(5);
```

```
footDist = 130;
legs = random(3)+3;
walkHeight = 100;
myBounds = _root.boundBox.getBounds(_root);
// -- set initial x pos and randomize breathing
gotoAndPlay (random(_totalframes));
_x = random(myBounds.xMax)+myBounds.xMin;
_y = myBounds.yMax-walkheight;
// -- attach clips
var kneeDist = (walkHeight/3)+random(walkheight/4);
for (i=0; i<legs; i++) {
  _parent.attachMovie("toe", "toe"+i, i+1000);
  myToe = _parent["toe"+i];
  myToe._x = (_x+(i*(footDist/legs)))-50;
  myToe._y = _y+walkHeight;
  myToe.num = i;
  _parent.attachMovie("knee", "knee"+i, i+2000);
  myKnee = _parent["knee"+i];
  myKnee._y = _y+kneeDist;
  myKnee._x = myToe._x;
  myKnee.num = i;
  _parent.attachMovie("line", "kline"+i, i+3000);
  _parent.attachMovie("line", "tline"+i, i+4000);
}
// -- lower the head to make them look cooler
_y += random(walkheight/1.2);
// -- hook up the head dot
_parent.attachMovie("headDot", "headDot", 10);
_parent.headDot.dot.newX = _parent.head._x;
_parent.headDot.dot.newY = _parent.head._y-20;
_parent.headDot._x = _parent.head._x;
_parent.headDot._y = _parent.head._y-20;
}
```

Note that I'm using the getBounds() method to get the coordinates of the boundBox movie clip on the main timeline. This creates an object called myBounds with four variables: xMin, xMax, yMin, and yMax. These variables correspond to the left, right, top, and bottom of the boundBox movie clip. I prefer using this method to find the Stage's dimensions instead of manually entering the variables, as it's easier to change the Stage's size: All I have to do is change the size of the boundBox movie clip. I also kept all of the attached movie clips inside the m-walker movie clip. This helps when there are multiple insects on the Stage because I don't have to keep track of the depth that each clip uses.

Adding Interactivity

The next section of code adds a bit of interactivity to the insect:

```
onClipEvent (mouseDown) {
  if (this.hitTest(_root._xmouse, _root._ymouse)) {
    startDrag (this);
    grabbed = true;
  }
}
onClipEvent (mouseUp) {
  if (grabbed) {
    stopDrag ();
    grabbed = false;
  }
}
```

Note that there are no buttons in this FLA file. Instead, I used the hitTest() method to add interactivity to the insect. A mouse click triggers this event. If the mouse's *x* and *y* positions are within the bounds of the head movie clip, it will call the actions inside the If statement associated with the hitTest(). I used the startDrag() method and a variable that's set to true or false. This will tell the insect to stop walking if the user is dragging it.

Controlling the Insect's Speed and Direction

This next section of code controls how quickly the insect walks and in which direction it walks. Here's the code:

```
onClipEvent (enterFrame) {
  if (!grabbed) {
    if (_x>myBounds.xMax) {
      goBack = true;
      goForth = false;
    }
    if (_x<myBounds.xMin) {
      goBack = false;
      goForth = true;
    }
    avgX = 0;
```

```
for (i=0; i<legs; i++) {
 avgX += _parent["toe"+i]._x;
}
_x = avgX/legs;
if (count) {
 backLeg.toe.newY = backLeg.toe.oYpos;
 frontLeg.toe.newY = frontLeg.toe.oYpos;
 walkDir = random(15);
 if (walkDir == 2) {
  goForth = true;
  goBack = false;
 } else if (!walkDir) {
  goBack = true;
  goForth = false;
 } else if (walkDir == 3) {
  goBack = false;
  goForth = false;
 }
 // -- forward movement
 if (goForth) {
  backLeg = _parent.toe0;
  for (i=0; i<legs; i++) {
   if (_parent["toe"+i]._x<backLeg._x) {
    backLeg = _parent["toe"+i];
   }
  }
  backLeg.toe.newX += footDist+random(7)-3;
  backLeg.toe.newY -= walkheight/3;
 }
 // --- backwards movement
 if (goBack) {
  frontLeg = _parent.toe0;
  for (i=0; i<legs; i++) {
   if (_parent["toe"+i]._x>frontLeg._x) {
    frontLeg = _parent["toe"+i];
   }
  }
  frontLeg.toe.newX -= footDist-random(7)-3;
  frontLeg.toe.newY -= walkheight/3;
 }
 count = false;
} else {
```

```
counter++;
if (counter>5) {
 count = true;
 counter = 0;
}
}
}
```

First, the code checks to see if the insect is being dragged. If it's not, the code checks the head's *x* position. If it's outside the boundBox movie clip, the code tells the insect to walk in the direction toward the box. Then it will position its head at the average *x* position of all the legs.

Once this is done, we can move the legs. First, an If statement checks to see if the count variable is true. I use the count variable to slow the insect's walking speed. Here, I set it to be true only once every five frames. (If I wanted to slow down the insect even further, I would increase the count limit.) If the count variable is true, the insect generates a random number between 0 and 15; then, depending on the value of this variable, it decides whether to change directions. Using random numbers ensures that the insect will behave differently every time.

 Using random numbers to choose actions is great way to add lifelike movement to your Flash projects. For example, you could randomize different parts of a Web site to give users a different experience each time.

Determining Leg Movement

Now let's look at the code in the previous section that controls which leg moves. This was probably the hardest part of the project to code. To make the insect walk forward and backwards and lift its feet, I added code that would find the leg that's either farthest in front or farthest in back, and then tell that leg to move.

Here's how the code works: To determine which leg is in front or back, the code checks the *x* position of each leg. Starting with leg0, it checks the *x* position of all the other legs. If the *x* position of another leg is greater or less than leg0, that leg becomes the chosen leg. After the code loops through all the legs, the chosen leg moves forward or backward, depending on the insect's current direction. The toe of the chosen leg is also told to change its *y* position, which causes the insect to raise its leg as it walks. On the next count cycle, this toe is told to move back down to the ground. The distance that each leg moves also has a small amount of random deviation, so the spacing between the legs will change as the insect moves around.

Updating the Leg and Antenna Lines

This last section of code simply loops through all the legs and antenna lines in the insect and updates their positions. This is the same method I used to draw the lines in the spider earlier in this chapter.

```
// -- draw the lines
for (i=0; i<legs; i++) {
  myKLine = _parent["kline"+i];
  myTLine = _parent["tline"+i];
  myKnee = _parent["knee"+i];
  myToe = _parent["toe"+i];
  myKLine._x = myKnee._x;
  myKLine._y = myKnee._y;
  myKline._xscale = _parent.head._x-myKnee._x;
  myKline._yscale = _parent.head._y-myKnee._y;
  // ----
  myTLine._x = myToe._x;
  myTLine._y = myToe._y;
  myTLine._xscale = myKnee._x-myToe._x;
  myTLine._yscale = myKnee._y-myToe._y;
}
// -- draw the head line
_parent.headline._x = _parent.headDot._x;
_parent.headline._y = _parent.headDot._y;
_parent.headline._xscale = _x-_parent.headDot._x;
_parent.headline._yscale = _y-_parent.headDot._y;
}
```

Conclusion

By now you should have a good grasp of some effective ways to use clip events and some pretty advanced programmatic movement. You should also understand the advantages of using generic code.

Play around with the code in the walking insect file to better understand how it works. Try adding or removing legs, or changing some of the movement variables in the toes and knees. You can achieve many different effects just by changing a few variables.

2: 3D and Flash

Michael Brandon Williams is a senior at Spring Woods High School in Houston, Texas, with many years of mathematics and computer science study in his curriculum vitae. His mathematics focus has been single and multivariable calculus, real analysis, linear algebra, ordinary differential equations, elementary combinatorics, and number theory. His computer science experience is based on programming design, object-oriented programming, and problem solving. His goal is to pursue a Ph.D. in Mathematics.

In his spare time, he helps run the math forum at Were-Here (www.were-here.com) under the name of ahab, and works for Eyeland Studios (www.eyeland.com) as a games programmer.

Danish freelance designer **Torben Nielsen** runs his own design company, SD Flash Studios, which specializes in Flash solutions for the Internet and other medias. He is based in Rome.

Throughout his childhood, Lego, Walt Disney cartoons, and his Comodore 64 computer sparked his interest in drawing and creativity. His popular comic strip for his high school newspaper reflected school life in a sarcastic way. Torben has never had formal design education, apart from a two-year art class in college.

When he discovered Flash 3 in 1998, that old Lego feeling came back to him, and it was love at first sight. Since then he has specialized in Flash; today it's the base of all of his projects.

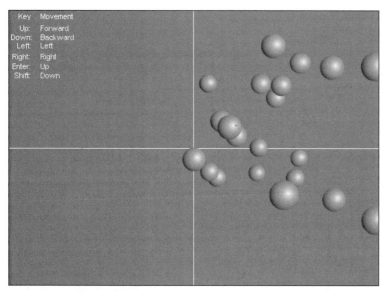

Figure 2.14 Navigate through a field of points.

 Open random_3D_points_trans2.fla from the CD-ROM.

In this file, we'll put all scripting, except for the duplicate preliminaries, in the point movie clip. We'll replace the three random translate increments we defined earlier with one value, which will be how much the points are translated when a key is held down. Therefore, the load clip event actions have changed slightly:

```
onClipEvent (load)
{
// position of origin
origin_x = 275;
origin_y = 200;
// used for perspective - distance from the viewer to
→ the screen
D = 400;
// size of movie clip at the origin
regular_size = this._width;
// random ordered triplet
x = Math.random () * 200 - 100;
y = Math.random () * 200 - 100;
z = Math.random () * 200 - 100;
// increment the point will move by when a key is down
inc = 4;
}
```

The constants, such as the position of the origin, the size of the movie clip, and the perspective distance, are still initialized first. The script gives the point a random ordered triplet and a constant value for the rate at which the point is translated when a key is down. In the previous file, we initialized a random value for the translation increments in the load clip event. Here, the translation increment is determined by which keys are pressed; this is done in the enterFrame clip event.

The enterFrame clip event actions take care of the rendering and movement. In our previous file, the random translation increments were added to the point's ordered triplet every frame. Here, we replace the old increment actions with actions that increment and decrement variables from key presses. Because we aren't dealing with 2D movement any more, I had to change which keys changed which translation axis. In this file, the Left and Right arrow keys control the x-movement, the Enter and Shift keys control the y-movement, and the Up and Down keys control the z-movement. The rendering part of the script remains unchanged.

```
onClipEvent (enterFrame)
{
// move the point according to which keys are pressed
x += Key.isDown (Key.LEFT) * inc - Key.isDown (Key.RIGHT)
→ * inc;
y += Key.isDown (Key.SHIFT) * inc - Key.isDown (Key.ENTER)
→ * inc;
z += Key.isDown (Key.DOWN) * inc - Key.isDown (Key.UP)
→ * inc;
// calculate the perspective ratio
perspective_ratio = D / (D + z);
// calculate position of point on computer screen
perspective_x = x * perspective_ratio;
perspective_y = y * perspective_ratio;
// update position of movie clip on stage
this._x = origin_x + perspective_x;
this._y = origin_y - perspective_y;
// update size of movie clip
this._xscale = this._yscale = regular_size *
→ perspective_ratio;
// set the depth of the clip based on its z-position
this.swapDepths (-z);
}
```

Although the script may not look like much, we've created a truly impressive file!

A problem with the rendering engine. When you give viewers complete control over the 3D environment, you're more likely to find small bugs in the rendering engine. A problem may arise if you try to move too far into the points. If a point's ordered triplet is behind you, its position on screen (ordered pair) goes out of whack. The points will come back out in front of you and will be flipped across each axis. The solution: Set the visibility of the movie clip to false when it's behind you and true when it's in front of you.

How do you check if a point is in front of or behind you? Let's refer to the picture that helped us derive the perspective equations earlier in this chapter (**Figure 2.15**).

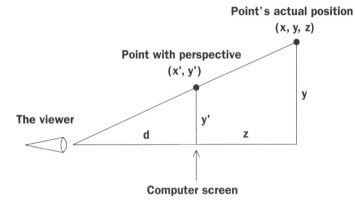

Point's actual position (x, y, z)

Point with perspective (x', y')

The viewer

Computer screen

Figure 2.15 A point is behind the viewer when it goes less than negative d.

The origin of 3D space is placed right on the surface of your computer screen. Anything on your side of the computer screen has a negative z-position; anything inside the computer has a positive z-position. The distance from your eye to the computer screen is d, the perspective distance. In other words, the z-position of your eye is $-d$. Therefore, if any point has a z-position less than $-d$, you know it has traveled behind you.

Using this information, we can make a conditional statement that tests to see if a point's z-position has gone behind you; if it has, then it makes the movie clip invisible. Because the clip doesn't have to be rendered on the Stage at all if it's behind you, you can save Flash a few processor calculations by placing the rendering script inside the `else` of the condition statement.

The following script will be more insightful than my words; it translates and renders the point in the enterFrame actions.

```
onClipEvent (enterFrame)
{
// move the point according to which keys are pressed
x += Key.isDown (Key.LEFT) * inc - Key.isDown (Key.RIGHT)
→ * inc;
y += Key.isDown (Key.SHIFT) * inc - Key.isDown (Key.ENTER)
→ * inc;
z += Key.isDown (Key.DOWN) * inc - Key.isDown (Key.UP)
→ * inc;
// check if point is behind viewer
if (z < -D)
{
// make clip invisible
this._visible = false;
}
else
{
// show and render clip
this._visible = true;
// calculate the perspective ratio
perspective_ratio = D / (D + z);
// calculate position of point on computer screen
perspective_x = x * perspective_ratio;
perspective_y = y * perspective_ratio;
// update position of movie clip on stage
this._x = origin_x + perspective_x;
this._y = origin_y - perspective_y;
// update size of movie clip
this._xscale = this._yscale = regular_size *
→ perspective_ratio;
// set the depth of the clip based on its z-position
this.swapDepths (-z);
}
}
```

 The following file is similar to the previous one, except for the conditional that removes points behind the viewer. You'll find it on the CD-ROM as random_3D_points_trans3.fla.

Rotation

Rotation is the epitome of 3D. It gives you the sense of truly being in a 3D environment because you can twist and turn inside it. Although it's by far the most complicated aspect of 3D covered in this chapter, it's easy for even math novices to understand.

Rotation Preliminaries

Before we get to the code, let's review a few underlying concepts, mainly based on trigonometry.

The two trigonometric functions that play the most important role from now on are sine and cosine. Both return ratios when given an input of an angle. To picture what type of ratio the functions return, you must create a right triangle from the angle (**Figure 2.16**).

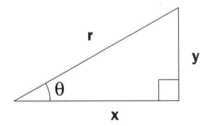

Figure 2.16 *The sine and cosine ratios are derived from a right triangle.*

The sine of the angle, θ, is the opposite side of the angle, *y*, divided by the hypotenuse, *r*. The cosine of the angle, θ, is the adjacent side to the angle, *x*, divided by the hypotenuse, *r*. These definitions are better understood with the following written mathematical equation (**Figure 2.17**):

$$\sin \theta = \frac{y}{r}$$

Figure 2.17 *Equations for calculating the sine and cosine ratios.*

$$\cos \theta = \frac{x}{r}$$

We can formulate our first applicable equations from these simple definitions. The quantities *x* and *y* represent the base and height of the right triangle made from the angle and *r*. Placing the origin at the vertex from which we're measuring the angle, we can also interpret *x* and *y* as the position of the non-right angle vertex (**Figure 2.18**).

Figure 2.18 *A right triangle as points on a graph.*

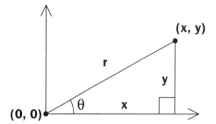

Figure 2.18 *A right triangle as points on a graph.*

Now, by rearranging the sine and cosine equations we can solve for *x* and *y* (**Figure 2.19**).

$$\cos \theta = \frac{x}{r} \quad \longrightarrow \quad x = r \cos \theta$$

Figure 2.19 *Solving the sine and cosine ratios for x and y presents two more useful equations.*

$$\sin \theta = \frac{y}{r} \quad \longrightarrow \quad y = r \sin \theta$$

This last set of equations is important for finding the *x* and *y* position of a point given *r* and θ. But what significance do *r* and θ hold? Picture a straight stick lying flat on the floor with one end at the origin (0, 0) and the other at the point (r, 0) where *r* is the length of the stick (**Figure 2.20**).

Figure 2.20 *Here's a stick with one end at the origin and the other at a point on the x-axis.*

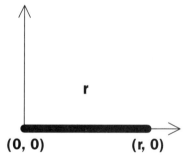

If you were to rotate the stick around the origin by an angle of θ, one end would stay at the origin while the other would move somewhere out into the coordinate plane. Where exactly in the plane is a question we can now answer. The sine and cosine equations we solved for *x* and *y* helps us find the position of the point by simply plugging in *r* and θ (**Figure 2.21**).

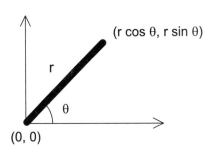

(r cos θ, r sin θ)

Figure 2.21 *You can use sine and cosine to find the position of the stick when it's rotated.*

r

θ

(0, 0)

From the picture above, we can conclude that if we were to go out a distance of *r* units in the direction of θ, we could find the position of that point by multiplying *r* with the sine or cosine of θ. In other words, another way of writing an ordered pair (x, y) is (r cos θ, r sin θ).

Trigonometric identities come up all the time in trigonometry and calculus. A trigonometric identity is an equation containing a trigonometric function that any angle will solve. They're particularly useful when you need a general formula for finding the sine and cosine of the sum, difference, or product of two angles. The two identities we're concerned with are called the sum identities for sine and cosine (**Figure 2.22**).

sin (a + b) = sin a cos b + cos a sin b
cos (a + b) = cos a cos b - sin a sin b

Figure 2.22 *Sum identities for sine and cosine.*

If you're curious, you can find the proofs to these identities in most textbooks. We'll apply these identities shortly.

Now that we're dealing with angles, sine, and cosine, I should mention Flash's idiosyncrasies in dealing with the trigonometric functions. There are two ways to measure an angle: in degrees and in radians. Almost everyone is familiar with degrees and knows there are 360° in a circle. Radians, however, aren't so straightforward. A radian is a ratio of the radius of a circle to an arc length of a circle (**Figure 2.23**).

radian measure of θ = s / r

Figure 2.23 *Measuring an angle with radians.*

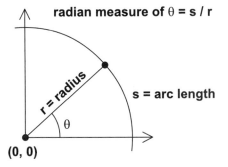

s = arc length

(0, 0)

To make things easier, let's assume that the radius of the circle is 1. That means the radian angle measure reduces to only the arc length *s*. The arc length for an entire circle (also known as the *circumference*) is 2πr. If the radius is 1, then the circumference is 2π. This implies that an angle of 360° is equal to 2π radians. So, if we were given 360°, we could convert that to radians by multiplying it by 2π divided by 360, which reduces to π divided by 180. This is your conversion factor to translate between angle units (**Figure 2.24**).

radians = degrees • π / 180

⇓ ⇑

degrees = radius • 180 / π

Figure 2.24 *Converting between degrees and radians.*

Flash's ActionScript uses radians so you must convert all angles before you can use the Math object. Later you'll see that it's better to keep track of our rotation angles in degrees, and then change to radians when we're ready to use Flash's sine and cosine functions.

What Rotation Boils Down To

If you want to derive equations to rotate a point in space, you must first know how you're going to formulate the problem. You must also know what is meant by a rotation around the *x*-axis, or any other axis for that matter.

When you rotate a point around the *x*-axis, you literally move a point around the *x*-axis; there's no other way to put it. The same goes for the other axes. It's important to note that a point rotated around the *x*-axis doesn't change its *x*-position; only the *y*- and *z*-positions change. When an object is rotated around the *z*-axis it doesn't change *z*-positions, either. A point rotating around the *z*-axis is the same as a point rotating around the origin in a regular 2D Cartesian graph (**Figure 2.25**).

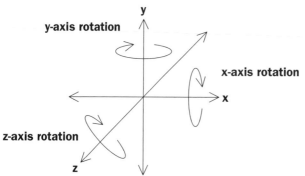

Figure 2.25 *How a point rotates around each of the three coordinate axes.*

Z-axis Rotation

Let's formulate the equation for rotating a point around the z-axis; the other axes will follow easily from that. Picture a point in the *xy*-plane with no z-position whatsoever. The point is placed at (x, y, 0), is at a distance of *r* from the origin, and makes up an angle of *a* with the origin and *x*-axis (**Figure 2.26**).

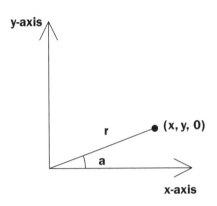

Figure 2.26 An ordered pair makes an angle with the x- and y-axes on a 2D graph.

Now, rotate that point by an angle of *b*, to the point (x', y', 0), while maintaining a distance of *r* from the origin (**Figure 2.27**).

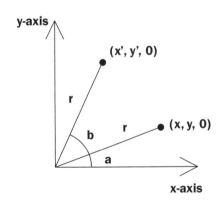

Figure 2.27 An ordered pair rotated by an angle around the z-axis.

Note that the angle made up from the rotated point and the *x*-axis is *a* plus *b* rather than just *b*. The angle *b* is by how much you rotated from the original position. So, the rotation problem boils down to finding (x', y', 0) by knowing *a*, *b*, *r*, and the original ordered triplet (x, y, 0).

Using Trigonometry for Rotations

Let's start by using our definitions of sine and cosine that were solved for *x* and *y* to find the position of the original point and the rotated point (**Figure 2.28**).

x = r cos a
y = r sin a
z = 0

Figure 2.28 Equations for calculating the original position and rotated position of the point.

x' = r cos (a + b)
y' = r sin (a + b)
z' = 0

If you're paying attention, you might start to see why the sum identities were shown earlier. These equations don't say much more than what we already know. It's important that you remember the rotated point makes an angle of *a* plus *b* with the *x*-axis. Although these equations might be of some use in rotating a point, they aren't as good as they could be. We'd have to constantly keep track of how far the point is from the distance and from the angle made from the original point and the *x*-axis. This is possible, but certainly not necessary. By substituting our sum identities, we come up with a few new equations (**Figure 2.29**).

x = r cos a
y = r sin a
z = 0

Figure 2.29 Substitute the sum identities for sine and cosine.

x' = r cos (a + b) = r (cos a cos b - sin a sin b)
y' = r sin (a + b) = r (sin a cos b + cos a sin b)
z' = 0

Remember that the sum identities had no quantities such as *r* involved, so *r* must stay outside the parentheses. But to simplify the expressions, we can distribute the *r* into the parentheses (**Figure 2.30**).

x = r cos a
y = r sin a
z = 0

Figure 2.30 *Distribute the term throughout the equation.*

x' = r cos (a + b) = r cos a cos b - r sin a sin b
y' = r sin (a + b) = r sin a cos b + r cos a sin b
z' = 0

If you've got a keen eye, you might see quite a few repetitions in this last set of equations. The equations that solve for (x', y', 0) have some terms that appear to be exactly the same as the equations for (x, y, 0). The terms of particular interest are those that involve the sine or cosine of *a* because these are the ratios used in (x, y, 0). Therefore, we can substitute all terms with an *r* and a sine or cosine with just *x* or *y* (**Figure 2.31**).

x = r cos a
y = r sin a
z = 0

Figure 2.31 *Simplify the equation by substituting like terms.*

x' = r cos (a + b) = x cos b - y sin b
y' = r sin (a + b) = y cos b + x sin b
z' = 0

⇓

x' = x cos b - y sin b
y' = y cos b + x sin b

You've just derived the equations for rotating a point around the *z*-axis. If you know the current position of a point (x, y, 0) and you want to rotate it around the *z*-axis by *b* degrees, simply use this last set of equations. Note that we got rid of all the awkward quantities like *r* and *a*.

Rotation Around the Z-axis

Rotation around the *z*-axis doesn't involve any 3D (because the points stay in the *xy*-plane), so let's go through a few small demos to get the hang of it.

 Open z_axis_rotation1.swf from the CD-ROM.

Every time you press the Rotate button, the point will rotate around the origin by the rotation angle (**Figure 2.32**).

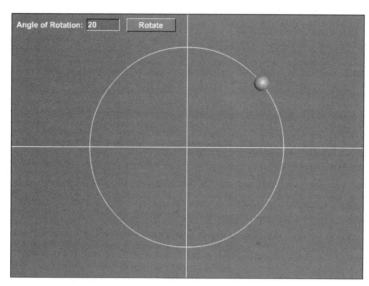

Figure 2.32 *Rotating a point around the z-axis by a user-defined angle.*

 Open z_axis_rotation1.fla from the CD-ROM.

I created a textbox (called rotation_angle) for entering the rotation angle, a button for rotating the point, and a movie clip (called point) to represent the point. The only actions in the entire movie are placed in the first frame of the _root for declaring the initial variables and in the button for the rotation actions.

I added another layer to the _root (used only for putting some actions), and declared the initial variables in the first frame. A variable translates degrees to radians for the Math object, two variables for the initial position of the point, and two variables for the position of the origin. I also positioned the point so it would be in the right place immediately when you open the file.

```
// used for translating between angle units
trans = Math.PI / 180;
// position of origin
origin_x = 275;
origin_y = 200;
// starting position of point
x = 150;
y = 0;
// place the point for the beginning
point._x = origin_x + x;
point._y = origin_y - y;
```

The rotation actions go in the button's on(release). When the button is pressed and released, you must first find the sine and cosine of the rotation angle (in the textbox). Because the angle needs to be in radians only when using the Math object, I do the conversion directly in the function's parameters.

```
// find the sine and cosine of the rotation angle
sin_angle = Math.sin (Number (rotation_angle) * trans);
cos_angle = Math.cos (Number (rotation_angle) * trans);
```

 Note that rotation_angle is run through the Number object before it's used. This is because numbers are taken from textboxes sometimes as strings, which means you can't perform mathematical operations on them. It's just a safety measure taken when dealing with textboxes.

The next few lines rotate the point. However, you can't directly change the x and y values with the equations we derived earlier. If you were to update the x-position of the point before you calculated the y-position, the identities wouldn't work. Therefore, two temporary variables are set to hold the rotated point's position, and then the x and y variables are updated.

```
// Calculate the rotated position of the point.
// Use sum identities for sine and cosine.
rotated_x = x * cos_angle - y * sin_angle;
rotated_y = y * cos_angle + x * sin_angle;
// update the position of the point
x = rotated_x;
y = rotated_y;
```

Once you've rotated the point's position, all you can do is render the point. Using the previously defined position of the origin, the code is the same as before:

```
// render point
point._x = origin_x + x;
point._y = origin_y - y;
```

Putting everything together, we have the actions for the button that will rotate a point (x, y) by the angle of rotation_angle around the origin:

```
on (release)
{
// find the sine and cosine of the rotation angle
sin_angle = Math.sin (rotation_angle * trans);
cos_angle = Math.cos (rotation_angle * trans);
// Calculate the rotated position of the point.
```

```
// Use sum identities for sine and cosine.
rotated_x = x * cos_angle - y * sin_angle;
rotated_y = y * cos_angle + x * sin_angle;
// update the position of the point
x = rotated_x;
y = rotated_y;
// render point
point._x = origin_x + x;
point._y = origin_y - y;
}
```

A variation of rotation around the z-axis. The next demo lets you use the Arrow keys to rotate a point continuously around the origin. The longer you hold down a key, the faster the point will spin in that direction. This file also uses what we learned about key presses earlier.

 Open z_axis_rotation2.swf from the CD-ROM.

Holding down the keys lets you speed up and slow down the point's rotation. Before you look at the code, think of how you might accomplish this. How would you extrapolate the rotation angle from the user's key presses and rotate the point?

 Open z_axis_rotation2.fla from the CD-ROM.

This file is similar to the first *z*-axis sample, as far as graphics go. For this file you can delete the button, the extra layer for the actions, and textbox; all the actions are placed in the movie's clip events.

The load clip event declares many variables. The constant that translates between angle units, the position of the origin, the initial position of the point, and the current rotation angle are all still declared. Also, the value that the rotation will increment by when a key is pressed down is initialized. Because we update *x* and *y* every time the point is rotated, you don't need to increment the rotation angle to keep the point moving. In other words, the rotation_angle quantity controls the angular speed at which the point goes around the origin. If you increment or decrement that value, you're only changing its speed.

```
onClipEvent (load)
{
// used for translating between angle units
trans = Math.PI / 180;
// position of the origin
origin_x = 275;
```

```
origin_y = 200;
// starting position of point
x = 150;
y = 0;
// increment the rotation will change by when a key is down
→ inc = .1;
// current rotation angle
rotation_angle = 0;
}
```

The enterFrame actions don't look much different than the actions that were in the button for the last file. Rather than jumping right into the rotation script, we must first increment the rotation angle. Because this is controlled by the user's keys, we resort to the script we used before. Once we've incremented the rotation angle, you find the sine and cosine of the angle, plug the numbers into the rotation equations, and render the point like before.

```
onClipEvent (enterFrame)
{
// increment rotation angle according to which key is down
rotation_angle += Key.isDown (Key.LEFT) * inc - Key.isDown
→ (Key.RIGHT) * inc;
// find the sine and cosine of the rotation angle
sin_angle = Math.sin (rotation_angle * trans);
cos_angle = Math.cos (rotation_angle * trans);
// Calculate the rotated position of the point.
// Use sum identities for sine and cosine.
rotated_x = x * cos_angle - y * sin_angle;
rotated_y = y * cos_angle + x * sin_angle;
// update the position of the point
x = rotated_x;
y = rotated_y;
// render the point
this._x = origin_x + x;
this._y = origin_y - y;
}
```

Rotation Around the Other Axes

The other axes don't need to be covered in as much depth as the z-axis because they're almost identical. Once the equations are derived for all three axes, you'll see that they differ only by a few values.

We concluded earlier that a rotation around the *x*-axis doesn't affect the *x*-position of a point. Therefore, to imagine a point rotating around the *x*-axis, we turn our view to the side so that the *x*-axis is pointing at us and the other axes are vertical and horizontal. Then, we have a point somewhere in the *yz*-plane that makes up an angle of *a* with the *x*-axis and we wish to rotate it to a new position by an angle of *b*. This is the same situation we came across before, except only the *y*- and *z*-positions are affected (**Figure 2.33**).

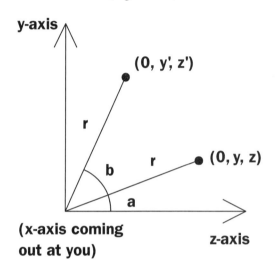

Figure 2.33 *A point rotated around the x-axis.*

From the picture above, we can formulate our first set of equations, much like we did before. Again, note that the angle created by the rotated point and the x-axis is *a* plus *b* (**Figure 2.34**).

Figure 2.34 *Position of the original and rotated point.*

$x = 0$
$y = r \sin a$
$z = r \cos a$

$x' = 0$
$y' = r \sin (a + b)$
$z' = r \cos (a + b)$

We'll skip most of the work here. By substituting in the sum identities again and simplifying, you get these steps (**Figure 2.35**):

$$x = r \cos a$$
$$y = r \sin a$$
$$z = 0$$

$$x' = 0$$
$$y' = r \sin (a + b) = r \sin a \cos b + r \cos a \sin b$$
$$z' = r \cos (a + b) = r \cos a \cos b - r \sin a \sin b$$

$$\Downarrow$$

$$y' = y \cos b - z \sin b$$
$$z' = z \cos b + y \sin b$$

Figure 2.35 *Equations used to rotate a point around the x-axis.*

You've now derived the equations for rotating a point around the *x*-axis. If you know the current position of a point (x, y, z) and you want to rotate it around the *z*-axis by *b* degrees, simply use this last set of equations. Once again, the *r* and *a* terms dropped out because they aren't necessary to rotate a point.

The derivations of the equations that rotate a point around the *y*-axis are almost entirely the same. Therefore, I've left out the geometric representations, and am showing only the algebraic work (**Figure 2.36**).

$$x = r \cos a$$
$$y = 0$$
$$z = r \sin a$$

$$\Downarrow$$

$$x' = r \cos (a + b)$$
$$y' = 0$$
$$z' = r \sin (a + b)$$

$$\Downarrow$$

$$x' = r \cos (a + b) = r \cos a \cos b - r \sin a \sin b$$
$$y' = 0$$
$$z' = r \sin (a + b) = r \sin a \cos b + r \cos a \sin b$$

$$\Downarrow$$

$$x' = x \cos b - z \sin a$$
$$z' = z \cos b + x \sin a$$

Figure 2.36 *Equations used to rotate a point around the y-axis.*

We've now derived all the equations for rotating a point around the three axes. In summary, here are all six equations (**Figure 2.37**).

Given Point: (x, y, z)
Point rotated around the x-axis: (x, y', z')
Point rotated around the y-axis: (x'', y', z'')
Point rotated around the z-axis: (x''', y''', z'')

Figure 2.37 A reference list of all the equations used to rotate a point around each of the three axes.

x-axis rotation

$y' = y \cos b - z \sin b$
$z' = z \cos b + y \sin b$

y-axis rotation

$x'' = x \cos b - z' \sin b$
$z'' = z' \cos b + x \sin b$

z-axis rotation

$x''' = x'' \cos b - y' \sin$
$y''' = y' \cos b + x'' \sin$

Although the apostrophes may be confusing, it's crucial that you understand what they mean. These equations demonstrate an important 3D concept: Use the newest position of a point when you want to rotate it. This means that if you want to rotate a point on the x- and y-axis, you would first rotate around the x-axis, and then use the rotated position in the equations to rotate around the y-axis.

The outline of a script that rotates many points around each axis by angles of a, b, and c might look something like this:

1. Find the sine and cosine of the rotation angles a, b, and c.

2. Use a loop to perform a rotation on and render each point.

   Translate the point on all three axes (if applicable).

3. Rotate the point by the x-axis.

4. Use the current position from the x-axis rotation and rotate the point by the y-axis.

5. Use the current position from the y-axis rotation and rotate the point by the z-axis.

6. Calculate the position of the point on the screen.

7. Set all the properties of the movie clip representing the point.

Optimizations

We now have all the information we need to create some spectacular effects in Flash. Making these effects run well in Flash, however, is equally important. Most sophisticated methods for reducing CPU calculations quickly become too burdensome in Flash for two reasons: Flash can't handle the optimization calculations, and there aren't enough objects in the environment to fully use the algorithms. We'll cover the few optimizations that are practical in Flash.

Hidden Objects

Our previous files adhered to a popular 3D optimization philosophy: *If you can't see it, don't render it.* When a point went behind the viewer, for instance, we didn't render it. This time, we'll remove a point if it goes off the viewing area.

An object is off the viewing area if its *x*- or *y*-position is greater than the Stage's width or height, and if its *x*- or *y*-position is less than 0. A few conditionals can test this problem and set the point's _visible property to either false or true, accordingly.

```
OnClipEvent (load)
{
// width and height of the stage
stage_width = 550;
stage_height = 400;
}
onClipEvent (enterFrame)
{
// check if clip has gone off the stage
if ((this._x > stage_width) || (this._x < 0))
{
 // clip is off the left or right side of the stage
 this._visible = false;
}
else if ((this._y > stage_height) || (this._y < 0))
{
 // clip is off the top or bottom of the stage
 this._visible = false;
}
else
{
```

```
   // clip is on the stage
   this._visible = true;
 }
}
```

Remember that you must do all the translations, rotations, and perspective calculations before you can check if the point is visible. Removing hidden objects may not save you some calculations, but it will minimize the number of objects that are simultaneously displayed on Flash's Stage.

Perform Fewer Calculations

This optimization applies to programming as a whole. To speed anything up, you must do the fewest calculations possible. This means using the Math object as little as possible, only doing actions that are absolutely necessary, and simplifying expressions to use fewer multiplies and divides.

The Math object. Although it's not incredibly slow, the Math object should only be called a few times as it can tax the user's CPU. Many people make the mistake of finding the sine and cosine of the rotation angles from within the loop that rotates all the points. Because the rotation angles shouldn't be changing from one point to the other, you need to find the sine and cosine loop only once.

Here's some code with comments that outlines this:

```
OnClipEvent (enterFrame)
{
// change rotation angles or translation increments
// calculate sine and cosine of rotation angles
for (var j = 0; j < num_points; j++)
{
// translate
// rotate
// calculate perspective
// check if on stage
// render
}
}
```

Some people create look-up tables for sine and cosine values so they don't have to use the Math object. While this used to be common practice in C++ and other computer languages, it's unnecessary with today's powerful personal computers.

Showcase 1: Rotating a Field of Points

My first showcase is similar to the demo we've been developing throughout the chapter. It creates a field of randomly placed points and lets you use buttons to control their rotation. The structure of the script and movie is entirely different, so let's start over with something new.

 Open demo_one1.swf from the CD-ROM.

The demo clearly displays the rotation angles around each axis and continuously rotates the points by those increments (**Figure 2.38**).

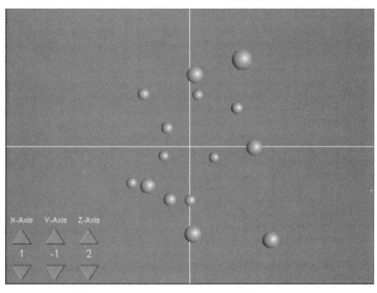

Figure 2.38 Rotation points around each axis through the use of buttons.

 Open demo_one1.fla from the CD-ROM.

The Layout

This file has seven main graphics. Six are buttons that control the increment and decrement of each of the three rotation angles. The last graphic is the movie clip that represents the point. Unlike before, most of the code isn't placed in the clip events of the point movie. Due to my experience in C++, I prefer to have as much of my code in one place as possible. Therefore, I created a movie clip named dummy to place all of the main actions.

Variable Scope

The code is mainly contained in the dummy's clip events, except for three variables: the rotation angles around each axis. These variables are kept on the _root of the movie so the buttons can easily change their values. The variables are accessed from the dummy movie clip to find the sine and cosine of the angles.

Getting Rid of an Unwanted Movie Clip

The movie clip named point is duplicated many times to create the field of points. We only want the duplicated clips to be visible, however, because the script that rotates the points won't affect the base movie clip. Therefore, I put the following actions in the load clip event of the point movie to make the base clip invisible and the duplicates visible:

```
OnClipEvent (load)
{
if (this._name == "point")
{
this._visible = false;
}
}
```

Initializing the Movie

In the first frame of the _root, the variables rotation_angle_x, rotation_angle_y, and rotation_angle_z have been initialized to represent the rotation angles around each axis. These values are changed when one of the six buttons are pressed and are accessed from the dummy movie clip. Because no rotation should be taking place initially, they are set to 0.

I placed the rest of the actions in the dummy movie clip. Keeping track of the ordered triplet wasn't a problem in our previous files because all of the point's information was contained in itself. This time we're controlling everything from an external script, which means we have to keep track of many points. We could simply create many variables named x1, x2, y1, y2 and so on for every point's ordered triplet, but that's not efficient as far as memory usage goes. Instead, I use an array of objects. Each element in the array represents a point and each member variable of the object represents a value of the ordered triplet.

Therefore, in the load clip event of the dummy movie, we create an array, loop through it, and create an object in each element. Then we set the initial ordered triplet for the point. In that same loop, the point movie clips are also duplicated.

```
onClipEvent (load)
{
// number of points to be placed out randomly
num_points = 15;
// array which will hold the position of the points
point_position = new Array (num_points);
// duplicate points and set initial position randomly
for (var j = 0; j < num_points; j++)
{
// duplicate new movie clip
  _parent.point.duplicateMovieClip ("point" + j, j);
// create object for x-, y-, and z-position of point
point_position[j] = new Object ();
// set point's initial position randomly
point_position[j].x = Math.random () * 200 - 100;
point_position[j].y = Math.random () * 200 - 100;
point_position[j].z = Math.random () * 200 - 100;
}
```

The rest of the actions in the load clip event declare all the variables we've used before: the position of the origin, the size of the point, the perspective distance, and a value for translating between angle units.

```
// position of origin
origin_x = 275;
origin_y = 200;
// used for perspective - distance from the viewer to
→ the screen
D = 300;
// size of movie clip at the origin
regular_size = this._width;
// used to translate between angle units
trans = Math.PI / 180;
}
```

Button Actions

The button actions are simple. When a button pointing upwards is pressed, the rotation value for that button is increased; when a button pointing downwards is pressed, the rotation value is decreased. It's up to you to decide by how much the rotation angles are incremented; I used the increment and decrement operators ++ and --, which will change the values by 1.

Here are the actions that are executed when the Up arrow for the *x*-axis rotation is pressed:

```
on (release)
{
// increase the x-axis rotation angle by one
rotation_angle_x++;
}
```

Main

The last set of actions in the movie clip is in the dummy's clip events. This takes care of all the rotations and renderings. Although there's nothing new in the 50 or so lines, there are a couple of pitfalls to watch out for. You'll also see one optimization technique used in this script.

 Although it may seem like common sense, too many people make the mistake of rotating around every axis whether they need to or not. On many occasions, you only need to rotate around one or two axis. Rotating on more axes than you need to only adds unnecessary calculations to your script.

Because the file doesn't deal with any translations, we'll skip right to rotational movement. At the very beginning, the sine and cosine of the rotation angles are defined. Make sure to translate the angle units from degrees to radians.

```
onClipEvent (enterFrame)
{
// calculate the sine and cosine of the rotation angles
sin_a = Math.sin (_parent.rotation_angle_x * trans);
cos_a = Math.cos (_parent.rotation_angle_x * trans);
sin_b = Math.sin (_parent.rotation_angle_y * trans);
cos_b = Math.cos (_parent.rotation_angle_y * trans);
sin_c = Math.sin (_parent.rotation_angle_z * trans);
cos_c = Math.cos (_parent.rotation_angle_z * trans);
```

Now you must loop through every element of the `point_position` array and rotate the ordered triplet around each axis. I prefer to use a `for` loop because the number of elements in the array is not likely to change and because you need integers to access the elements.

```
// loop through all the points and rotate and render
for (var j = 0; j < num_points; j++)
{
// actions
}
```

The first things to be carried out in the `for` loop are the rotations. Remember that the rotation around the *x*-axis is done first, the *y*-axis second, and the *z*-axis last. Also, use the most current position of the point to do your next rotation and don't update the `point_position` array until you've performed all rotations. It's OK to refer back to the equation reference picture from earlier—it's not easy to memorize six equations!

```
// rotate around the x-axis
rx1 = point_position[j].x;
ry1 = point_position[j].y * cos_a - point_position[j].z
 → * sin_a;
rz1 = point_position[j].z * cos_a + point_position[j].y
V* sin_a; // rotate around the y-axis
rx2 = rx1 * cos_b - rz1 * sin_b;
ry2 = ry1;
rz2 = rz1 * cos_b + rx1 * sin_b;
// rotate around the z-axis
rx3 = rx2 * cos_c - ry2 * sin_c;
ry3 = ry2 * cos_c + rx2 * sin_c;
rz3 = rz2;
// update array that holds the position of the points
point_position[j].x = rx3;
point_position[j].y = ry3;
point_position[j].z = rz3;
```

The script has so far taken every point's ordered triplet and rotated it around the *x*-, *y*-, and *z*-axes. When all 3D movement is done, you're only left with rendering the point. The perspective ratio is calculated first and the position of the point on a 2D screen is calculated next.

```
// calculate the perspective ratio
perspective_ratio = D / (D + rz3);
// calculate the position of point on computer screen
perspective_x = rx3 * perspective_ratio;
perspective_y = ry3 * perspective_ratio;
```

You might wonder what you're supposed to do after all these calculations. The perspective ratio is key to finding the position of the point on the Stage and sizing it appropriately. To calculate the perspective ratio, you need to know the point's ordered triplet. To find the most current ordered triplet, you must translate and rotate it by various values. So, once you get it down to the perspective ratio and the ordered pair, you simply set a few properties.

```
// update position of movie clip on stage
_parent["point" + j]._x = origin_x + perspective_x;
_parent["point" + j]._y = origin_y - perspective_y;
// update size of movie clip
_parent["point" + j]._xscale = _parent["point" + j]._yscale
→ = regular_size * perspective_ratio;
// set the depth of the clip based on its z-position
    _parent["point" + j].swapDepths (-rz3);
```

A Simple Variation

Instead of controlling the rotations with buttons, this time we use certain keys. Pressing the Up or Down arrow keys changes the *x*-axis rotation, pressing the Left or Right arrow keys changes the *y*-axis rotation, and pressing the Control key or the 0 key on the number pad changes the *z*-axis rotation.

 Open demo_one2.fla from the CD-ROM.

We use the same technique from earlier, but we must slightly change our script from demo_one1.fla. First, take out the buttons and the actions on the first frame of the _root. The variables for the rotation angles will be kept in the dummy movie clip from now on. Therefore, the following lines need to be placed in the load clip event of the dummy movie:

```
// rotation angles of each axis
rotation_angle_x = 0;
rotation_angle_y = 0;
rotation_angle_z = 0;
```

We also need to initialize a variable in the load clip event to determine how much the rotation angles should increment or decrement by when a key is pressed. Play around with different values to find what you like best.

```
// increment the rotation angles will change when a key
→ is down
rotation_inc = .5;
```

Another variable that's initialized might not make sense at first. In the Key object there are many variables set. The variables have the names of various keys and hold numerical values. For instance, Key.LEFT has a numerical value of 37. The values are used to check if certain keys are being held down with the isDown() method. The Key object has predefined variables for every key we could use in this sample except for number pad 0. You'd have to pass the numerical value of 96 to the isDown() method. However, if you're following good programming practice, you should be using as few numerical values in your code as possible. Therefore, I set a member variable in the Key object for number pad 0 and simply pass that variable to the method.

```
// key code value for the number pad zero
Key.NUMPAD_0 = 96;
```

That's all of the extra variables this variation uses. In the enterFrame clip event we need to add the actions that increment or decrement the rotation angles, depending on which key is pressed. This is done before the sine and cosine of the angles are calculated because we want only the newest angles when calculating those ratios.

```
// increment rotation values according to which keys
→ are pressed
rotation_angle_x += Key.isDown (Key.UP) * rotation_inc -
→ Key.isDown (Key.DOWN) * rotation_inc;
rotation_angle_y += Key.isDown (Key.RIGHT) * rotation_inc -
→ Key.isDown (Key.LEFT) * rotation_inc;
rotation_angle_z += Key.isDown (Key.CONTROL) * rotation_inc
→ - Key.isDown (Key.NUMPAD_0) * rotation_inc;
```

The last thing to be changed is when using the Math object. Before, we had to access the rotation angles from the _root, which means we had to use a target path. This time, the rotation angles are in the same timeline so we can drop the _parent path.

```
// calculate the sine and cosine of the rotation angles
sin_a = Math.sin (rotation_angle_x * trans);
cos_a = Math.cos (rotation_angle_x * trans);
sin_b = Math.sin (rotation_angle_y * trans);
cos_b = Math.cos (rotation_angle_y * trans);
sin_c = Math.sin (rotation_angle_z * trans);
cos_c = Math.cos (rotation_angle_z * trans);
```

That's it for the variation. You can control the rotation of the points around each axis with six keys.

Showcase 2: 3D World

The effects in this showcase may seem complex, but they're easy to create. We'll use all of the 3D knowledge we've gained so far, along with some extra information, to create a 3D world in Flash.

 Open demo_two1.swf from the CD-ROM.

Use the arrow keys to explore the world (**Figure 2.39**). Take a second to ponder how you might achieve this effect without looking on. What kind of rotation is taking place? What kinds of translations are taking place?

Figure 2.39
A 3D world created in Flash.

 Open demo_two1.fla from the CD-ROM.

3D World in Flash

A 3D world in Flash must be simple in all aspects. Its objects should be static and look the same from all perspectives. It's possible to have an object pre-rendered from different angles so that, depending on your location in the world, the image could be set to a different frame. This is rarely worth doing, however, as it will great increase your file size and slow performance.

Due to these limitations, creating a 3D world in Flash requires using only a few techniques that we've learned. Because you want the world to encapsulate you from the sides, the only rotation possible in the xz-plane is around the y-axis. Also, the only axes you can move through are the x- and z-axes. Moving along the y-axis would mean to go up above the world, which would not look right because the objects are static.

In this showcase, a graphic of one tree is placed multiple times at random throughout the world. The instance name of the movie clip with the tree inside is objects. It's kind of hard to decide how to represent this tree in 3D space, as it's composed of an infinite number of points. To keep a sense of continuity in our world, we must choose only one point to represent the tree. The most defining point of the tree and the world is where the two meet. Therefore, the bottom of the tree is placed at the center of the movie clip and the ordered triplet will be the position of the bottom of the tree.

3D World Trickery

We use two simple translations to create the illusion of objects surrounding us. When we derived the equations for finding the position of a 3D point on a 2D surface, we assumed that the viewer was sitting at a distance (d) away from the screen. In an immersive environment, however, there's no distance between the viewer and computer screen. So, for our first translation, we'll translate every point in the world toward the viewer by an increment of d. Because this translation is for rendering purposes only, it shouldn't affect the points' actual positions.

The second translation gives the viewer height in the 3D world. Because the tree's position is determined by the position of its bottom, the viewer would see the world from ground level. To fix this, you translate all the points down the y-axis by a certain amount to make the trees' bottoms seem slightly below the viewer. This translation is also temporary and shouldn't affect the points' actual positions. Play around with height's value until you find what you like.

3D World Idiosyncrasies

A few things in the file can cause havoc in the overall production. The first is the background image. I drew a simple green ground that meets the sky in the middle of the Stage. The ground and sky don't meet in the middle by chance; the horizon is the vanishing point for all the objects in the world. This means that as the objects move farther away, they move closer to the horizon. The vanishing point is chosen when you pick a value for the *y*-coordinate of the origin. In general, make the horizon's *y*-position the same as the origin's.

This file also uses the technique we used last time by placing all the code in a dummy movie clip that does all the main calculations. All variables are kept in this movie clip and all 3D calculations and rendering actions are done in its clip events.

All the trees placed in the world will be duplicated from a main tree. We place actions in clip events to remove this original tree, as it's the only one that doesn't need to be rendered. The actions are similar to the ones we used before.

```
OnClipEvent (load)
{
if (this._name == "objects")
{
this._visible = false;
}
}
```

Initializing the 3D World

The variables, objects, duplicate movie clips, and initial conditions are set in the load clip event of the dummy movie clip. All of the values initialized are what we've already been using, with a few exceptions.

Our first task is to duplicate the trees and place them randomly. Each tree is also given a random size to create a more natural-looking forest. First, we initialize a variable for the number of objects to be duplicated and the array that will hold the position of each object:

```
onClipEvent (load)
{
// number of objects to create num_objects = 20;
// array which will hold the position of the objects
object_position = new Array (num_objects);
```

The script loops through and duplicates the trees. An object is created for each element in the `object_position` array. The object will have a variable for the *x*-, *y*-, and *z*-position of the point as well as a value that will hold the size of the regular size tree.

```
// duplicate objects and initialize random properties
for (var j = 0; j < num_objects; j++)
{
// duplicate object
_parent.objects.duplicateMovieClip ("objects" + j, j);
// create object for ordered triplet and size of object
object_position[j] = new Object ();
// set object's initial position randomly
object_position[j].x = Math.random () * 1500 - 750;
object_position[j].y = 0;
object_position[j].z = Math.random () * 1500 - 750;
// size of movie clip at the origin - set randomly
object_position[j].regular_size = Math.random () * 50 + 50;
}
```

The rest of the variables set are the constants of the world, the current rotation angle, and translation increment. Like all other 3D demos, you need values for the position of the origin, the distance from the viewer to the computer screen for perspective, and a constant for translating between angle units.

```
// position of origin
origin_x = 275;
origin_y = 200;
// used for perspective - distance from the viewer to
→ the screen
D = 500;
// used to translate between angle units
trans = Math.PI / 180;
```

A new value set is for the viewer's height. Play around with this value to see what you like best. You might want to let the viewer control this value. For instance, when the viewer holds down the space bar the value could be set to something smaller, which would create the effect of crouching down in the world.

```
// height of player walking around in world
player_height = 30;
```

The next three values help handle the translation movement. The first value is the increment at which the viewer moves when a key is pressed. Note that it's not the value that the viewer *is* moving at along the axes, but rather what the viewer *will* move at when a key is down. The other two values are the rates at which the viewer is currently moving along the *x*- and *z*-axes. These values are added to the viewer's *x*- and *z*-positions every frame.

```
// increment to move along the x- and z-axes when a key
→ is pressed
translation_inc = 10;
// current translation across the x- and z-axes
translation_x = 0;
translation_z = 0;
```

Basically, the same thing is done for the rotational movement as for the translations. A value is set for the rate at which the viewer will turn when a key is down. The second, however, is the increment at which the viewer is currently turning around the *y*-axis.

```
// increment to rotate around the y-axis when a key
→ is pressed
rotation_inc = 2;
// current rotation angle around the y-axis
rotation_angle_y = 0;
```

Finally, another value is set in the Key object for number pad zero. The key layout of the demo will be covered shortly.

```
// key code value for the number pad zero
Key.NUMPAD_0 = 96;
}
```

Key Layout

The key layout of the demo is important because it lets viewers easily navigate the world. We must let them control their turns around the *y*-axis, as well as their movement back and forth along the *z*-axis, and side to side along the *x*-axis. Choosing keys to control the *y*-axis rotation and *z*-axis translation movement is pretty straightforward: The Arrow keys make the most sense. Side-to-side movement is less obvious: I chose the Control and the number pad 0 keys.

Main

The rest of the actions in the demo are carried out in the dummy's clip events. These final 70 to 80 lines use every technique we've talked about so far, including the optimizations.

Before we can translate, rotate, or render any points, we must change the current translation and rotation increments. Once again, we'll use the technique from before.

```
onClipEvent (enterFrame)
{
// change the x- and z-axis translation of the objects
→ according to which keys are pressed
translation_x = Key.isDown (Key.CONTROL) * translation_inc -
→ Key.isDown (Key.NUMPAD_0) * translation_inc;
translation_z = Key.isDown (Key.DOWN) * translation_inc -
→ Key.isDown (Key.UP) * translation_inc;
// change the y-axis rotation angle according to which keys
→ are pressed
rotation_angle_y = Key.isDown (Key.RIGHT) * rotation_inc -
→ Key.isDown (Key.LEFT) * rotation_inc;
```

Once the current rotation angle is known you must find its sine and cosine for the rotation equations. Remember that these values need to be calculated only once before the rotation equations are used. Don't take the sine and cosine of the rotation angle in the for loop that rotates and renders all the points.

```
// sine and cosine of rotation angle
sin_y = Math.sin (rotation_angle_y * trans);
cos_y = Math.cos (rotation_angle_y * trans);
```

After the script calculates all the increments at which the world will be translated and rotated, it loops through every point and perform these transformations. I used a for loop again.

```
for (var j = 0; j < num_objects; j++)
{
// other actions
}
```

Inside the for loop is the meatiest part of the entire script. Before we can start rendering or checking if a point is off the Stage, we must translate and rotate the point. First, the object's position is translated and the translated values are placed in temporary variables; the object_position array is still not changed. Then, the translated point is rotated around the *y*-axis. Once the point has been translated and rotated, we update the values in the object_position array.

```
// translate the object across the x- and z-axes
tx = object_position[j].x + translation_x;
ty = object_position[j].y;
tz = object_position[j].z + translation_z;
// rotate the translated point around the y-axis
rx = tx * cos_y - tz * sin_y;
ry = ty;
rz = tz * cos_y + tx * sin_y;
// update object position array
object_position[j].x = rx;
object_position[j].y = ry;
object_position[j].z = rz;
```

In the earlier files, this was as far as we had to go to render a point. A 3D world, however, must completely surround the viewer. This calls for the two extra translations we discussed earlier. The translations affect only the *ry* and *rz* variables. The object_position should not be changed because you only want to temporarily translate the points for rendering purposes.

```
// translations used for making the world surround the
→ viewer
// and rendering — doesn't affect the point's actual
→ position.
// shift the rotated and translated point down the y-axis
→ to give user height
ry -= player_height;
// shift the rotated and translated point down the z-axis
→ to make first person perspective
rz -= D;
```

The points are now in their final positions; the script has performed all of the transformations needed. All we need to do now is render everything.

When rendering, we want to take every shortcut possible. The first shortcut is one we've used before: Check if an object is behind the view. If the most current value of the z-position of the point is less than the negative value of the perspective distance, then you don't need to render the point.

```
// check if object has gone behind viewer
if (rz < -D)
{
// object is behind viewer, make invisible
_parent["objects" + j]._visible = false;
}
else
{
// other actions
}
```

Even if the object is in front of the viewer, you should still check if it is on the Stage. If the object is placed far off screen, you still don't want the code to render it on the Stage. Before we can determine if the object is off the Stage, however, we must first calculate the values used in rendering, such as the point's position on the Stage and the size of the point with perspective. Remember that these actions are performed in the else of the conditional and are only executed when the object is in front of the viewer.

```
// object is not behind viewer but still may be off
→ the screen,
// so don't make visible yet
// calculate perspective ratio
perspective_ratio = D / (D + rz);
// calculate the position of point on computer screen
perspective_x = origin_x + rx * perspective_ratio;
perspective_y = origin_y - ry * perspective_ratio;
// perspective scale of object
perspective_scale = object_position[j].regular_size *
→ perspective_ratio;
```

Once the perspective values have all been calculated, you can check if the object is on the Stage or not. An object is off the left side of the Stage if its right-most point is less than 0; an object is off the right side of the Stage if its left-most point is greater than the Stage width. By taking the object's *x*-position, adding or subtracting the size of the object, and checking if it has gone out of the bounds, you can determine whether the object is still on the Stage.

```
// check if object is off the side of the screen
if (((perspective_x + perspective_scale) < 0) ||
 ⇥ ((perspective_x - perspective_scale) > origin_x*2)))
{
// object is off the screen, make invisible
_parent["objects" + j]._visible = false;
}
else
{
// other actions
}
```

All the rendering actions go in the actions of the else of this conditional. First, the object's visibility should be set to true because it's in front of the viewer and on the Stage. After that, all the set properties are the same as before.

```
// the object is on the screen and in front of the view,
 ⇥ make visible
_parent["objects" + j]._visible = true;
// update position of movie clip on stage
_parent["objects" + j]._x = perspective_x;
_parent["objects" + j]._y = perspective_y;
// update size of movie clip
_parent["objects" + j]._xscale = _parent["objects" +
 ⇥ j]._yscale = perspective_scale;
// set the depth of the clip based on its z-position
_parent["objects" + j].swapDepths (-rz);
```

Close all the curvy braces to end your script, and you're done: You've just created a 3D Flash world. The number of lines for the entire script did not go above 150 and the effect is mesmerizing.

Showcase 3: 3D Menu System

The final showcase is a 3D-menu system with buttons that open new browser windows via URLs that you define in the code. This project works equally well for a gallery showcase.

 Open demo_three1.swf from the CD-ROM.

This file randomly places a few menu items in 3D space and lets you navigate through them. We won't add any rotation to the environment because we can't control what the menu items look like at different angles (**Figure 2.40**).

Figure 2.40 Navigable menu items placed randomly in space.

 Open demo_three1.fla from the CD-ROM.

Starting the Demo

This demo has very few components to it and no tricks in its mechanics. You'll probably want to create a background to cover the entire Stage. If you want to create the illusion of a horizon, be sure to make the Stage's *y*-position the same as the *y*-position of the origin. You should also create a movie clip (called menu_item) for the menu item names. I chose to create a long textbox (to accommodate long names) named field. I also created an invisible button behind it so that an URL is brought up when the item is clicked. A dummy movie clip handles the main actions.

Actions

There are only three places to look for code: the button inside the menu_item movie clip, the clip events of the menu_item movie clip, and the clip events of the dummy movie clip. The most important scripting is in the latter clip; only a few lines are in the other two.

Because the menu_item movie clip will be duplicated many times, I put actions in it to remove the clip if it's not a duplicated clip. This prevents you from having extra movie clips on the Stage.

```
onClipEvent (load)
{
// remove base menu item
if (this._name == "menu_item")
{
this._visible = false;
}
}
```

The main actions in the dummy clip events are slightly different from what we've been working with so far. First, we initialize a variable for the number of menu items we expect to have. For each menu item we must keep track of information like its name, the URL it's linked to, and its ordered triplet. To organize this information, we create an array with an object in each of its elements. The array elements will hold the menu items' information and the object will hold the miscellaneous pieces of information.

```
onClipEvent (load)
{
// number of menu items
num_menu_items = 9;
// array that will hold the information for each menu item
→ menu_item_info = new Array (num_menu_items);
// create an object in each element of the information
→ array for (var j = 0; j < num_menu_items; j++)
{
menu_item_info[j] = new Object ();
}
```

Next, we initialize the names and URLs of all the menu items. You can choose to enter them directly into Flash, or load them from an external text file. However you do it, make sure the information is put into the menu_item_info array so it can be used in the rest of the script. I picked 10 random names and URLs.

```
// names of menu items
menu_item_info[0].name = "Home";
menu_item_info[1].name = "News";
menu_item_info[2].name = "Portfolio";
menu_item_info[3].name = "Locations";
menu_item_info[4].name = "Staff";
menu_item_info[5].name = "History";
menu_item_info[6].name = "Awards";
menu_item_info[7].name = "Business";
menu_item_info[8].name = "About";
menu_item_info[9].name = "Contact";
// urls to be executed when a button is pressed
menu_item_info[0].url = "http://www.home.com";
menu_item_info[1].url = "http://www.news.com";
menu_item_info[2].url = "http://www.portfolio.com";
menu_item_info[3].url = "http://www.locations.com";
menu_item_info[4].url = "http://www.staff.com";
menu_item_info[5].url = "http://www.history.com";
menu_item_info[6].url = "http://www.awards.com";
menu_item_info[7].url = "http://www.business.com";
menu_item_info[8].url = "http://www.about.com";
menu_item_info[9].url = "http://www.contact.com";
```

Once all the information is gathered, you must duplicate the menu items and set the initial conditions. Each item's name and URL values are sent to the movie clip so they can be displayed and used with the button's actions.

The items' ordered triplets are initialized in a certain way. The effect we're going for is to have items spread out in front of the viewer. This means the items should be placed along the x- and z-axes only. I added a small amount of random y-position, however, to space things out better.

```
// duplicate menu items and set out randomly
for (var j = 0; j < num_menu_items; j++)
{
// duplicate menu item
_parent.menu_item.duplicateMovieClip ("menu_item" + j, j);
// set text field inside movie clip for menu item name
→ parent["menu_item" + j].field = menu_item_info[j].name;
```

```
// pass url to movie clip for when the button is pressed
→ parent["menu_item" + j].url = menu_item_info[j].url;
// place randomly on the x- and z-axis
menu_item_info[j].x = Math.random () * 1000 - 500;
menu_item_info[j].y = Math.random () * 100 - 50;
menu_item_info[j].z = Math.random () * 500;
}
```

The only variables left to be initialized are the constants and values that change the position of the items. A variable for the size of the menu item at the origin has also been set. You most likely want the size of all the menu items to be the same at the origin, so you don't have to keep track of that value in the menu_item_info array.

```
// position of the origin
origin_x = 275;
origin_y = 200;
// used for perspective - distance from the viewer to
→ the screen
D = 300;
// used to translate between angle units
trans = Math.PI / 180;
// increment to move along the x- and z-axes when a key
→ is pressed
translation_inc = 10;
// current translation across the x- and z-axes
translation_x = 0;
translation_z = 0;
// size of menu items
menu_item_size = 200;
}
```

The rest of the actions in the dummy movie clip are in the enterFrame clip event. These actions take care of the translations and rendering. There are no rotations in this showcase, so there's no need to keep track of rotation angles and the sine and cosine of the angles.

First, we change the current translation increment along the x- and z-axes, depending on which keys are pressed. (You could also let viewers move along the y-axis if you don't think that would be too cumbersome.)

```
onClipEvent (enterFrame)
{
// change the x- and z-axis translation of the items
→ according to which keys are pressed
translation_x = Key.isDown (Key.LEFT) * translation_inc -
→ Key.isDown (Key.RIGHT) * translation_inc;
translation_z = Key.isDown (Key.DOWN) * translation_inc -
→ Key.isDown (Key.UP) * translation_inc;
```

When all the information is calculated for moving the points, the script will loop through every point and translate and render it. The translated points' positions are first put into two temporary variables, tx and tz, and then the menu_item_info array is updated. Putting the translated values into two new variables helps shorten the rest of the code because you don't need to type "menu_item_info" every time; using temporary variables also keeps you from having to index the array many times.

```
// loop through all the points and translate and render them
for (var j = 0; j < num_menu_items; j++)
{
// translate the object across the x- and z-axes
tx = menu_item_info[j].x + translation_x;
tz = menu_item_info[j].z + translation_z;
// update the array with all the item's information
menu_item_info[j].x = tx;
menu_item_info[j].z = tz;
```

Once the point has been translated, you do the first visibility check. When the point goes behind the viewer, there's no need to render it and calculate its position on the Stage. If it's in front of the viewer, you still have one more check left to do depending on whether or not the point is on the Stage.

```
// check if menu item has gone behind the viewer
if (tz < -D)
{
// item is behind viewer, make invisible
_parent["menu_item" + j]._visible = false;
}
else
{
// other actions
}
```

Inside the `else` of the conditional, the script will calculate the point's perspective position and size. Once you have this information, you can check if the point is still on Flash's Stage. Because the *y*-position of the items' will never change, we use the value in the `menu_item_info` array to calculate the perspective corrected *y*-position.

```
// object is not behind viewer but still may be off
➝ the screen,
// so don't make visible yet
// calculate perspective ratio
perspective_ratio = D / (D + tz);
// calculate the position of point on computer screen
perspective_x = origin_x + tx * perspective_ratio;
perspective_y = origin_y - menu_item_info[j].y *
➝ perspective_ratio;
// perspective scale of object
perspective_scale = menu_item_size * perspective_ratio;
```

We use the same method as before to determine if the point is on Flash's Stage. The right-most point of the object is used to determine if it has gone off the left side of the Stage, and the left-most point is used to determine if the object has gone off the right side.

```
// check if object is off the side of the screen
if (((perspective_x + perspective_scale) < 0) ||
➝ ((perspective_x - perspective_scale) > origin_x*2)))
{
// object is off the screen, make invisible
_parent["menu_item" + j]._visible = false;
}
else
{
// other actions
}
```

If the script has gotten this far, it means the object is somewhere in front of the viewer. If the object is still on the Stage then you can set its visibility to true and carry on with setting its properties to render it.

```
// the object is on the screen and in front of the view,
➝ make visible
_parent["menu_item" + j]._visible = true;
// update position of movie clip on stage
```

```
_parent["menu_item" + j]._x = perspective_x;
_parent["menu_item" + j]._y = perspective_y;
// update size of movie clip
_parent["menu_item" + j]._xscale = _parent["menu_item" +
→ j]._yscale = perspective_scale;
// set the depth of the clip based on its z-position
_parent["menu_item" + j].swapDepths (-tz);
```

After you close a few curvy braces, you can test your demo.

A Variation

There are plenty of ways to add even more interactivity to your menu system or gallery showcase. In this variation, we'll let viewers use their mouse to navigate the menu items.

 Open demo_three2.swf from the CD-ROM.

Moving the mouse up and down the Stage lets viewers to go in and out of the world; moving the mouse to the sides lets them slide along the world (**Figure 2.41**).

Figure 2.41 Try moving the authors' names with your pointer.

 Open demo_three2.fla from the CD-ROM.

The engine we've written so far is easy to adapt to this small variation. In fact, we only need to change the few lines that calculate the translation increments, which were previously created from the key presses. This time, the increments will be calculated for the mouse position.

It's key that your navigation controls are intuitive. I chose to have the world slide along the x-axis in the opposite direction of the pointer. So, when the pointer is on the left side of the origin, the translation increment should be negative so the items move to the left. When on the right, the increment should be positive so the items move to the right. These simple statements are coded like this:

```
translation_x = origin_x - _parent._xmouse;
```

If the pointer is above the origin, then the translation increment for the z-axis should be negative so that the items slide toward the viewer. The items should slide away from the viewer when the pointer is below the origin, so the translation increment should be negative. This is expressed with the following line:

```
translation_y = _parent._ymouse - origin_y;
```

When you replace the previous method with these lines, you'll notice that the items move too fast. The lines calculate large numbers because the Stage is measured in pixels. To make the world move more slowly, divide the difference of the pointer and origin position by a certain number. The number depends on what kind of control you want to give the viewer. Experiment until you find something you like. Also, to keep from having too many numerical values in our code, I first set a variable in the load clip event to regulate the translation increments.

```
// used to regulate the translation increments based on the
→ mouse position
trans_regulate = 20;
```

With this variable defined, you can replace the two lines that calculated the translation increments with these two lines.

```
// change the x- and z-axis translation of the items based
→ on mouse position
translation_x = (origin_x - _parent._xmouse) /
→ trans_regulate;
translation_z = (_parent._ymouse - origin_y) /
→ trans_regulate;
```

That's it!

Open demo_three3.swf from the CD-ROM.

Here's another variation—one of the multitude of options left to explore. This one lines up all the items in a row down the *z*-axis and lets the viewer travel through them. The Up and Down keys control the *z*-axis movement and the pointer controls the slight movements along the *x*- and *y*-axes (**Figure 2.42**).

Figure 2.42 *You can create a multitude of variations on a simple theme.*

More Examples

 I've included a few more examples of 3D in Flash on the CD-ROM. One demo is a rotating 3D menu with a sample site layout; another is a terrain generator with a ball rolling around on the terrain. I hope you enjoy exploring them. You'll find these files in the Extra Examples sub-folder in the chapter 2 folder.

Closing Thoughts

Congratulations: You're now in a position to create new and awe-inspiring effects. No doubt you'll have 3D questions or issues that you'd like to discuss with others in the Flash community. A good place to start is Were-Here (www.were-here.com). You can interact with some of the best Flash demo creators around at Were-Here's math forum; members have been known to discuss just about every aspect of 3D.

Rendered 3D

The second half of this chapter will take you on a tour of the Rendered 3D world. I hope this tour gives you a glimpse of the many possibilities that 3D and Flash provide, and I hope it offers you some insight and inspiration for your own future projects.

Third-Party 3D Software

Although there are many 3D applications on the market, two programs are particularly well suited for preparing 3D objects for use in Flash: Swift 3D from Electric Rain (www.swift3d.com) and Vecta3D from Idea Works (www.vecta3d.com). These two inexpensive programs are a boon for Flash developers. They let you modify and animate 3D objects, import files from more full-featured (and more expensive) 3D programs like 3ds max (formerly known as 3D Studio Max) or LightWave 3D, and import vector shapes from illustration applications like Macromedia FreeHand. More importantly, they're the only two applications I know of that can export SWF files. Both programs export SWFs as a series of vector images, which can be brought into Flash in individual keyframes (much as you see in cel animation).

Both Swift 3D and Vecta3D come in standalone versions for Windows and Mac. Swift 3D also ships as a plug-in for 3ds max (Windows) and LightWave 3D (Mac and Windows); Vecta3D comes as a Windows-only plug-in for 3ds max.

Aside from this, the similarities between the two programs are few. Each has a different workflow.

Swift 3D

Swift 3D employs a familiar 3D interface (**Figure 2.43**).

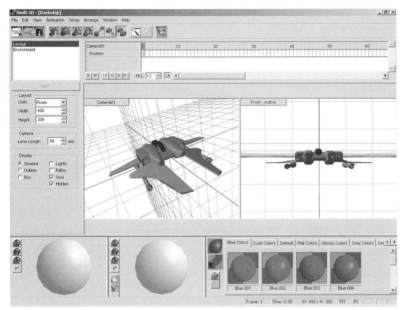

Figure 2.43 The
Swift 3D interface.

Swift 3D lets you create animations in three ways. You can import a 3D
mesh made with 3D Studio Max (.3DS); import vector shapes from programs such as FreeHand (.EPS) and convert them to 3D objects via Swift
3D's editing tools; and create 3D objects (including primitives such as
spheres, cones, and toruses, as well as text) from scratch.

The program's easy-to-use interface offers controls for specifying colors,
bevel types, depth, rotation, and position. Swift 3D comes with predefined
color schemes and animation sequences that you can apply via drag and
drop. It also offers an interesting rotating camera feature that lets you
animate the camera instead of the object. (A good tutorial for this feature
is at www.erain.com/tutorial.asp.)

Vecta3D

The Vecta3D interface is quite different from Swift 3D's (**Figure 2.44**).

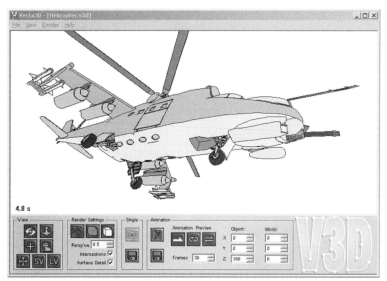

Figure 2.44 *The Vecta3D interface.*

Vecta3D doesn't let you create 3D objects from scratch and doesn't offer preinstalled animation schemes, so it requires a different workflow. The program displays a 3D object as a group of dots. To see the object with fills, you must render it.

Showcase 1: Spaceship

My first showcase is an animation of a spaceship that dives from the sky, levels out, fires a few shots, and then banks left and disappears from the screen. This animation is a trailer to a project of mine called the Stargate Interface.

 To see the animation, open Spaceship_final.swf from the CD-ROM (**Figure 2.45**). You can also see the completed project at www.sdflash.net/trailer.htm.

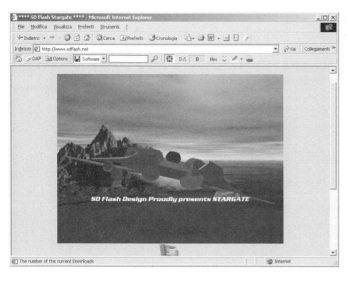

Figure 2.45 The Stargate Interface.

The animation is fairly straightforward with very little ActionScript—proof that you don't need to write tons of code to create cool 3D.

Storyboarding the Animation

Storyboarding your 3D animation is a crucial step to take before you begin your project. Seeing your project laid out in frames will help you analyze the action and decide which parts should be created with a rendering program and which should be created with Flash. This will save you lots of time and frustration later on.

 In general, limit the number of frames that you render in a third-party application. This will help you minimize your Flash file size. (Each frame in a rendered animation is a separate drawing, which can quickly increase file size.)

Here's the storyboard of my animation (**Figure 2.46**):

Figure 2.46 Hand-drawn layout of the animation sequence.

It's clear from the storyboard that Flash will run into problems when creating the spaceship's turns: specifically, when the spaceship changes from an almost vertical position to a frontal view, and later, when it banks to the left.

Flash can't create these different views because it can't change the visible part of the spaceship. With that in mind, here's how I divided the animation tasks between Swift 3D and Flash:

1. Spaceship turns from vertical to level flight. (Swift 3D)

2. Spaceship, while turning, dives towards ground level and moves towards viewer. (Flash)

3. Spaceship shoots at viewer. (Flash)

4. Spaceship banks left. (Swift 3D)

5. Spaceship, while banking left, moves toward the top right angle of the screen and disappears. (Flash)

Let's discuss the sequence that was created within Swift 3D.

Starting the Project in Swift 3D

Open Spaceship_Final.t3d from the CD-ROM (**Figure 2.47**). This is a Swift 3D file; you'll also find a demo version of Swift 3D on the CD-ROM.

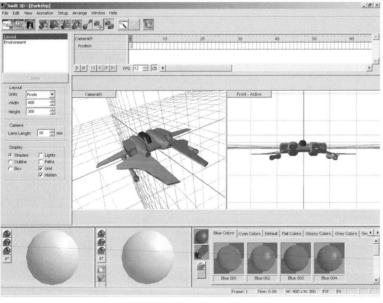

Figure 2.47
The final Swift 3D file that we'll export to Flash.

Press the Play button on the timeline to preview the animation. You'll see the spaceship go from vertical to level flight and then bank to the left. This covers the exact movement that I specified in the list above.

Note that the active viewpoint is called camera01. When Swift 3D imports a 3D Studio file, it inherits some of the 3D Studio preferences, such as camera views, lights, and colors, If you're a 3D Studio user, this is a big advantage because you can prepare your object completely before switching to Swift 3D.

 The Internet offers plenty of free 3D meshes for users who don't have the time, patience or ability to create their own. Check out www.3dcafe.com or www.highend3d.com. I found the spaceship model for my showcase on 3dcafe.com.

As you can see in the timeline below, my animation has three keyframes (**Figure 2.48**). I used Swift3D's Object Trackball to flip and rotate the model into each position.

Frame 1   Frame 20   Frame 35

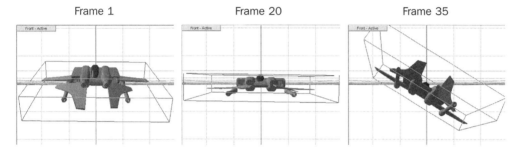

Figure 2.48 *Position of the spaceship in the three keyframes.*

After I set up my animation, it was time to export it as a SWF file. There are two important factors to consider during the export process: the number of polygons the renderer needs to draw each frame, and the type of fill you chose. Using more complex fills will increase your object's detail, but it will also create larger file sizes for each frame. **Figure 2.49** clearly illustrates this. You might need to experiment to find the optimal resolution.

FLAT FILL (1,77 KB)   AVERAGE FILL (7,03 KB)   AREA SHADING (13,2 KB)   MESH SHADING (70,0 KB)

Figure 2.49 *The same object exported with various fill options.*

 Open Spaceship_rendered.swf from the CD-ROM to see the exported SWF.

Flash is not the place for complex 3D objects. Import a 70,000-polygon object into your Flash project and you'll see what I mean—that is, if you can get the animation to load! Finding the right balance between file size and image quality requires patience: Sometimes you'll have to render an object several times before you find the optimal solution.

Finishing the Project in Flash

Once I brought the file intro Flash, my goal was to do a kind of cloning—to take the 3D genes from the Swift 3D file and clone them with the powerful Flash genes.

 Open Spaceship_final.fla from the CD-ROM (Figure 2.50).

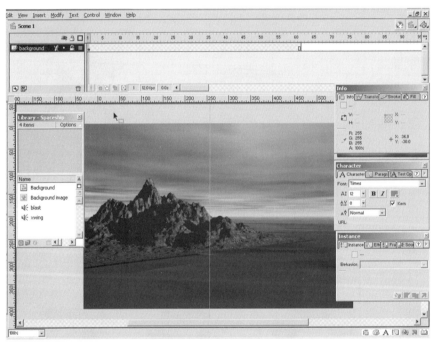

Figure 2.50 *Continuing the project in Flash.*

Importing the animation. In Flash, I began by creating a movie clip called ClipSpaceship to contain the rendered 3D object. I put the rendered animation on the movie clip's default layer, renamed the layer Spaceship and imported the rendered SWF file from Swift 3D. This brought 34 keyframes into the layer (**Figure 2.51**).

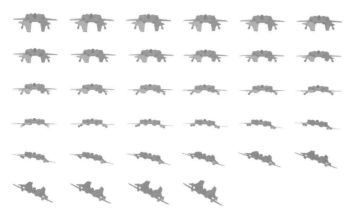

Figure 2.51 *The spaceship animation sequence.*

Creating the engine exhaust and laser shots. Next, I made a graphic symbol (a circle with a radial fill) that I used to create to some engine exhaust and laser shot effects for my movie. I placed this Laser symbol in the Engine Exhaust layer in the ClipSpaceship movie clip. It was important for this layer to be below the Spaceship layer in the timeline because it had to look like it was behind the spaceship. I scaled the symbol to make it look like realistic engine exhaust emitting from the spaceship (**Figure 2.52**). I was going for the effect seen in the Star Wars spaceships—that clear white-blue glowing light from the engines, just like on the Millennium Falcon with Han Solo and Chewie.

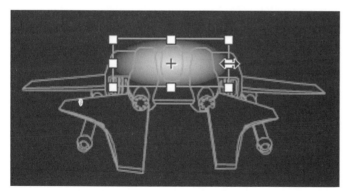

Figure 2.52 *Scaling the engine exhaust to fit the spaceship.*

The spaceship's movement is pretty linear over the first 20 frames of the movie clip, so I was able to use a normal tweened animation to make the exhaust follow the spaceship. In the last 15 frames, the spaceship moves more irregularly, so it becomes more difficult to control. Therefore, I made a new keyframe for each of the remaining frames, scaling and rotating the laser symbol into the right position in each frame.

Figure 2.53 shows how the timeline and animation appeared at this point.

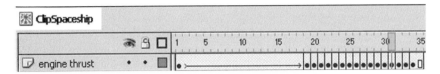

Figure 2.53 *The animation of the engine exhaust is a combination of tweens and keyframes.*

Next, I created the lasers that would shoot at the viewer. I created a movieclip symbol called ClipLaserRight, then positioned an instance of the Laser symbol at the center of the Stage and resized it (height: 13.6. width: 13.6). I made a new keyframe on frame 4 and resized the laser again (height 272, width: 272) and changed the *x*-position to -128. As a final step, I created a third keyframe on frame 7 and modified the laser again (height: 340, width 340, *x*-position: 176). By moving the *x*-position, I was able to achieve a more realistic effect in the final movie.

I then attached the following ActionScript to frame 7:

```
gotoAndPlay(1);
```

To make the laser for the left side. all I had to do was duplicate it and call the copy ClipLaserLeft. I then edited this duplicated movie clip, changed the *x*-position of the laser shot on frames 4 and 7, and changed the values in the Info panel from the current negative values to the equivalent positive values. This made the laser shot move in the opposite direction.

Adding sound. The final step was to add the sound of the laser cannon. Note that I added sound to only one of the two laser shot movie clips—because they fire simultaneously it's not necessary to insert sound into both. I prefer to use ActionScript to control my sounds, as Flash 5's Sound object offers excellent control. (For more information on using audio with Flash, see Chapter 4.)

I normally define all my sounds on the first frame of the main timeline of the movie. This makes it easier when debugging code. I made the sound symbols in my library available to ActionScript by setting the linkage option for each sound symbol. The identifier name that you give a sound symbol in the Linkage menu works like the instance name of a movie clip: You refer to it when you call it from within ActionScript. To keep things simple, I prefer to use the same name as the symbol has in the library.

I put the following script into the first keyframe in the timeline:

```
_root.blastSound.start();
```

Wrapping up the spaceship clip. Now back to the final preparations on the spaceship movie clip. I inserted a new layer above the Spaceship layer and called it Lasers. The lasers will fire their shots when the Spaceship levels out at horizontal flight, which means that they must appear on frame 19 of the movieclip timeline.

I created an empty keyframe in frame 19 and positioned the two lasershot movie clips exactly above each laser cannon. Here's how frame 19 looked at this point (**Figure 2.54**):

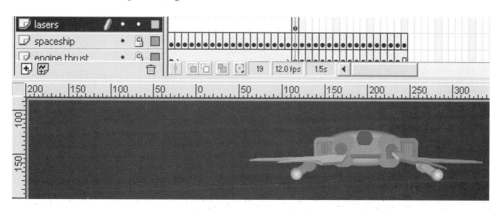

Figure 2.54 *The spaceship is now locked and loaded.*

Lastly, I inserted a few simple frame actions to help control the animation later on. I created a new layer called Frame scripts and created two empty keyframes, one on frame 19 and the other on frame 35. I inserted a stop()action in each one. (I know it may be difficult to see the logic in these two actions, but when I show you how I put together the animation on the Stage, it will become much clearer.)

Putting it all together. Now that the Spaceship movie clip was complete, it was time to put it all together on the Stage. In Scene 1, I created a new layer above the Background layer and named it Spaceship. To help me more precisely lay out the animation, I used Flash 5's ruler and guide tools. (If you're familiar with FreeHand, you've probably used these tools before.)

I positioned a guide centrally on the stage and locked it (**Figure 2.55**):

With the spaceship layer active, I selected the ClipSpaceship movie clip from the library, dragged it onto the Stage and named it darkship_mc in the Instance panel.

 I always append the names of my movie clip instances with _mc. This makes it easy to tell whether I'm referring to a movie clip or a variable. It also makes code more readable, which is a big help during debugging.

I scaled the movie clip to 10 percent of its original size, and then placed the spaceship's center exactly on the guide. I also put the spaceship close to the top of the screen setting the coordinates like this:

```
X position: 237.1
Y Posistion: 0.1
```

I made a new keyframe on frame 20. This is where the spaceship finishes its dive and reaches horizontal flight level.

When I putted the spaceship movieclip on the Stage, only the first frame of it is visible. This made it pretty difficult to position the spaceship because I had to imagine what frame of the spaceship movieclip would be visible at that specific moment of the animation. I have a trick for situations like this: I selected the ClipSpaceship movie clip and edited it. Then I created a new layer at the top of the movie clip timeline. I copied the spaceship from frame 19 in the Spaceship layer and pasted it into the first frame of the new layer.

Back to the Stage in Scene 1. Here's how the spaceship movie clip looked at this point (**Figure 2.56**):

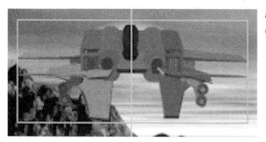

Figure 2.56 *Special editing view of the spaceship.*

In frame 20, I scaled the spaceship to 65 percent and changed the coordinates to this:

```
X position: 128.2
Y position: 54.0
```

I selected motion tween in the frame panel and kept the other default settings. Then I created the third keyframe on frame 40, scaled the spaceship to 150 percent, and changed the coordinates to this:

```
X position: -38.9
Y position: 43.9
```

Again, I selected motion tween and kept the other default settings. At this point, I needed to insert an action to tell the spaceship to move onto the first frame after the Stop command that I inserted in the movie clip on frame 19. I created a new layer in Scene 1 and named it Frame scripts.

I made a new keyframe on frame 1 and inserted the following script that defines the sounds used in the movie:

```
blastSound = new sound();
blastSound.attachsound("blast");
xwingSound = new sound();
xwingSound.attachsound("xwing");
```

To play the spaceship's sound, I created a new keyframe on frame 6 and inserted the following script:

```
xwingSound.start();
```

To control the spaceship, I insert an empty keyframe on frame 40 and added the following script:

```
_root.darkship_mc.gotoAndPlay(20);
```

This makes the movie clip begin the part of the animation where the space-ship banks to the left.

To ease the positioning of the spaceship in the next keyframe (frame 54), I used the same method as before. I replaced the graphic in frame 1 in the spaceship movie clip with frame 35 of the spaceship layer (**Figure 2.57**).

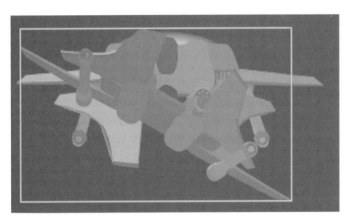

Figure 2.57 Dragging and positioning a new guide on the Stage.

Back at Scene 1, I created a new keyframe in the spaceship layer on frame 54, scaled the spaceship to 300 percent, and changed the coordinates to this:

```
X position: -252.8
Y position: -347.0
```

I created the last keyframe on frame 60 and gave the spaceship the following coordinates:

```
X position: -9.8
Y position: -499.0
```

That's it. Although this showcase may not seem that complex from a coding point of view, there are many other aspects to consider.

This showcase has taught you the basics, but I'm not finished yet. I want to show you how you can incorporate the principles of rendered 3D as seen in this showcase into a larger project.

Showcase 2: Stargate Interface

The science fiction movie Stargate inspired me to create the following project, called the Stargate Interface. This interface is a prototype, but it shows what you can do with a little more ActionScript and a lot of imagination. By the time this book hits the shelves, the project should be published on my site, www.sdflash.net.

The site's concept is built around a round gate with eight symbols, a Star Navigator that searches and finds the symbols for a specific code sequence, and a menu with six options. Each menu option has a code sequence of four symbols that must be activated by the gate to jump to one of the menu options. The symbols are individualized by the Star Navigator, which finds each symbol and tells the gate to lock on it. Once all the symbols in the code sequence have been locked, the movie takes you to the option you've selected.

 Open Stargate.swf from the CD-ROM to see the final file.

All the 3D objects in this prototype were made with Swift 3D. I designed the Stargate as a flat vector drawing in FreeHand and then imported it into Swift 3D. All of the symbols on the gate made the output file kind of big, but I decided to go with it anyway because I really liked the result.

The interface is constructed around four movie clips that work together (**Figure 2.58**).

Star navigator (starnav_mc)

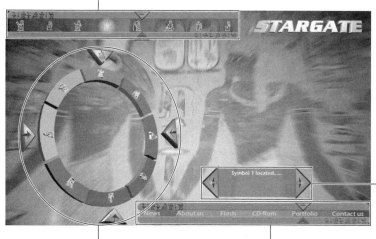

Figure 2.58 The basic navigation setup.

Status message (status_mc)

Stargate (stargate_mc)   Menu navigator (menunav_mc)

Initialization

All navigation begins in the Menu Navigator movie clip, where the viewer selects a destination. Each destination has its own code sequence of four symbols, which have been defined in six arrays at the beginning of the movie:

```
newsarray = new Array(5, 7, 4, 3);
aboutarray = new Array(3, 5, 6, 7);
flasharray = new Array(4, 1, 5, 3);
cdromarray = new Array(2, 5, 7, 3);
portfolioarray = new Array(2, 6, 1, 3);
contactarray = new Array(1, 5, 2, 6);
```

These arrays control the entire animation scheme. In the beginning of the movie, I defined some variables that are also crucial in controlling the interface:

```
//sets the value of the first symbol in the code sequence;
var symbol0 = 0;
//sets the value of the second symbol in the code sequence;
var symbol1 = 0;
//sets the value of the third symbol in the code sequence;
var symbol2 = 0;
//sets the value of the fourth symbol in the code sequence;
var symbol3 = 0;
//tells the stargate which of the four symbols in the code
sequence must be set; var step;
```

Selecting from the Menu

When a viewer clicks a button in the Menu Navigator, the two trace arrows search for the destination selected. A variable is set upon click; this tells the arrows where to stop. When they find the right destination, the following script is executed:

```
//first we check if the variable is set to the right value;
if (this.menuitem == "news") {
//Then we assign the values of the right array to the 4
→ symbol variables;
for (counter=0; counter<=3; counter++) {
root["symbol"+counter] = _root.newsarray[this.counter];
}
```

```
//tell the stargate to lock for the first symbol in the
→ code sequence;
root.step = 1;
//tell the star navigator to look for the first symbol in
→ the code sequence;
root.starnav_mc.counter = 0;
//activate the star navigator;
root.starnav_mc.play();
//set the right status message;
root.status_mc.message = "Symbol tracking  initiated......";
stop ();
}
```

The Star Navigator

As you can see in the code, we have activated the Star Navigator. In the Star Navigator I've defined a function that's being reused every time the trace arrows pass over a symbol. Here's the function:

```
//lock is used to define which symbol the trace arrows are
→ passing over;
function funcStarlock (lock) {
//check if the symbol is the right one and if step has the
→ right value;
if (_root["symbol"+counter] == lock && _root.step==1) {
//set the status message;
root.status_mc.message = "Symbol "+_root.step+"
→ located......";
//activate the stargate movieclip;
root.stargate_mc.play();
// activate the flashing light over the symbol;
setProperty (_root.starnav_mc["lock"+lock+"_mc"], _
→ visible, true);
root.locksound.start();
counter++;
stop ();
//this repeats itself for each symbol;
} else if (_root["symbol"+counter] == lock && _
→ root.step==2) {
root.status_mc.message = _ root.status_mc.message+"\nSymbol
→ "+_root.step+" located......";
```

```
root.stargate_mc.play();
setProperty (_root.starnav_mc["lock"+lock+"_mc"], _
→ visible, true);
root.locksound.start();
counter++;
stop ();
} else if (_root["symbol"+counter] == lock &&
→ root.step==3) {
root.status_mc.message = _root.status_mc.message+"\nSymbol
→ "+_root.step+" located......";
root.stargate_mc.play();
setProperty (_root.starnav_mc["lock"+lock+"_mc"], _
→ visible, true);
root.locksound.start();
counter++;
stop ();
} else if (_root["symbol"+counter] == lock &&
→ root.step==4) {
root.status_mc.message = "Symbol "+_root.step+"
→ located......\nLaunch sequence activated!!!!!";
root.stargate_mc.play();
setProperty (_root.starnav_mc["lock"+lock+"_mc"], _
→ visible, true);
root.locksound.start();
counter++;
stop ();
}
}
```

Each time the trace arrows reach a symbol, I put a reference to the code and
assign a value for the lock variable like this:

```
funcStarlock(1);
//1 is the value that are being assigned to the lock
variable
```

Whenever a symbol is found, the Stargate (stargate_mc) is activated. Again,
I use the powerful Function action. This time I have two different functions: one for the first three symbols, and the other for the last symbol in

the code sequence. I did this because the actions executed on the first three and the last symbol are different. Here are the two functions:

```
//Function for the first three symbols in the code sequence;
function funcStargate (symnum,symvalue,stepnum,clipname) {
if (_root["symbol"+symnum] == symvalue && _root.step ==
→ stepnum) {
//activate the right lock arrow on the Stargate;
root.stargate_mc[clipname+"_mc"].gotoAndPlay(10);
root.gatelocksound.start();
//restart the Star Navigator;
root.starnav_mc.play();
root.step++;
stop ();
}
}
//Function for the final symbol of the code sequence;
//notice the differences from the other function;
function funcStargate2 (symnum,symvalue,stepnum,clipname) {
if (_root["symbol"+symnum] == symvalue && _root.step ==
→ stepnum) {
root.stargate_mc[clipname+"_mc"].gotoAndPlay(10);
root.gatelocksound.start();
//jump to the beginning of the travelsequence;
root.gotoAndPlay("travelstart");
root.step++;
stop ();
}
}
stop ();
```

In the stargate_mc these functions are called when needed, and provide the right arguments. Their positions depend on the position of the symbols on the Stargate compared to the lock arrows next to it. The actions inserted into one of the frames look like this:

```
//calls the function for the first three symbols;
funcStargate(0,1,1,"topnav");
funcStargate(1,7,2,"rightnav"); //idem
funcStargate(2,5,3,"bottomnav"); //idem
//calls the function for the last symbol;
funcStargate2(3,3,4,"leftnav");
```

This ends the code sequence part. Now it's time to start the travel sequence.

The Travel Sequence

In the travel sequence, the star travel is mapped, similar to using a GPS unit in a car. You choose a destination and the computer maps your route. I made six destinations and 14 hubs that you can pass through on the way to the destinations. In a movieclip called mapping_mc I made six routes, one for each destination (**Figure 2.59**).

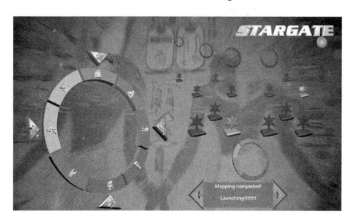

Figure 2.59 The mapping_mc that maps our star travel.

In the function funcStargate2, I send the playhead in the main timeline to a label called travelstart. In this frame I lay out the groundwork for the mapping sequence. Again, I defined a function earlier in the timeline that sorts out the route. The function script looks like this:

```
var destination;
var label="route";
function funcTravelstart () {
//sets  destination to a random integreter between 1 and 6;
destination = math.floor(math.random()*6)+1;
//set destination to a string that is made of a combination
→ of the variable label and itself;
destination = label+destination;
}
```

The function is called in the main timeline, and sends the playhead in the mapping_mc movieclip to the label that the function specifies. Here's the script:

```
funcTravelstart();
root.mapping_mc.gotoAndPlay(destination);
```

The mapping takes place, and off we go. At least that's my idea—I haven't gotten any further. For this reason, my little tour of the Stargate prototype finishes here. I hope this not only gives you a practical example of how you can combine rendered 3D with ActionScript in a real project, but also inspires you to create your own.

By the time this book hits the shelves I will have finished the entire project. You'll be able to go to www.sdflash.net and see which path I took toward the stars.

Conclusion

We have now reached the end of the line. I hope you've gained some knowledge about working with rendered 3D, and have learned how to create some nice visual effects to make your movies look more realistic. Happy 3D-ing!

3: Flash Physics

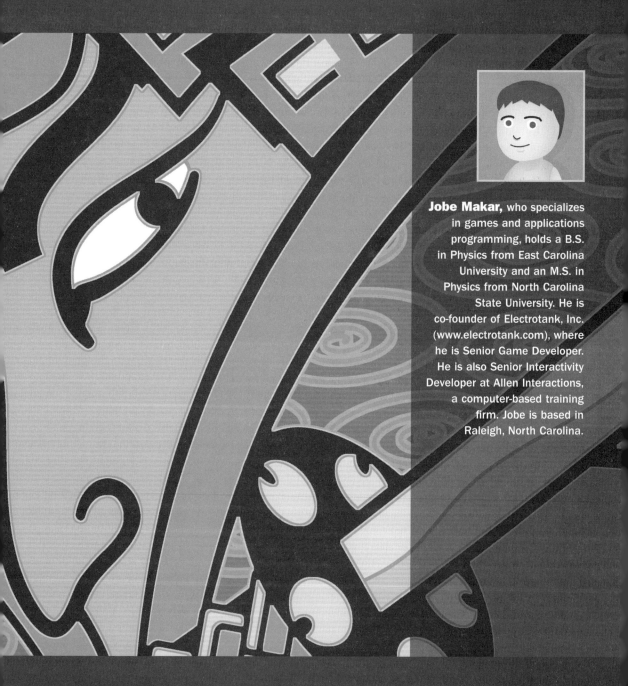

Jobe Makar, who specializes in games and applications programming, holds a B.S. in Physics from East Carolina University and an M.S. in Physics from North Carolina State University. He is co-founder of Electrotank, Inc. (www.electrotank.com), where he is Senior Game Developer. He is also Senior Interactivity Developer at Allen Interactions, a computer-based training firm. Jobe is based in Raleigh, North Carolina.

Flash, by definition, brings 2D drawing to life. But it lets you do even more: To give your Flash animations a sense of realistic movement, you can apply the laws of physics and mimic the way objects behave in nature.

Flash physics draws mainly upon classical mechanics, which describes familiar concepts such as speed, velocity, momentum, friction, and movement in a gravitational field. Some real-world examples of classical mechanics include the behavior of a thrown baseball, a falling object, a car skidding to a stop, billiard balls colliding, and a spring oscillating.

Flash designers are using physics in surprisingly creative ways to simulate realistic movement. Many Flash-created navigation systems now feature windows or buttons that slide onto a page, slow down, and stop. Other animations simulate pool table-like collisions. Games are a great proving ground for Flash physics.

This chapter will give you the mathematical background you need to begin using Flash physics in your animations. It will also show you how to use ActionScript to apply Flash physics to create motion in a straight line, motion under gravity, collisions, and collision reactions of simple objects.

Math Basics

Using physics in Flash is easy. In fact, many developers already use physics intuitively, because much of it is common sense. This section presents the mathematical concepts you'll need to work with physics in Flash.

Flash Coordinate System

A good understanding of the Flash coordinate system will help you apply physics to your Flash animations.

Most people know the Cartesian coordinate system (**Figure 3.1**). It has a vertical *y*-axis with its positive side above the horizontal and its negative side below. The horizontal *x*-axis has its positive side to the right of the *y*-axis and its negative side to the left.

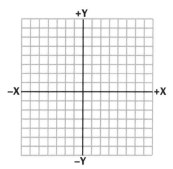

Figure 3.1
The Cartesian coordinate system as seen in your high school math book.

In Flash the *y*-axis is reversed: The negative side is on top and the positive side is on the bottom. This variety of Cartesian representation is standard in computer applications because the upper left corner of the screen is a fixed point. If the origin point (where *x*=0 and *y*=0) is placed in the upper left corner of the application, then the working area is where both *x* and *y* are positive. This is still a Cartesian coordinate system—just imagine that you're looking at it standing on your head: The *y*-axis is reversed but the *x*-axis is the same. Nothing has changed except the way you're looking at it.

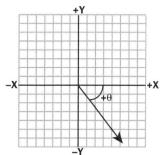

Figure 3.2
The Cartesian coordinate system as seen in Flash.

Rotation in the Flash coordinate system is measured from the *x* axis and is positive when rotated in a clockwise direction (**Figure 3.2**). The maximum rotation around any point in a Cartesian coordinate system is 360°. Flash sees this as −180° to +180° (still a total of 360°).

 You can use 0°-360° when working with the rotation property in Flash; it sees 270° and −90° as the same angle.

Trigonometry 101

In this section we'll review some basic trigonometric functions and discuss how they work in Flash. Contrary to popular belief, trigonometry is quite straightforward if you remember a few simple rules.

Trig functions, which are derived from the relationship between the sides and angles of a right triangle, can be used to solve many types of problems. For example, using trig you can calculate the distance between two arbitrary points, calculate the amplitude of a wave, or calculate the new trajectory of a certain objects at the moment of a collision.

In this section we'll use the following methods of the math object:

```
Math.sin()
Math.cos()
Math.sqrt()
```

The methods `Math.sin()` and `Math.cos()` are the ActionScript versions of the trig functions sine and cosine.

 You can employ trigonometry without actually using trig functions. Simple mathematical ratios can sometimes be used in place of trig functions.

Converting Degrees to Radians (and Vice Versa)

Just as distance can be measured in several ways (such as meters, miles, and inches), angles have more than one unit of measurement. Although angles are usually measured in degrees, they are measured in radians in physics, math, and Flash. It's simple to convert a number from one to the other (**Figure 3.3**).

Radians to Degrees	**Degrees to Radians**
$\theta = \theta * 180 / \pi$	$\theta = \theta * \pi / 180$

Figure 3.3 *A simple conversion chart for moving between degrees and radians.*

 Flash trigonometric functions recognize angles in radians, except for the `_rotation` property, which recognizes angles in degrees.

Right Triangles and the Pythagorean Theorem

A right triangle is any triangle that has one 90° angle. When using trigonometry to solve a problem, it's often helpful to draw a right triangle.

The Pythagorean theorem draws a relationship between the sides of a right triangle, such that if the lengths of two sides are known, then the length of the third side can be determined. This is also used to find the distance between two points. In **Figure 3.4**, *a* is the length of the side along the *x*-axis, *b* is the length of the side along the *y*-axis, and *c* is the line that connects the two points (called the *hypotenuse*).

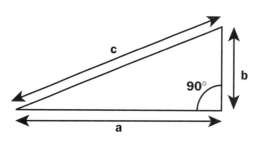

Figure 3.4 *The length of the sides of a right triangle are related to each other via the Pythagorean theorem.*

The Pythagorean theorem states this relationship as follows:

$a^2 + b^2 = c^2$

The distance between point 1 and point 2 is found by solving for *c*, where

$c = \sqrt{(a^2 + b^2)}$

which, in ActionScript is

```
C=math.sqrt(a*a+b*b)
```

Now let's make this a bit more general. The ActionScript that we've just created will tell you the distance between any two points, provided you know the values of *a* and *b*. The next step is to extend this equation for *c*—the distance between two points—so that you can input the coordinates of your points and have the distance between them as the output. The current equation will only return the distance between two points if one of the two points is the origin (*x*=0, *y*=0). **Figure 3.5** shows a typical set of two points for which you may need to know the distance.

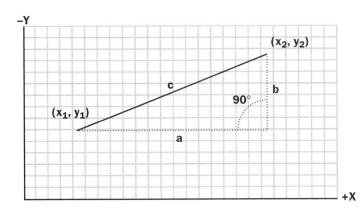

Figure 3.5 *It's easy to find the distance between two points by using the Pythagorean theorem.*

If the coordinates of point 1 are x_1 and y_1, and the coordinates of point 2 are x_2 and y_2, then a is the difference between x_2 and x_1, and b is the difference between y_2 and y_1.

$$a = x_2 - x_1$$
$$b = y_2 - y_1$$
$$c = \sqrt{a*a + b*b}$$

Renaming c to the more descriptive word *distance* and renaming the coordinates in a way that can be used in ActionScript gives us:

```
a=x2-x1;
b=y2-y1;
Distance=math.sqrt(a*a+b*b);
```

Those three lines of code are enough to give you the distance between any two points. As you can see, the Pythagorean theorem is quite simple and useful.

 When finding the distance between two points in three dimensions you can use the same formula with one added term:
Distance=math.sqrt($a*a+b*b+k*k$), where $k=z2-z1$, the difference between the two points' z-coordinates.

Projection

You may be familiar with some trig functions, such as `math.sin()` and `math.cos()`, but what do these functions do? In the previous section we used the Pythagorean theorem to calculate the distance between two points if we knew the coordinates of the other two sides. What if you know the

distance between two points and the angle they form, and you want to know their distance apart along the *x*-or *y*-axis? Using `math.sin()` or `math.cos()` you can easily find these values.

Figure 3.6 shows a light source projecting a shadow onto the *x*-axis.

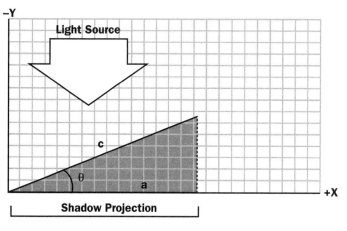

Figure 3.6 The mathematical projection of a line can be conceptualized by a light source casting a shadow off of a rod. This casted shadow is the projection of the rod onto the floor.

$$a = c*cos(\theta)$$

Now let's apply this concept to a real-world example. The person in **Figure 3.7** has walked 10 miles at a direction of 30 degrees and wants to know how far he is from the river.

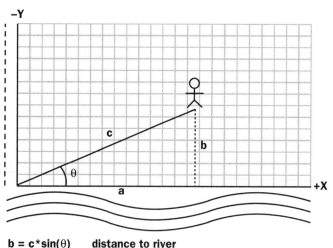

Figure 3.7 This is a simple example of using projection to solve a problem.

$b = c*sin(\theta)$ **distance to river**

$a = c*cos(\theta)$ **distance to road**

To find the *y* distance, you must project the distance walked onto the *y*-axis. This sounds complicated, but it's not:

```
Angle=30;
Distance=10;
//We must convert the angle to radians
Angle=Angle*math.pi/180;
xDisplacement=distance*math.sin(angle);
```

If you wanted to know how far the person is from the road, you must project the distance walked onto the *x*-axis. This is done in the same way, only with a different trigonometric function:

```
Angle=30;
Distance=10;
//We must convert the angle to radians
Angle=Angle*math.pi/180;
yDisplacement=distance*math.cos(angle)
```

Vectors

A vector is a mathematical object that has both *magnitude* (a numeric value) and *direction*. Velocity is a vector because it has both magnitude and direction. For example, a velocity of 33 miles per hour Northeast has a magnitude of 33 and a direction of Northeast. Speed by itself is not a vector, nor is direction, but speed and direction together modifying the same object form a vector.

Here are some other examples of vectors:

Displacement. Displacement can be a vector when it describes where one point is in relation to another. For example, New York is 500 miles North of Virginia.

Force. Force can be a vector. The gravitational force that pulls you toward the Earth has both a magnitude and a direction.

You can use vectors in Flash to apply different forces to an object. These vectors can then be added to find the total force acting on an object. Gravity, wind, and friction can be added to a movie clip as vectors and the final trajectory motion will be automatically accurate. Adding vectors is called *superposition*.

Graphically, a vector is seen as an arrow. Mathematically, a vector's direction is often specified by an angle. To use the example above, 33 mph Northeast may alternatively be described as 33 mph at 45 degrees. An angle means nothing by itself; it needs a reference point to take on meaning. As discussed earlier, angles in the Flash coordinate system are measured from the positive *x*-axis. **Figure 3.8** shows the angles of a compass in Flash.

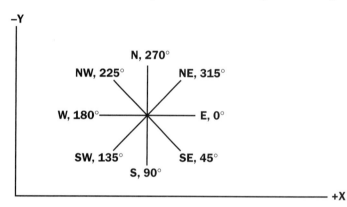

Figure 3.8 *The angles of a compass as measured in Flash.*

Vector Addition

It's often useful to add two vectors together. Imagine a game of tug-of-war: Both sides are pulling on a rope, but who will win? By adding the force vectors, you can predict a winner.

Let's take a one-dimensional example to ease into vector addition, and then we'll move on to a two-dimensional example. Imagine a train traveling 30 miles per hour East (**Figure 3.9**). On this train is a man who is running 10 miles per hour West (as measured by an observer on the train). What is this man's velocity with respect to the ground? Common sense tells you that he's moving 20 miles per hour East, but let's use math to back it up.

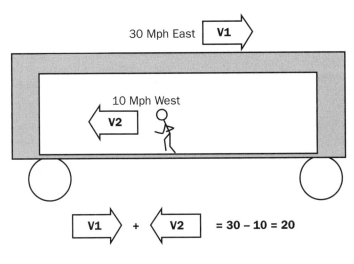

Figure 3.9 *A man runs West on a train moving East. The velocity vectors of each are shown here.*

East and West have no mathematical value; we must swap them for + and –, respectively. Here's how the vector addition works in ActionScript:

```
//Train velocity vector
trainVector=30;
//Man's velocity vector with respect to the train
manTrainVector=-10;
//Man's velocity with respect to the ground. Vector
→ addition.
ManGroundVector=trainVector+manTrainVector;
```

A vector can be dissected into two other vectors: a *y*-component vector and an *x*-component vector (**Figure 3.10**). This is called *resolving*. You must resolve a vector into its *x* and *y* components if you're going to add two vectors that don't already point along an axis.

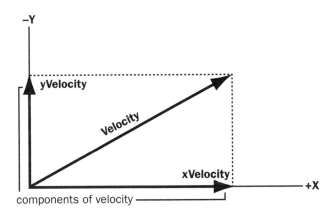

Figure 3.10 *This vector has been resolved into its x and y components.*

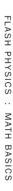

You've already learned how to do this in the previous Projection section. Resolving and projection are the same. For instance, if wind is blowing 3 mph at a direction of 30 degrees, then its *x* and *y* components are found as follows:

```
angle=30;
windSpeed=3;
//Convert angle to radians
angle=angle*Math.pi/180;
//Get the X component
xWind=windSpeed*math.cos(angle);
//Get the Y component
yWind=windSpeed*math.sin(angle);
```

Now, imagine wind is coming from two separate directions (hence, two vectors) and you'd like to know what resulting wind to expect. Here's what you do:

1. Resolve both vectors into their *x* and *y* components.

2. Add the *x* components.

3. Add the *y* components.

Here's an example:

```
//Set the winds
windSpeed1=10;
angle1=20;
windSpeed2=-40;
angle2=120;
//convert the angles
angle1=angle1*math.pi/180;
angle2=angle2*math.pi/180;
//Step 1: resolve wind2 into their X and Y components
xWind1=windSpeed1*math.cos(angle1);
yWind1=windSpeed1*math.sin(angle);
xWind2=windSpeed2*math.cos(angle2);
yWind2=windSpeed2*math.sin(angle2);
//Step 2: Add the X components
xWindFinal=xWind1+xWind2;
//Step 3: Add the Y components
yWindFinal=yWind1+yWind2;
```

This works the same way for any two vectors.

 TIP You can add any number of vectors this way. If you have 30 vectors, resolve all 30 into their x and y components, add all the x's and y's, and you're done.

Basic Physics

Now that we've covered the basic math, let's use it to mimic movement in nature. In the following sections, I'll introduce basic physics concepts and their associated equations, and then show you how to apply them using ActionScript. Along the way I'll share some tricks that will make things easier. (To see an example of physics in Flash, check out this Mini-Golf game that I programmed: www.electrotank.com/games/playGames.cfm?gameID=31.)

Velocity and Acceleration

In this section you'll learn the basics of programming movement in Flash. It's easy to program velocity and acceleration, so it's a great place to start.

Time-Based Animation vs. Frame-Based Animation

There are two primary types of animation: *time-based animation* (TBA) and *frame-based animation* (FBA). With TBA, an animation lasts a certain amount of time; with FBA, the animation lasts a certain number of frames. TBA ensures that an animation will play at the same speed on all computers, but it may drop frames to make up for processor speed on less powerful machines. Conversely, FBA will always play every single frame of an animation, but the playback speed may slow down on less powerful machines.

In nature, physics is time-based. In this chapter, however, we'll use frame-based animation because we want the playback and interactions to be the same on all machines—even if it takes longer to play back. Therefore, we'll replace time variables in all physics equations with frame variables. And because we'll be performing calculations on every frame, the frame variable will always be 1.

Note: The Flash examples that I've included on the CD-ROM use a frame rate of 24. This is fast enough for smooth animations, but slow enough to ensure consistent performance across a wide range of processors.

Moving at a Constant Velocity

We're all familiar with the term speed, which we know as *distance/time*. Because we're using frame-based animation, we're going to see speed as *distance/frame*. This makes things simple because we update positions every frame. If an object has a velocity of 3, that means the object moves 3 pixels every frame. Because we're not dealing with unit variations like kilopixels or megaframes, it's OK to forget about the units from now on. (My physics professors would slap me if they read this.) So, a speed of 3 pixels/frame can just be seen as 3 with no units.

The following physics equation gives you the position of an object if you know its initial position, its velocity, and the time elapsed since it was at its initial position (**Figure 3.11**):

In Physics

$$X = X_{original} + xVelocity*time$$

In Flash

$$X = X_{original} + xVelocity*frames$$

Figure 3.11 *Comparing a position equation using time and frames.*

In Flash, because we calculate a new position every frame, the value used for frames is always 1. The initial position in this equation is always where the object was in the previous frame. By replacing *time* in the first equation in the figure with *frames*, we arrive at the second equation in the figure.

Because velocity is a vector, it has a magnitude and direction. This magnitude is called *speed*. In Flash, we give direction to a vector either by modifying the magnitude with a sign (+ or −) or by giving it an angular direction. For example:

```
xVelocity=-3;
```

could be used as a vector because its magnitude is 3 and its direction is −.

Also:

```
angle=120;
speed=2;
```

could be used as together a vector. If given this second example, you'd most likely want to convert it to the first example—it's easier to use the projection method discussed earlier with the first example.

Now let's move on to some real Flash examples. Here's how you create a movie clip that moves at a constant velocity:

1. Create a movie clip.

2. Define velocity and position variables.

3. Update the position of the movie clip every frame, based on the velocity.

 Although there are several ways to accomplish these steps, here's how I recommend doing it. You can perform these steps in Flash, or open velocity_no_acceleration.fla from the Chapter 3 folder on the CD-ROM to follow along:

1. Draw a simple shape and convert it to a movie clip.

2. Give this movie clip an instance name of Ball.

3. Click on Ball and open the Actions window so you can add clip events to it.

4. Define a variable called xVelocity and one called yVelocity in an onLoad clip event. These variables control the amount that the movie clip will move on the stage every frame in both the x and y directions.

   ```
   xVelocity=2;
   yVelocity=3;
   ```

5. Define position variables in the onLoad clip event established in the previous step. These variables will be updated every frame and will store the position of the movie clip. This is good practice; you'll see its power later on.

   ```
   xPos=_x;
   yPos=_y;
   ```

6. Update the position variables by adding the velocities in an enterFrame clip event.

   ```
   xPos+=xVelocity;
   yPos+=yVelocity;
   ```

7. Update the position of the movie clip on the stage in the enterFrame clip event.

   ```
   _x=xPos;
   _y=yPos;
   ```

When finished, the code on your movie clip should look like this:

```
onClipEvent (load) {
    xVelocity=2;
    yVelocity=3;
    xPos=_x;
    yPos=_y;
}
onClipEvent (enterFrame) {
    xPos+=xVelocity;
    yPos+=yVelocity;
    _x=xPos;
    _y=yPos;
}
```

When you test the movie, you'll see the movie clip move toward the bottom right of the screen.

As we've seen, velocity is *distance/time* with a direction to modify it. Well, acceleration is *change in velocity/time* with a direction to modify it. Therefore, whenever the velocity changes (either magnitude or direction), acceleration has occurred. Although the word "acceleration" can also mean deceleration, in physics, it's used whether velocity is increasing or decreasing.

It's easy to modify the previous code example to include acceleration. We know acceleration occurs when velocity changes, so if we change the velocity variables xVelocity and yVelocity every frame, we have acceleration.

 You can edit the previous example or view the file velocity_and_acceleration.fla from the CD-ROM.

1. Define an acceleration variable in the onLoad clip event on the Ball movie clip.

    ```
    accel=1;
    ```

2. Change the Velocity variables every frame in the enterFrame clip event.

    ```
    xVelocity+=accel;
    yVelocity+=accel;
    ```

The entire code should look like this:

```
onClipEvent (load) {
    xVelocity=2;
    yVelocity=3;
    accel=1;
    xPos=_x;
    yPos=_y;
}
onClipEvent (enterFrame) {
    xVelocity+=accel;
    yVelocity+=accel;
    xPos+=xVelocity;
    yPos+=yVelocity;
    _x=xPos;
    _y=yPos;
}
```

Now when you play this movie, you should see the movie clip velocity change as frames pass.

Most of the cool effects you can create using Flash physics involve acceleration. Many of these use acceleration that changes every frame, which is known as *jerk* (change in acceleration/time). The acceleration in the code we have just written is based on a variable, so we can change it as often as we like.

Newton's Second Law

Perhaps the most well-known equation in all of physics is Newton's second law, which states:

TotalForce=mass*acceleration

This law, abbreviated $F=m*a$, lets you sum up all of the forces acting on an object (vector addition) and use that to find the object's acceleration. Consider the following example (**Figure 3.12**):

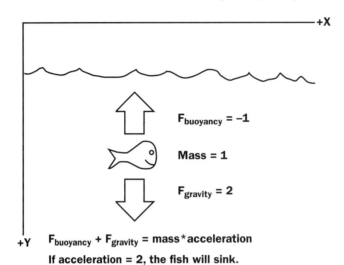

Figure 3.12 *The water exerts a buoyancy force upward on the fish while gravity exerts a force downward.*

Water exerts a buoyancy force upward on the fish and the Earth exerts a gravitational force downward on the fish. How can you tell if the fish will float or sink? You can use common sense by looking at the image to see which force is larger, or you can use Newton's second law. When there are more than two forces and these forces are at angles other than vertical or horizontal, common sense is less reliable and you'll need to use math.

To determine which direction the fish will go, do the following,

1. Sum all of the forces acting on the fish.

2. Solve for the acceleration.

3. Use this acceleration with the velocity and acceleration equations used earlier in this chapter.

Here it is in ActionScript:

```
GravitationalForce=2;
BouyancyForce=-1;
TotalForce=GravitationalForce+BouyancyForce;
Mass=1;
Accel=TotalForce/mass;
```

The accel variable can now be used with the equations for position and velocity that we've been using throughout this chapter.

Note: The gravitational force and buoyant force were selected at random for this example. You'll learn how to calculate these forces later in the chapter.

Simple Gravity

Note: Wind resistance, which accounts for the difference in acceleration for dropped objects, is beyond the scope of this chapter. Therefore, we've eliminated it from this section's examples.

The Earth exerts a gravitational force on all objects. This force, which varies depending on the object's mass, is what we all know as *weight*. The acceleration of a dropped object is independent of its mass. **Figure 3.13** shows the direction of the gravitational force.

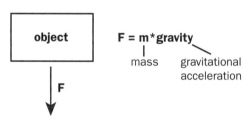

Figure 3.13 *The gravitational force acts downward and is dependent on an object's mass.*

If gravity is the only force acting on an object, then by applying Newton's second law we see that:

F=m*accel

F=m*g

So,

accel=g

Notice that the accel variable has no dependence on mass. This means that the acceleration of any dropped object is the same. For instance, a feather and a brick would hit the ground at the same time if dropped simultaneously from a rooftop and there was no wind resistance.

With this in mind, what does it take to add gravity to a movie clip? It takes nothing that you haven't already learned in this chapter. Let's use the earlier acceleration example and convert it to look like gravity.

Open simple gravity.fla from the CD-ROM.

Here's what we're going to do:

1. Define a gravity variable.

2. Set the acceleration variable to be the gravity variable.

3. Remove the *x* acceleration (because we're only concerned with the *y* acceleration).

Here's the final code:

```
onClipEvent (load) {
    xVelocity=0;
    yVelocity=3;
    gravity=1;
    accel=gravity;
    xPos=_x;
    yPos=_y;
}
onClipEvent (enterFrame) {
    yVelocity+=accel;
    xPos+=xVelocity;
    yPos+=yVelocity;
    _x=xPos;
    _y=yPos;
}
```

If you test the movie you'll see that this clip accelerates downward. You can now adjust the initial values to see what happens. You can already start to see the power of this method. By setting the xVelocity to an arbitrary value, you can see projectile motion start to take effect. Coding physics this way lets us create physically realistic results.

Friction

Friction is a concept we all know well. A frictional force is a force that opposes the direction of motion. If you slide a box to the right across the floor, a frictional force points to the left, opposing the velocity vector. The velocity of the box will approach 0 with a constant deceleration. The equation for sliding friction is:

$F=u^*m^*g$

Figure 3.14 shows the direction of the velocity and the frictional force.

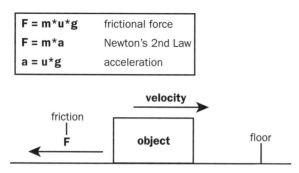

Figure 3.14 *Frictional force acts in a direction opposite to the direction of motion.*

Remember that $m*g$ is the weight of an object. Thus, the friction equation makes sense: The greater the weight, the greater the friction that will oppose the motion of a sliding object. The u factor is known as the *coefficient of sliding friction*.

A *frictional coefficient* is a numerical value between 0 and 1. This factor is found experimentally and is different for each surface/object interaction. For instance, a wet ice cube on a rubber floor may have a very low frictional coefficient (such as 0.01) whereas a tennis shoe on the same floor may have a high frictional coefficient (such as 0.2). This should give you a feel for what the coefficient does. In ActionScript, you simply choose a value for u depending on the type of surface.

Using Newton's second law, we can determine the deceleration due to friction:

$F=m*accel$

$F=u*m*g$

$m*accel=u*m*g$

$accel=u*g$

You can use this `accel` variable with the velocity equations we covered earlier. If you're emulating only friction in your Flash project, you can skip all of the Newton's second law steps in your ActionScript and pick any `accel` variable that works for you. If your velocity is positive, a negative acceleration will slow down the object.

In Flash, there are two methods for applying friction to moving objects:

1. The physically correct way, which, using the equation above, approaches the velocity toward 0 in unchanging constant increments.

2. The easy but not physically correct way, which multiplies the velocity by a factor smaller than 1 every frame. This continually decreases the

velocity, slowing the movie clip down. This "faked" method uses only one line of code.

Although the first method isn't difficult, it requires some conditional statements. Because we're stepping the velocity toward zero in definite increments, what happens when we get close to zero? If we don't put in detection to know when the velocity decreasing should cease, we can have an object that rattles back and forth around the zero velocity point every frame. Therefore, we need to detect if it has reached zero and then discontinue the calculations.

Here are the steps for applying friction the physically correct way:

1. Define a friction variable and set `accel` to be that variable.

2. Create conditional logic that knows whether to add to or subtract from the velocity. If the velocity is negative, we must add to it to move closer to zero, and vice versa.

3. Update the position on the screen.

 Open friction.fla from the CD-ROM.

We've removed the *y*-component from this code example to simplify things. We'll just deal with friction in the *x* direction. Here's the ActionScript:

```
onClipEvent (load) {
    xVelocity=20;
    xPos=_x;
    friction=1;
    accel=friction;
}
onClipEvent (enterFrame) {
    if (xVelocity>0) {
        xVelocity-=accel;
        if (xVelocity<=0) {
            xVelocity=0;
        }
    } else if (xVelocity<0) {
        xVelocity+=accel;
        if (xVelocity>=0) {
            xVelocity=0;
        }
    }
    xPos+=xVelocity;
    _x=xPos;
}
```

The conditional statement checks to see if the xVelocity variable is less than or greater than zero. If it equals zero, it does nothing and the conditions are not fulfilled. If the velocity is greater than zero, it subtracts accel increment from that variable. If the velocity at that point is now on the other side of zero, we've reached a stopping point and the velocity becomes zero. The Else If statement works in a similar fashion.

Because the second method for applying friction uses only one line of code, you might want to consider using it. Unless you add some additional logic, however, the object will never stop. Why? Because every frame its multiplied by a number greater than zero, and multiplying two non-zero numbers is always greater than zero.

Here are the steps for applying friction the easy but not physically correct way:

1. Define a frictional coefficient that can have a value between 0 and 1.

2. Every frame, multiply the velocity by the frictional coefficient.

3. Update the position on the screen.

Here's the code:

```
onClipEvent (load) {
    xVelocity=20;
    xPos=_x;
    friction=.91;
}
onClipEvent (enterFrame) {
    xVelocity*=friction;
    xPos+=xVelocity;
    _x=xPos;
}
```

This slows down the movie clip in a non-linear fashion. The deceleration changes continually—it isn't constant as in Method 1. The result is an animation that looks smooth and eases to what appears to be a stop (although it's just moving very slowly). If you like the way this not-true-to-physics method looks in your game or application, then use it. It's faster than the alternative.

Hooke's Law: The Spring Equation

Imagine a mass attached to a spring. If you pull this mass to extend the length of the spring and then let go, the spring will pull the mass back toward the starting position and will continue to oscillate around the starting position. This is called Hooke's Law. Coding this type of spring behavior with ActionScript is easy—and it's useful for many games and applications.

Hooke's law is seen in physics as:

$F=-k*(y2-y1)$

F is the force that the spring is exerting on the mass and is known as the *force of restitution*; *y*2 is the current position of the mass; *y*1 is the initial position (the equilibrium position) of the mass; and *k* is the spring constant. The latter depends on the material of the spring and its geometry; its constant is a number between 0 and 1 and is found experimentally in real life. **Figure 3.15** shows a graphical representation of this.

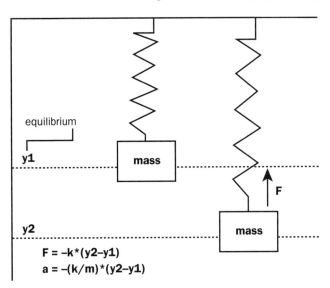

Figure 3.15 The mass on the left is at equilibrium, meaning it is not displaced at all. The mass on the right has been moved from equilibrium and is being forced back toward the equilibrium position.

Remembering Newton's second law, *F=mass*acceleration*, we find that:

Mass*acceleration=-k*(y2-y1) and,

Acceleration=-(k/m)*(y2-y1)

Here, $y1$ is the equilibrium position of the spring. For the purpose of our calculations, we'll consider $y1$ to be a constant. If we ignore gravity, then the equilibrium position, $y1$, is the same for all masses. (If we include gravitational forces, it gets more complicated, so we'll ignore them in this example.) The *mass* is an arbitrary value. In fact, if you have only one movie clip, you can combine k and m into a single new constant. This equation can be used to find force separately in the x and y directions.

Here's how to create a mass on a spring in Flash:

1. Create a movie clip and paste the ActionScript for velocity and acceleration that we've been using.

2. Define a spring constant between 0 and 1.

3. Define a mass variable (for now, just set it to 1).

4. Define an equilibrium variable, x1 and y1, to be the starting position.

5. Set the acceleration variable to accept the spring equation.

6. Make the spring draggable. (To test this, you need a way to displace the mass from equilibrium.)

 Open hookes_law.fla from the CD-ROM.

Here's the ActionScript for the onLoad clip event:

```
onClipEvent (load) {
    xVelocity=0;
    yVelocity=0;
    xAccel=0;
    yAccel=0;
    xPos=_x;
    yPos=_y;
    k=.3;
    x1=_x;
    y1=_y;
    m=1;
    mouseUp=true;
}
```

The ActionScript starts by setting the velocities to zero because we don't want to start with the movie clip in motion. Note that we're treating the x and y accelerations separately; that's because the force of restitution in the *x* direction has nothing to do with how much the mass is displaced in the *y* direction, and vice versa. For testing purposes we're tracking a variable called mouseUp. You'll see why in the enterFrame clip event. Here's the ActionScript in the enterFrame event:

```
onClipEvent (enterFrame) {
    if (mouseUp) {
        xAccel=-(k/m)*(xPos-x1);
        yAccel=-(k/m)*(yPos-y1);
        xVelocity+=xAccel;
        yVelocity+=yAccel;
        xPos+=xVelocity;
        yPos+=yVelocity;
        _x=xPos;
        _y=yPos;
    } else {
        xPos=_x;
        yPos=_y;
        xVelocity=0;
        yVelocity=0;
    }
}
```

This movie clip contains a button that lets us drag the clip away from its equilibrium position. During the drag operation, mouseUp is set to false and the spring equation isn't used. When the drag operation stops, mouseUp is set back to true and the calculations resume.

Notice how xAccel and yAccel are being used separately. Test the file: Drag the movie clip around and let it go. You'll see the spring-like behavior and you may notice that this mass never stops oscillating. In real life, the mass would eventually slow to a stop. It's easy to add that feature by introducing a decay variable. This works by taking the velocity of the previous frame and multiplying it by a number between 0 and 1 in the current frame. Thus, in every frame, the velocity decreases. It's very much like the previous friction example.

Add this to the onLoad clip event:

```
decay=.8;
```

and these two lines to the enterFrame clip event just below the xAccel and yAccel equations:

```
xVelocity*=decay;
yVelocity*=decay;
```

 Test the movie again: You'll see that the mass now behaves more like a mass would in nature. You can see this in action in hookes_law_with_decay.fla on the CD-ROM.

If you set decay to zero, then drag the mass anywhere on screen and let go, it will slide back into place with no oscillations. This effect, called *critical damping*, is seen in many Flash navigation systems. You can view this effect in critical_damping.fla on the CD-ROM.

Collision Detection

Flash physics gets fun when we start creating applications where objects interact. When objects detect each other they can react in realistic ways. A reaction can be triggered by a variety of events; the most common are collisions and proximity. In this section, we'll focus on collisions.

A collision must be detected before a collision reaction can be executed. There are many types of collision detection; we'll cover the following:

- Rectangular or circular object with a wall

- Rectangular object with another rectangular object

- Circular object with another circular object

There are two common methods used to calculate if a collision is taking place:

1. `MovieClip.hitTest()`. This is an easy and useful way to determine some collisions, but it's less powerful than using math.

2. Mathematically. This is the most powerful way to calculate collisions. We'll focus mostly on this method in this chapter.

MovieClip.hitTest()

HitTest() is a method that lets you programmatically determine collisions between movie clips or collisions between a point and a movie clip. This method can detect the following collision types:

1. If the bounding boxes of two movie clips are overlapping.

2. If any single point on the screen is overlapping the bounding box of a movie clip.

3. If any single point on screen is overlapping a shape contained within a movie clip.

Figure 3.16 shows the three types of hitTest.

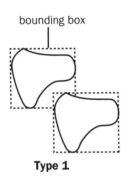 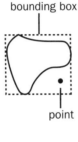 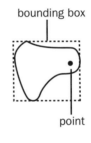

bounding box   bounding box   bounding box

point   point

Type 1   **Type 2**   **Type 3**

Figure 3.16 *These shapes are arbitrary and organically shaped. The dotted lines mark the movie clip bounding boxes.*

HitTest() returns a Boolean value of true or false. If a collision is occurring, the returned value is true; if a collision is not occurring, the returned value is false.

 Open box_box_hitTest.fla from the CD-ROM. This file shows an example of how to use hitTest() to determine if the bounding boxes of two movie clips are overlapping.

There are two movie clips on the Stage. The movie clip with an instance name of Projectile contains ActionScript that moves it upward. This is the same code we've been using throughout this chapter. The other movie clip, with an instance name of Ball, contains no ActionScript. A text field displays the value of a variable called colliding, which is updated every frame. This visual display lets you know if the hitTest() is true or false.

The only new ActionScript on this movie clip is an If statement that determines if a collision is taking place. This code, contained in the enterFrame clip event, is as follows:

```
if (_parent.ball.hitTest(this)) {
    _parent.colliding="colliding";
} else {
    _parent.colliding="not colliding";
}
```

The argument of the conditional statement looks to the parent of Projectile and performs collision detection on Ball and This. This collision detection is very simple.

 To see the second use of hitTest(), open point_box_hitTest.fla from the CD-ROM. The ActionScript in this file illustrates how to use hitTest() to determine if a point as seen in any timeline is overlapping the bounding box of a movie clip in that same timeline.

The movie clip on the Stage contains a mouseMove clip event, which lets us know if the mouse is colliding with the movie clip. A text field lets us know if a collision is taking place. Here's the ActionScript on the movie clip:

```
onClipEvent (mouseMove) {
    //collision detection;
    xPoint=_parent._xMouse;
    yPoint=_parent._yMouse;
    if (this.hitTest(xPoint,yPoint)) {
        _parent.colliding="colliding";
    } else {
        _parent.colliding="not colliding";
    }
}
```

This function of hitTest() is used by first targeting the movie clip of interest and then, in the argument, supplying the *x* and *y* coordinates to test against it.

The third use of hitTest() employs a shape flag. Shape flag is the name of a parameter passed into the movieClip.hitTest() method. It can either be true or false; if left blank, it defaults to false. The parameter compares the *x* and *y* coordinates of a point to a movie clip and sees if that point is covering any visual part of the movie clip, not the bounding box. This allows collision detection between a point and organic shapes.

To use this function, simply use the same code as in the previous method, but add this argument:

```
this.hitTest(xPoint,yPoint,true)
```

True tells Flash to test for a shape flag.

 To see an example of this, open point_shape_hitTest.fla from the CD-ROM.

Mathematical Collision Detection

Using math to detect collisions is much more powerful for collision detection. With `hitTest()`, two movie clips must be already colliding for a collision to be detected. With math, you can detect if two objects are colliding, or even if they are about to collide. Here, we'll show some of the basic mathematical collision detection techniques.

Object-Wall Detection

It's simple to detect if a rectangle or a circle is colliding with a vertical or horizontal wall. First, you must calculate the bounds of the object. The bounds are nothing more than how far left, right, up, and down an object goes. Then, you must check to see if the bounds overlap the walls. **Figure 3.17** shows the bounds of a movie clip.

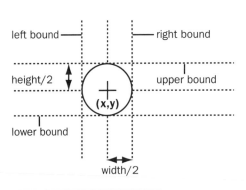

Figure 3.17 *The dotted lines show the object's four bounds.*

left bound = x−width/2
right bound = x+width/2
upper bound = y−height/2
lower bound = y+height/2

To perform object-wall detection, you must do the following:

1. Define walls as variables.

2. Create a movie clip that can be moved around.

3. Center the graphic in the movie clip for symmetry.

4. Add the velocity ActionScript that we've been using to the movie clip.

5. Add collision detection conditional statements.

We'll write one conditional statement for each wall. Because the object has a width and height, we must not just check where the center of the object is, but also see if any of the sides are outside of the walls. These four conditionals are:

■ If the x position of the object minus one-half its width is less than the x position of the left wall, the object is colliding with the left wall.

■ If the x position of the object plus one-half its width is greater than the x position of the right wall, the object is colliding with the right wall.

■ If the y position of the object minus one-half its height is less than the y position of the top wall, the object is colliding with the top wall.

■ If the y position of the object plus one-half its height is greater than the y position of the bottom wall, the object is colliding with the bottom wall.

The collision detection for a rectangle or circle is the same. A circle has the same height as it does width, so we can use just one variable instead of two to define its bounds.

 Open object_wall.fla from the CD-ROM. You'll see six movie clips on the Stage: a rectangle, circle, left wall, right wall, top wall, and bottom wall.

The ActionScript on the circle and rectangle is identical except the circle's height and the width are equal. Open the Actions panel on the rectangle movie clip. Let's look at the code in the onLoad clip event:

```
width=_width;
height=_height;
left=_parent.left._x;
right=_parent.right._x;
top=_parent.top._y;
bottom=_parent.bottom._y;
```

First, we set the `height` and `width` variables for the rectangle based on the movie clip properties `_height` and `_width`. Then we set four wall variables that store the position of each wall.

Now, let's look at the enterFrame clip event:

```
if (xPos-width/2<left) {
    xPos=left+width/2;
    xVelocity*=-1;
} else if (xPos+width/2>right) {
    xPos=right-width/2;
    xVelocity*=-1;
}
if (yPos-height/2<top) {
    yPos=top+height/2;
    yVelocity*=-1;
} else if (yPos+height/2>bottom) {
    yPos=bottom-height/2;
    yVelocity*=-1;
}
```

Using the conditional logic mentioned earlier, this ActionScript detects collisions with any of the walls. If the argument of any of the conditionals above is fulfilled (true), then a collision has been detected. Each time a collision is detected there's also a collision reaction. Collision reactions will be explained later in this chapter.

Rectangle-Rectangle Collision Detection

In this section you'll learn how to mathematically determine if two rectangles are colliding. But first we need to modify our approach a bit to more efficiently apply the ActionScript.

Until now, the ActionScript controlling an object's movement has been included on the object itself. This is a convenient method when dealing with single objects, and this method will serve you well in many games and applications. But imagine creating a game of 8-ball, a pool game that actually has 15 balls. In such a game, rather than maintaining collision detection and velocity code on each separate ball, it's more convenient to create a central controlling movie clip to define the rules of your environment. This controlling movie clip is a popular way to control an application. We'll call this movie clip the *controller*.

As we progress through this chapter, we'll store most information about each object in arrays. We'll start by storing the object names themselves.

For a rectangle-rectangle collision to occur, four conditions must be met simultaneously:

- The *x* position of the right bound (right edge) of one object must be greater in *x* position than the left bound of the other object.

- The *x* position of the left bound of one object must be less than the *x* position of the right bound of the other object.

- The *y* position of the top bound of one object must be less than the *y* position of the lower bound of the other object.

- The *y* position of the lower bound of one object must be greater than the *y* position of the top bound of the other object.

Now that we've moved the ActionScript to the controller, here's how to detect a collision in this way:

1. Build an array to store the object names.

2. Build a collision detection function.

3. Add actions to the collision detection function to create variables for the left, right, top, and bottom bounds of each object.

4. Use the bounds to detect if a collision is taking place.

 Open rectangle_rectangle.fla from the CD-ROM. You'll see three movie clips on the Stage: the controller, Box1, and Box2.

Box1 and Box2 contain only enough code to make them draggable. The controller contains all of the collision detection code. Open the Actions panel and select the controller. You'll see this ActionScript in the onLoad clip event:

```
path=_parent;
objects=["box1","box2"];
path.colliding="";
function collisionDetection (num1,num2) {
    var object1=objects[num1];
    var object2=objects[num2];
    var x1=path[object1]._x;
    var y1=path[object1]._y;
    var w1=path[object1]._width;
    var h1=path[object1]._height;
    var rightBound1=x1+w1/2;
    var leftBound1=x1-w1/2;
    var topBound1=y1-h1/2;
```

```
            var bottomBound1=y1+h1/2;
            var x2=path[object2]._x;
            var y2=path[object2]._y;
            var w2=path[object2]._width;
            var h2=path[object2]._height;
            var rightBound2=x2+w2/2;
            var leftBound2=x2-w2/2;
            var topBound2=y2-h2/2;
            var bottomBound2=y2+h2/2;
            if ((rightBound1>leftBound2 &&
    leftBound1<rightBound2) && bottomBound1>topBound2 &&
  → topBound1<bottomBound2) {
                path.colliding="yes";
            } else {
                path.colliding="no";
            }
        }
```

First, we define a variable called path that stores the path to a timeline. This is a handy trick. If we later decide to change the timeline of Box1 and Box2, we can just change the path variable to reflect this. Next, we define an array called objects and set the first two elements of that array to be the names of the movie clips that we're using on the Stage. This technique isn't necessary for collision detection, but it's good practice and will become handy if you deal with many movie clips. The colliding variable lets us know if a collision has taken place. It corresponds to a text field on the Stage and will either show Yes or No.

Next, we define a function called collisionDetection(). This has two arguments that are used to pull names out of the object's array. Collision detection will be performed on the two names that were pulled out of the array. The next eight lines of code determine the properties of object1 with the goal of finding its four bounds. The same is done for object2. After all of the bounds are found, the conditional statement explained earlier is executed to determine if a collision is taking place. If this statement is true, the colliding variable is set to Yes; if not, colliding is set to No.

Open rectangle_rectangle_many.fla from the CD-ROM. This file has collision detection for four rectangles and slightly extends the code seen here. The detection technique is the same, but the `collisionDetection()` function is called differently.

Circle-Circle Collision Detection

Collision detection between two circles is easy. There's only one condition that must be met for a collision to take place: If the distance between the centers of two circles is less than the sum of their radii, they're colliding (**Figure 3.18**).

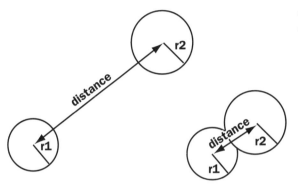

Figure 3.18 *It's easy to detect a collision between two circles.*

distance>r1+r2
no collision

distance<r1+r2
no collision

As in the previous section, we're using a controller movie clip (we'll continue to use one in all the following files). The code is set up in the same way, with an array to store the movie clip names and a function to be called for collision detection.

Here's how we determine if a collision is taking place between two circles:

1. Get the *x* and *y* position of each circle.

2. Get the width/2 of each circle to find its radius.

3. Use the Pythagorean theorem to find the distance between the two sets of coordinates.

4. Compare the distance with the sum of the radii to determine if a collision is taking place.

Open circle_circle.fla from the CD-ROM. You'll see three movie clips on the Stage: Ball1, Ball2, and the controller. Open the Actions panel and view the actions on the controller. Here's where the code differs from the previous example:

```
var object1=objects[num1];
var object2=objects[num2];
var x1=path[object1]._x;
var y1=path[object1]._y;
var r1=path[object1]._width/2;
var x2=path[object2]._x;
var y2=path[object2]._y;
var r2=path[object2]._width/2;
var distance=math.sqrt((x2-x1)*(x2-x1)+(y2-y1)*
↝ (y2-y1));
if (distance<=r1+r2) {
    path.colliding="yes";
} else {
    path.colliding="no";
}
```

The *x*, *y*, and radius for each circle are found first. Then, using the Pythagorean theorem, we find the distance between the two circles. Finally, we see if the distance is less than or equal to the sum of the two radii.

Collision Reactions

So far we've seen how you can move objects and how you can detect if they're colliding. The next logical step is to make these objects react when a collision occurs. There are two common types of collision reactions:

1. Non-physical reactions: These can be completely random or arbitrary.

2. Physical reactions: These are based on physics equations or mimic nature in some way.

Some reactions fall in a gray area between these two types. For instance, a paper blowing in the wind or a bomb exploding can be programmed with no knowledge of physics and still may look acceptable.

In this section we'll quickly cover two common, easy-to-use non-physical reactions. Then we'll proceed to the physical reactions, which are based on *conservation of momentum*.

Common Non-Physical Reactions

The two most common non-physical reaction methods for rectangles or circles are:

1. Reverse the velocities when a collision is detected: The objects go back the direction from which they came.

2. Swap the velocities when a collision is detected: An object will take on the velocity of the object with which it collided.

 Open non_physical_type1.fla from the CD-ROM. This file, which shows the reversing velocities technique, uses the same movie clips as the circle-circle collision detection example earlier in this chapter. The velocities are now stored in arrays called xVelocity and yVelocity in the controller. A function has been added that moves the objects on the Stage every frame. It's the same velocity concept that we've used, but now it's referencing the velocity from an array.

Open the Actions panel and select the controller. In the conditional statement for collision detection you'll see this code:

```
xVelocity[num1]*=-1;
yVelocity[num1]*=-1;
xVelocity[num2]*=-1;
yVelocity[num2]*=-1;
```

When a collision is detected, the velocity reverses. That's all these four lines of code do. Test the movie to see this in action.

 Now, open non_physical_type2.fla from the CD-ROM. This file, which shows the swapping velocities technique, is set up in the same manner as the preceding file.

Open the Actions panel to view the ActionScript on the controller. In the conditional statement for collision detection you'll see this code:

```
tempXvelocity=xVelocity[num1];
tempYvelocity=yVelocity[num1];
xVelocity[num1]=xVelocity[num2];
yVelocity[num1]=yVelocity[num2];
xVelocity[num2]=tempXvelocity;
yVelocity[num2]=tempYvelocity;
```

First, we store the x and y velocity for object1 in temporary variables. Then, we set the x and y velocity of object1 to equal those of object2. Finally, the x and y velocities of object2 are set from the temporary variables that stored the x and y velocities of object1. When you test this movie you'll see that after collision, a circle takes on the velocity of the circle with which it collided.

Conservation of Momentum and Conservation of Kinetic Energy

For the rest of this chapter we'll determine how the velocity of objects changes after a collision. We'll only consider *elastic collisions*—that is, collisions where no energy is lost. Therefore, we'll use the information available to us—velocities and masses—to determine what the new velocities are. When objects collide elastically, *momentum* and *kinetic energy* are conserved.

The momentum of an object is defined as the product of its mass and its velocity. If two people are ice-skating at the same velocity, the person who is more massive has more momentum. Mathematically, momentum is this:

Momentum=mass*velocity

Momentum is a vector because *velocity* is a vector.

Let's consider a collision of two hockey pucks sliding on an ice rink. Both pucks have a momentum associated with them. The velocity of each puck will change at the moment of impact, which means the momentum of each puck also will change. The Law of Conservation of Momentum says that *the total momentum before a collision is equal to the total momentum after a collision* (for perfectly elastic collisions) (**Figure 3.19**).

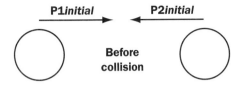

Before collision

Ptotal = P1initial + P2initial

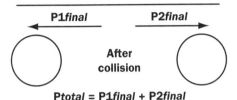

After collision

Ptotal = P1final + P2final

P1final + P2final = P1initial + P2initial

Figure 3.19 *The before and after of a collision. The total momentum of the system is the same after the collision as it was before.*

P1*before* + P2*before*=P1*after* + P2*after*

Remember, the goal is to find the two final velocities. This equation has two unknown values, so it requires two equations that contain those unknowns to find a solution. We turn to kinetic energy, which is energy associated with the motion of an object. Mathematically, it is:

KE=1/2*mass*speed*speed*

Kinetic energy is not a vector. Remember that speed is the magnitude of the velocity vector; for example, if velocity is −31.2, then the speed is 31.2. The kinetic energy before the collision is the same as it is after the collision, but the kinetic energy of each object separately is not the same.

KE1*initial* + KE2*initial*=KE1*final* + KE2*final*

Now we have two independent equations that have the same two unknown variables. We can solve for the final velocities to get:

V=V1*initial* − V2*initial*

P=m1*V1*initial*+m2*V2*initial*

V1*final*=(P-m2*V)/(m1+m2)

V2*final*=V+V1*final*

With this result you can start to build very cool physics into your Flash applications and games. We'll use these equations in the next few sections. The result will be a physics engine for a billiards game.

Collision with Immovable Object

If you throw a tennis ball against a wall, the ball bounces back without moving the wall. The wall is considered to be an *immovable object*. In Flash, we can treat this one of two ways. We can either use our newly found conservation of mass and energy equations (setting *V2=0* and *m2=infinity*) or we can just jump to the obvious result and reverse the velocity that's perpendicular to the plane of collision. For us, this usually means a vertical or horizontal wall. The logic works like this:

If an object collides with a horizontal wall, reverse the *y* component of the velocity.

If an object collides with a vertical wall, reverse the *x* component of the velocity.

 Open ball_immovable.fla from the CD-ROM. In this file you'll see a movie clip with a circular graphic, controller clip, and four walls. This file contains the same ActionScript that was used earlier for object-wall detection.

Open the Actions panel and view the actions on the controller. Near the bottom you'll see four conditional statements, one for each wall:

```
if (xPos-width/2<left) {
    xPos=left+width/2;
    xVelocity*=-1;
} else if (xPos+width/2>right) {
    xPos=right-width/2;
    xVelocity*=-1;
}
if (yPos-height/2<top) {
    yPos=top+height/2;
    yVelocity*=-1;
} else if (yPos+height/2>bottom) {
    yPos=bottom-height/2;
    yVelocity*=-1;
}
```

This ActionScript detects a collision and then applies the appropriate reactions. If a collision is detected, then mathematically, the ball is out of the boundaries created by the walls. The ActionScript moves the ball back in bounds so it's snug against the wall with which it collided; then it reverses the velocity component that points along the axis perpendicular to the collision wall. Although it sounds complicated, it just boils down to just multiplying the velocity by −1.

Objects Along an Axis

Now let's look at a more complicated example that uses the conservation of energy and momentum equations discussed above. Imagine four carts on a railroad track each carrying a different amount of mass. They're trapped between two walls and an initial velocity is given to each of them. Assuming elastic collisions, how would this animation play out? We have four carts bumping back and forth off each other transferring momentum to one another.

This sounds like a complicated problem, but we've already figured out the hard part. Each time a collision takes place we employ our conservation equations to figure out the new velocities. We don't ever have to know that there are a bunch of other carts in the picture; we only deal with the two that collide.

 Open railroad.fla from the CD-ROM. You'll see four movie clips that contain graphics to represent four railroad carts (named cart0 – cart3) and a controller clip.

The controller clip contains actions that initialize the look of the movie and initialize arrays that contain information about carts such as mass, velocity, and position. It also contains functions that get the position of the carts, check for collisions with other carts and with the walls, and update the position on the Stage.

Most of this code should be familiar by now. We'll focus on what happens when a collision is detected. We store each cart's mass in an array called mass in the element that corresponds with its name. For instance, the mass of cart2 is found by referencing mass[2]. The velocity and position arrays are set up identically. The collision detection is performed by calling a function that loops through mathematically checking each cart to see if it's colliding with another cart. If a collision is detected, a function named reaction() is called. The content of this function is the focus of this section.

Here's a reaction function:

```
function reaction (i,j) {
    P=mass[i]*xVelocity[i]+mass[j]*xVelocity[j];
    V=xVelocity[i]-xVelocity[j];
    var v1f=(P-mass[j]*V)/(mass[i]+mass[j]);
    var v2f=V+v1f;
    xVelocity[i]=v1f;
    xVelocity[j]=v2f;
}
```

The object of this function is to use the masses and velocities of the colliding carts to set a new velocity for each cart. This function accepts two arguments, i and j, which refer to the number of each cart involved in the collision. To see the relationship between the conservation equations and this code, compare the first four lines to those four equations. xVelocity[i] refers to V1initial, xVelocity[j] to V2initial, and mass[i] and mass[j] refer to mass1 and mass2. The final result is v1f and v2f. We then set the velocities in the velocity array to the new velocities that we calculated.

Billiard Ball Physics

In this section you'll see how a billiard ball reacts when it collides with another.

We've learned how to use conservation of momentum and energy to determine the final velocities of two colliding objects. When two billiard balls collide, their velocities most likely are not along the same axis as they were in the previous example. The imaginary line between the center of one ball and the center of the other ball at the moment of impact is called the *line of collision* (**Figure 3.20**). The only components of the velocities that are affected in a ball-to-ball collision are those along this line. Once we know those velocities, we can apply the conservation method already used to determine the final velocity.

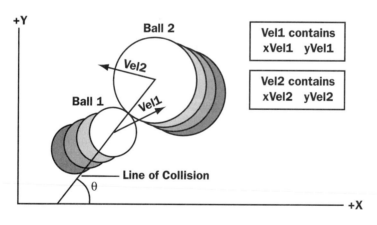

Figure 3.20
The balls just before they collide. Notice the line of collision.

We'll refer to the initial velocity of ball1 as Vel1 and the initial velocity of ball2 as Vel2. The x and y components of these two velocities are xVel1, yVel1, xVel2, and yVel2. Figure 3.20 displays balls of two different sizes to illustrate that our math is more general than for balls of equal size and mass. (This is important for projects that require spherical objects of different sizes and masses. For billiard physics, we use balls of equal mass and radius.)

Now we need to find the piece of each ball's velocity along the line of collision. We can employ the projection method using trigonometry to determine this by using the angle (**Figure 3.21**).

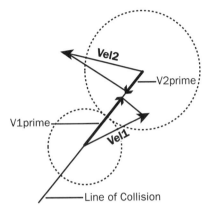

Figure 3.21 *The two black vectors are the components projected onto the line of collision. They are affected by the collision.*

This angle is found from the slope of the line of collision shown in the ActionScript below. We'll refer to the components along this line as V1prime and V2prime. By knowing these velocity components and the masses, we can determine the velocity after collision. The new velocities will also be along the line of collision; we'll have to project them back onto Flash's coordinate system to obtain mathematical values that we can use (**Figure 3.22**).

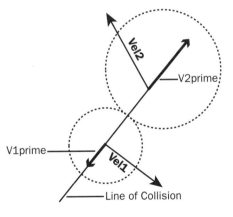

Figure 3.22 *The system post-collision. The projected components have been affected.*

Before digging into the example file, let's recap this process. Remember, this is at the moment of collision.

1. Use the position of both balls to get the angle of the line of collision.

2. Project the xVelocity and yVelocity of each ball onto the line of collision.

3. Perform conservation of momentum and energy method to obtain the new prime velocities.

4. Translate these velocities back to Flash's coordinate system.

 Open billiards.fla from the CD-ROM. This file contains 11 movie clips: 10 balls (named ball0 - ball9) and a controller.

The controller is set up in a familiar way: It divides the tasks into separate functions. We're only going to focus on what happens if a collision is detected. If a collision is detected, a reaction function is called that calculates the new velocities. This function is fed six parameters, the *x* and *y* position of each ball, and the number of each ball.

Let's look at the ActionScript in four steps to correspond to the procedure listed above.

1. The difference in position of the two balls separately along the *x*- and *y*-axis determines the slope of the line of collision. The inverse tangent of that slope is Theta.

```
var run=(x1-x2);
var rise=(y1-y2);
var Theta=Math.atan2 ( y, x );
```

2. We project the velocities into the coordinate system defined by the line of collision and a line perpendicular to it. xVel1prime and xVel2prime are to be used when calculating the new velocities.

```
var cosTheta=math.cos(Theta);
var sinTheta=math.sin(Theta);
var xVel1prime=xVel1*cosTheta+yVel1*sinTheta;
var xVel2prime=xVel2*cosTheta+yVel2*sinTheta;
var yVel1prime=yVel1*cosTheta-xVel1*sinTheta;
var yVel2prime=yVel2*cosTheta-xVel2*sinTheta;
```

3. Next we move on to conservation of momentum. This step should be familiar to you from the previous section: It uses the laws of conservation of momentum and energy. These are the velocities in the prime coordinate system after the collision.

```
P=(mass[n]*xVel1prime+mass[m]*xVel2prime);
V=(xVel1prime-xVel2prime);
var v1f=(P-mass[m]*V)/(mass[n]+mass[m]);
var v2f=(V+v1f);
var xVel1prime=v1f;
var xVel2prime=v2f;
```

4. This final step takes the prime velocities and translates them back into Flash's coordinate system using projection.

```
var xVel1=xVel1prime*cosTheta-yVel1prime*sinTheta;
var xVel2=xVel2prime*cosTheta-yVel2prime*sinTheta;
var yVel1=yVel1prime*cosTheta+xVel1prime*sinTheta;
var yVel2=yVel2prime*cosTheta+xVel2prime*sinTheta;
```

Test the movie and you'll see how this interaction plays out. I used the "faked" friction method, but you can easily use the real method.

You can use these powerful physics reaction formulae in a number of ways. Some of the most obvious applications are game-related ones such as Pool and Air Hockey, but there are many other potential uses such as creative application navigation systems.

There's a problem with this interaction, however. The physics in this section is valid for two balls colliding at the moment of collision. In pool, if you hit the cue ball forcefully, it's not going to go halfway through the eight-ball before a collision takes place. Consider this scenario: A 20-pixel-wide ball is moving toward another ball of the same diameter at a speed of 10. If on one frame, ball1 is 2 pixels from ball2, then on the next frame, ball1 will be over-lapping ball2 by 8 pixels. In real life, the ball would have collided at some point between the two frames. If we increase Flash's frame rate to 100, this problem would be negligible, but Flash can't run the code at that rate.

There are two solutions. One is very advanced so I'll just mention it; the other is a workaround that keeps the interaction looking good.

1. Write an equation for the distance between the two balls as a function of time, and then set this distance equal to the sum of their radii and solve for the time. If the time falls between the previous frame and the current frame, a collision has happened. This method is exact and is frame-independent, although it requires more logic to be coded and it takes longer for the computer to calculate.

2. This solution uses our current ActionScript. If a collision is detected, run the collision detection function a second time. If you don't do this—and you don't make any other modifications to the code—it's possible for two balls to get stuck. Running the detection twice kicks any stuck balls apart before the frame has ended. (I've already added this method to the file as conditional in the enterFrame clip event on the controller.)

Last Notes

If you want to explore more advanced physics topics to use with Flash, just remember to use Newton's second law. You can create numerous complicated, yet easy-to-use forces in your Flash environment if you:

1. Add all of the forces on an object together, one equation for the x direction and one for the y direction.

2. Divide by the mass of the object to get the acceleration.

3. Use the velocity and acceleration equations developed in this chapter.

In this chapter we've only discussed how to mathematically describe gravity as we're used to seeing it, very close to the surface on an extremely massive object. But how do the gravitational forces of the planets affect each other? The equation isn't difficult, but the result has limited use for most projects. Still, with a little creative imagination you may find a use for it. **Figure 3.23** shows the equation for gravitational force between two masses.

$$F = G\frac{m1*m2}{R^2}$$

Figure 3.23 *This equation represents the gravitational force that two objects exert on each other. This force is dependent on the masses of the two objects and the distance between them.*

This equation gives the force that both objects experience. Any two objects feel the same force, although they each experience a different acceleration. When you jump, you actually push the earth a little bit away from you, and when you fall, both you and the earth accelerate toward each other.

 Check out realGravity.fla on the CD-ROM to see this in action.

If you want to create large applications with many objects—or if you're just looking for a challenge—consider taking an object-oriented programming approach to physics in Flash. Developing in this fashion will most likely lower Flash's performance, but it will yield physics or math chunks that you can reuse. Check the Flash resource sites for the latest in this type of Flash programming. Two Web sites with excellent user boards are Ultrashock (www.ultrashock.com) and We're Here (www.were-here.com). Both of these sites have knowledgeable users who can answer questions on Flash physics.

Although we've only covered 2D examples in this chapter, everything you've learned for 2D Flash physics holds up in 3D. Vectors can be resolved into three components instead of two. The distance between two points is now:

$$Distance = \sqrt{(x2\text{-}x1)\text{\textasciicircum}2 + (y2\text{-}y1)\text{\textasciicircum}2 + (z2\text{-}z1)\text{\textasciicircum}2}$$

A couple of topics take a little more effort in 3D, however. Mapping 3D coordinates onto a 2D screen is one. See Chapter 2: 3D and Flash, for help with this. Also, collision detection in 3D takes more planning because there are more edges and walls. The Ultrashock and We're Here user boards are also great resources for 3D Flash physics.

4: Programming Sound in Flash

Allan Kennedy is a Flash and Director developer and digital media instructor at Toronto's award-winning zinc Roe design team (www.zincroe.com). In his first career as a cellist, Allan won several national and international awards, performed at Carnegie Hall, and toured Europe and North America as a soloist and chamber musician. Through his doctoral studies at McGill University, he was able to combine his lifelong interests in music and computers.

Allan is a contributor to www.ultrashock.com and has given seminars on Flash and Director throughout the U.S. and Canada. He has worked on traditional CD-ROM- and kiosk-based projects as well as online Flash and Shockwave content for companies such as the Family Channel, Cage Digital, Teletoon, and CN Rail.

Sound can have a dramatic impact on Flash projects. By using sound effectively, you can add richness and excitement to animation sequences, interactive games, and other Flash creations.

This chapter will focus on ways to program sound in Flash 5. We'll begin by discussing the fundamentals of sound and a few relevant digital audio concepts. Then, we'll examine various scenarios that use spatial relationships to control sound during runtime. Many of the programming techniques used throughout this chapter will be incorporated into the final showcase project.

After reading this chapter, you should understand how Flash's Sound object works, how to individually control multiple sounds, and how to control sound through unusual techniques such as spatial relationships and the rotational values of symbols.

What Is Sound?

Sound is a wave created by a vibrating object. A wave, in turn, can be described as a disturbance that transports energy through a medium—whether it's air, water, or any other material. It's this disturbance that we, as humans, perceive as an aural sensation or sound.

Frequency and Amplitude

A sound wave has two main properties: *frequency* and *amplitude*. Frequency, measured in hertz (Hz), refers to the number of repetitions, or cycles, a sound wave completes each second. Frequency also determines a sound's pitch—the higher the frequency, the higher the pitch. The human ear can detect sounds in an approximate frequency range from 20 to 20,000 Hz.

Figure 4.1 shows how sound appears in an oscilloscope, a mechanical tool or application that graphically displays a waveform.

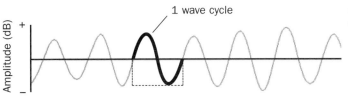

Figure 4.1 An oscilloscope view of a waveform.

Amplitude, represented by the waveform's height, refers to the volume of a sound wave and is measured in relative units of sound pressure known as decibels (dB). If 0 dB is interpreted by the human ear as silence, then 120 dB would be the approximate volume of a jet at takeoff.

Digital Audio Concepts

Understanding a few basic concepts of digital audio will help you create smaller and better-sounding audio files for your Flash projects.

Sample Rate and Bit Resolution

Sample rate, measured in kilohertz (kHz), is the number of times per second that sound wave information is gathered, or *sampled*, during the sound recording process. Flash can import sounds with sample rates of 11.025 kHz, 22.05 kHz, or 44.1 kHz. The sample rate used to record a sound determines its frequency range and thus, its accuracy. A basic rule of digital audio recording, the Nyquist Theorem, states that sample rate should be twice the value of a sound's highest frequency component for true reproducibility. We often capture frequency ranges outside of our hearing range, which influence the fundamental of a sound or note. That's why CD audio is sampled at 44.1kHz, while our hearing range only extends to 20 kHz. Of course, the higher the sample rate, the greater the file size.

Bit resolution is the number of bits used to describe each individual sound sample taken during recording. Flash can import either 8- or 16-bit audio. Bit resolution directly affects file size: A 16-bit audio file is twice the size of an 8-bit audio file. A 16-bit sound also has a broader volume range, greater clarity, and less background hiss than an 8-bit sound.

Both sample rate and bit resolution can be decreased to reduce file size; this process is called *downsampling*. Increasing a file's sample rate or resolution after it has been recorded at lower resolutions, however, won't improve its sound quality—it will only increase its file size. Instead of downsampling files and decreasing their quality, we can use clever compression formats such as the MP3 compression format, which Flash 5 supports. I highly recommend using it.

MP3 Compression

MP3 is an audio compression format that lets you reduce audio file sizes with minimal perceived loss in audio quality. It uses a complex psycho-acoustic model that retains only sound data perceived as important to the human ear. MP3 compression is measured in bit rate. Bit rate, measured in kilobits per second (kbps), is the number of bits played per second. Higher bit rates produce higher-quality MP3s and larger file sizes. For example, an MP3 encoded at 160 kbps will be far superior to an MP3 encoded at 8 kbps.

The Sound Object

The Sound object, one of Flash 5's built-in or predefined objects, lets you control sound using ActionScript. Although you can still attach sound to a keyframe or button, the Sound object lets you play sounds directly from the library, and controls playback in various ways in sync with programmatic events.

Think of the Sound object as an invisible blanket that wraps itself around sound assets in order to control them. Like other predefined objects, it comes with a set of predefined abilities or methods. The Sound object's methods allow it to start and stop a sound, set volume and pan levels, and retrieve information on current volume and pan levels. It can even isolate and control the volume of individual stereo channels.

The Sound object does have some limitations, however. For instance, it doesn't offer a method that identifies the current position of a sound during playback, or one that determines the length of a sound. But we can extend the capabilities of the Sound object by creating our own functions.

Controlling a Single Sound

Let's begin by examining an interface that controls a sound's pan and volume levels. As we review this project, I'll introduce you to a number of the Sound object's methods.

 Open sndObj_single.swf from the CD-ROM.

This interface controls a single sound during runtime and repeats part or all of a sound file based on the values we set. Play around with the volume and pan sliders to see how it works (**Figure 4.2**).

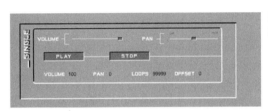

Figure 4.2 *The interface used to control a single sound.*

 Open sndObj_single.fla from the CD-ROM.

Attaching Sounds

Because this project doesn't use sound in the traditional timeline sense, we have to tell Flash to export the sound when we publish the movie. If we don't, the sound file won't be included in our compiled movie. Our first step, therefore, is to set the symbol linkage properties for the imported sound asset in the Library. To do this, we must supply an identifier string for the sound file. This linkage identifier requires a unique name, different from any other symbols set for export. In this file, it's called *loop*; we'll use it to programmatically attach sound from the Library.

Like some of the other predefined objects, the Sound object requires a more formal treatment, as it uses a constructor function. We do this by using new Sound(). We must also refer to the Sound object through a variable. This is done during the onClipEvent(load) event:

```
globalSnd1 = new Sound();
```

We'll begin by instantiating (creating an instance) a Sound object without a parameter. This creates a global Sound object, which can control all the sounds in a player, including timeline-based ones. It can even stop sounds in other SWF files playing in the browser environment.

Next, we'll attach the sound from the Library using the loop linkage identifier. This forces the sound to be exported when the movie is compiled. The imported sound file is now controlled by the global Sound object. The following code is attached to a load clip event on the movie clip symbol acting as the entire interface:

```
globalSnd1 = new Sound();
globalSnd1.attachSound("loop");
```

Note that the attachSound() method is applied to the variable name assigned to the Sound object. This sound will load at runtime before the first frame is rendered.

Starting Playback

Two of the Sound object's most basic methods are start() and stop(). I applied these methods respectively to the two buttons inside the main movie clip symbol.

The Play button has the following code attached to it:

```
on (press) {
if (!globalSnd1.playing) {
 globalSnd1.start(secondOffset,loops);
 globalSnd1.playing = true;
 }
}
```

We don't want to restart the sound every time someone clicks the Play button; that would create overlapping audio chaos. To prevent this, we'll use a conditional statement to test if it's already playing. The Stop button sets the playing variable's Boolean value to false.

The start() method can accept two optional parameters: secondOffset and loops. The secondOffset value is an integer or floating point number that tells the start() method when to begin playback (measured in seconds). In other words, if we have a 5-second sound file in our Library and we set the value of secondOffset to 2.5, we begin playback halfway through our sound.

TIP Make sure your offset value doesn't exceed the total duration of your sound file—otherwise you won't hear anything. If you omit this parameter, the default value is 0.

The second parameter, loops, accepts a positive integer value that tells the Sound object how many times the sound should play back based on its secondOffset value. (If it's the default value of 0, the sound will playback only once).

```
globalSnd1 = new Sound();
globalSnd1.attachSound("loop");
globalSnd1.playing= false;
var loops = 99999;
```

If you'd like to play around with these parameter values, initialize different values for the secondOffset and loops variables in the onClipEvent(load) event handler.

Stopping Playback

Now that we can start the sound, let's stop it. (Depending on your mindset, this may be more important!) Here's the code on the Stop button:

```
on (press) {
  globalSnd1.stop();
  globalSnd1.playing = false;
}
```

The stop() method, as invoked here, stops the playback of the global Sound object. It can also accept an optional parameter, which is useful when working with multiple sounds. We can include the sound's unique identifier to stop a specific sound regardless of how many sounds exist at that symbol's nesting level. The following code shows the stop() method using a linkage identifier as a parameter value:

```
globalSnd1.stop("loop");
```

Creating Volume and Pan Sliders

The sliders in the interface let you control the sound's volume and pan. They rely on two additional methods and their own local coordinate systems to accomplish this.

Adjusting Volume

The Sound object uses the setVolume() method to adjust the volume of the sound controlled by the object. Its related method, getVolume(), determines the volume of the sound controlled by the object. It's wise to use the two in conjunction to determine the current volume level before setting a new value. We'll use the setVolume() method in an enterFrame clip event that reads its parameter value based on slider values.

The setVolume() method generally accepts a parameter value between 0 and 100, although it can receive values beyond this range with both positive and negative numbers. It also has a reflective nature (based on an absolute distance from 0). For example, a parameter value between 5 and - 5 has the same volume output. Anything above 100 or below – 100, however, tends to distort the sound to some degree.

Panning Sound

Although a mono sound file contains a single channel with the same information sent to both the left and right speakers, we can still control the balance or distribution of volume between the speakers. The Sound object uses the setPan() method to do this. Its related method is getPan(). Like the two volume methods, these two methods are often used together.

The setPan() method accepts a number usually between - 100 and 100. Negative 100 controls the sound so it plays entirely in the left speaker, 0 distributes the balance evenly between the left and right speakers, and 100 plays the sound entirely in the right speaker. Anything between these values outputs a proportional mix of balance between left and right.

When you exceed this range, the effect is similar to rotating an object by an amount greater than 360 degrees. For example, using a value of 150 will give the same result as using a value of - 50. In other words, by exceeding these ranges you aren't giving more dominance to one speaker, but requesting additional sound information from the other speaker.

Programming the Sliders

Our interface project also demonstrates an easy way to use a slider's local coordinate system and some simple mathematical formulas to output value ranges appropriate to the setPan() and setVolume() methods. The slider, which is 100 pixels in length, has a local coordinate range between - 50 and 50 (**Figure 4.3**).

Figure 4.3 The slider's local coordinate system.

Because setVolume() works with values between 0 and 100, we simply add 50 to the slider button's local _x coordinate and round it off:

```
_parent.volume = Math.round(slider._x + 50);
```

Likewise, we can use the −50 to 50 coordinate range multiplied by two to generate an appropriate value for setPan(), as this statement demonstrates:

```
_parent.pan = Math.round(slider._x)*2;
```

As you can see, sliders provide a simple and traditional means of providing values for both the setVolume() and setPan() methods.

Asynchronous Events and Sound

Equally important as controlling the volume and pan of the Sound object is the ability to trigger a sound in response to a programmatic event.

Open sndObj_asynch.swf from the CD-ROM.

In this file, a draggable movie clip symbol plays a single sound when it collides with a boundary, which is represented by a white dotted line (**Figure 4.4**).

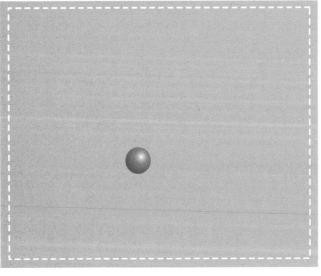

Figure 4.4 Drag the ball around until it collides with the boundary to hear what happens.

Open sndObj_asynch.fla from the CD-ROM.

The following code, called from an enterFrame clip event, moves the movie clip symbol around the Stage and detects boundary interceptions:

```
function move() {
oldX = _x;
oldY = _y;
newX = oldX + xSpeed;
newY = oldY + ySpeed;
// degrade the speed of the symbol
xSpeed *= energyLoss;
ySpeed *= energyLoss;
// check for boundary hit
if (newX < minX   || newX > maxX) {
 xSpeed = -xSpeed * energyLoss;
// trigger sound on impact with left or right boundary
 hitSound.start();
 newX = oldX;
}
if (newY < minY || newY > maxY) {
 ySpeed = -ySpeed * energyLoss;
// trigger sound on impact with top or bottom boundary
 hitSound.start();
 newY = oldY;
 }
x = newX;
y = newY;
 }
```

The Sound object is instantiated in the ball movie clip symbol's timeline along with its functions. The move() function is called repeatedly from an enterFrame clip event. This function moves the ball and checks whether it has collided with a boundary. If it has, we use the start() method to trigger playback of the sound. The sound will play only once, so there is no need for parameter values—it's as simple as that.

Controlling Multiple Sounds

As we've seen, controlling the playback of a single sound in the Flash player is quite easy. Controlling multiple sounds independently, however, can be considerably more complicated. This is mostly due to the way the Sound object is instantiated with its constructor function and corresponding parameter value. You'd think that simply referring to the Sound object with two separate variables would let you independently control the respectively attached sounds, but this is not the case, as seen below.

```
// bad example of sound programming
function soundInit(){
  sound1= new Sound(); // global Sound object
  sound2= new Sound(); // another global Sound object
  sound1.attachSound("soundId1");
  sound2.attachSound("soundId2");
  sound1.start(0,500);
  sound2.start(0,500);
  sound1.stop(); // stops both sounds!
}
```

Here, the first invocation of the stop() method terminates playback of both sounds, not just sound1. The stop() method refers to a global Sound object (sound1 is attached to _level0 and highest in the chain of command), and controls all sounds in the player, even those placed within nested timelines and set to stream or event sync types. Sound1 also controls the volume and pan of all these sounds as well. Why?

When the Sound object is instantiated without a parameter value (and sound is attached) it's by default scoped to _level0, and we create a global Sound object that can control all sound in nested timelines. This object prevents other Sound objects from maintaining complete individual control over volume and pan, as well. Once you understand that simply assigning different variable names to instances of the Sound object won't always give you the independent control you seek, you'll be one step closer to controlling multiple sounds.

Figure 4.5 illustrates the chain of command resulting from Sound objects being instantiated in a nested hierarchy. If the sounds attached to movie clip symbols on the main timeline currently have their volume set to 50 and the global Sound object changes its volume level from 100 to 50, the Sound objects under its control will drop to 25. There is a proportional relationship in this nested hierarchy. This volume change also affects other Sound objects on the same timeline.

Pathways to each Sound Object

Figure 4.5 *A visual representation of Sound objects instantiated within a nested hierarchy.*

Let's take a closer look at some parameters of the Sound object's methods that allow us to target individual sounds.

```
new Sound(target);
```

The Sound object's constructor function can receive an optional target parameter (a valid movie clip symbol reference) essential for dealing with multiple sounds. This parameter value lets you break away from a global Sound object that controls all the sounds in your player. Think of it as a chain of command: The closer the instantiated object is to the _root time-line, the more authority it has.

```
sound1.stop("soundId1");
```

You can use the stop() method to pinpoint and stop individual sounds that exist in the same timeline. You do this by using the linkage identifier as a parameter value for the stop() method.

Building a Mixer

We've had enough background theory on the sound object in relation to multiple sounds. Let's put this information to use.

 Open sndObj_multiple.swf from the CD-ROM.

This example, a sound mixer, demonstrates a simple yet effective way to control multiple sounds in your Flash movie while avoiding the headaches of using a global Sound object. You can change the volume and pan values for three sounds playing at the same time (**Figure 4.6**).

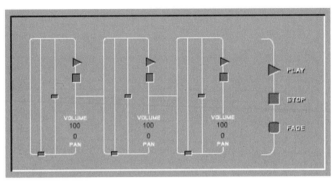

Figure 4.6 *Use the buttons to control and mix the sounds.*

 Open sndObj_multiple.fla from the CD-ROM.

This file uses three movie clip symbol instances, each containing two sliders: one for volume and the other for pan control. Each Sound object is instantiated within these movie clip symbols. This lets you control each sound separately, or all three sounds at once, by using the larger buttons to the right. The code attached to each movie clip symbol lets you individually control each Sound object. Here's the code:

```
onClipEvent (load) {
    sComponent = new Sound(this);
    sComponent.attachSound(this._name);
    sComponent.playing = false;
    var loops = 500;
    var secondOffset = 0;
    var volume = 100;
    var pan = 0;
}
```

Notice that the Sound object is instantiated with our new Sound() constructor function using this as a parameter value. The this keyword is a reference to the movie clip symbol instance and associates each Sound object with a unique timeline. Once the new Sound object is referenced through the variable sComponent, we can attach each sound from the Library by passing the movie clip symbol's instance name as the parameter for the attachSound() method. (All three movie clip symbols use the same variable name for the Sound object because each exists in different scopes.)

I find it convenient to match my movie clip symbols' instance names to the identifier string used in linkage properties. In this case, I used s1, s2, and s3 for each movie clip symbol and linkage identifiers.

The following statements declare and initialize values that are needed by our start(), setVolume(), and setPan() methods. If the fadeOut() function hasn't been triggered by a button on the main timeline, the enterFrame clip event checks for any change in the volume and pan values.

```
onClipEvent (enterFrame) {
 sComponent.setPan(pan);
 if(fadeTrig) {
  fadeOut();
 }else {
  sComponent.setVolume(volume);
 }
}
```

If the fadeOut() function has been triggered, the enterFrame clip event repeatedly calls a function inside each movie clip symbol. This function looks at the current volume level for each Sound object and decreases it until volume is set to 0. When this occurs, the fade trigger is deactivated, and playing for that individual sound is set to false.

This code is placed in the first frame of each movie clip's timeline:

```
function fadeOut () {
if (sComponent.getVolume()>=0) {
 sComponent.setVolume(sComponent.getVolume()-4);
} else {
 sComponent.setVolume(0);
 sComponent.stop();
 fadeTrig = sComponent.playing = false;
 }
}
```

We control each Sound object (starting, stopping, and use of sliders) just as we did with the single sound example, except we're no longer using a global Sound object. We now have three sounds that can be controlled independently via the sliders and buttons.

TIP The maximum number of sounds that can safely be controlled simultaneously via the Sound object is debatable: Some say four; others insist on six. Ultimately, this depends on the capabilities of your sound card. Some low-end cards can play only eight individual sounds simultaneously. I recommend using no more than eight sounds, which is what I have safely worked with to date.

Master Controls for Multiple Sounds

What if we want to start all the sounds together? First, to avoid playback of two instances of the same sound, we use a short script to check which sounds aren't currently playing. We then tell each sound to begin playing by executing the following code attached to a Master Control button on the main timeline:

```
on (release) {
for (var i=1; i<=3; i++) {
 mcRef = _root["s"+i];
 if (!mcRef.sComponent.playing) {
 mcRef.sComponent.start(mcRef.secondOffset, mcRef.loops);
 mcRef.sComponent.playing = true;
   }
  }
 }
```

We use the array access operator to dynamically generate the names of each symbol containing the sound and then conveniently access the same variable within the scope that refers to that Sound object. We also set each instance's playing value to true.

We can use a similar, yet simpler approach to stop all the sounds at once. This approach doesn't check to see what sounds are currently playing—it just stops them all.

```
on (release) {
for (var i=1; i<=3; i++) {
 mcRef = _root["s"+i];
 mcRef.sComponent.stop();
 mcRef.sComponent.playing = false;
  }
 }
```

 Note that I used the variable mcRef extensively. We use it frequently in our shop as a placeholder for passing around movie clip symbol references.

Synchronization

The previous example had three sounds with independent and general controls. What if we had three sounds with corresponding rhythms at the same beats per minute (bpm), and we wanted to synchronize them so their beats matched up during playback? Most programmatically controlled sounds are attached at runtime as event sync sounds, so they don't have the built-in global buffer of 5 seconds of playback time that stream sync sounds have. This buffer is needed to synchronize the sounds' beats at the same bpm. If you try to use three timeline-based event sounds with the same bpm and corresponding rhythmic material, they won't be synchronized either (stream sync types will, however).

To handle this issue for programmatic event syncs, I use a function that simulates a buffer for each sound and extends its capability. To create the buffer, we start each sound at 0 volume, stop all the sounds, and then restart them at the desired volume level.

The following sample code, which creates this buffer effect, uses a script similar to the previous code sequence:

```
function sync() {
var mcRef;
for (var i=3; i>0; i--) {
 mcRef = _root["s"+i];
 mcRef.playing = true;
 mcRef.sComponent.setVolume(0);
 mcRef.sComponent.start();
 mcRef.sComponent.stop();
 mcRef.sComponent.start(0, 500);
 mcRef.sComponent.setVolume(100);
 }
}
```

The sync() function above will safely synchronize three event sounds with the same tempo or bpm. It's possible to extend the power of this function by creating synchronized groupings within larger sets of sounds. The showcase project at the end of this chapter uses a similar sync() function and puts this technique to work.

Beyond Traditional Input Techniques

Now that we understand the fundamentals of the Sound object, let's extend this knowledge by looking at different ways to feed input values to our methods. The next two examples will do just that.

Using Coordinate Systems

The following example uses the coordinate systems of a movie clip symbol to control the volume and pan values of the Sound object's methods. This project is the foundation for the more complex scenarios used in the show-case project.

 Open sndObj_beyond1.swf from the CD-ROM.

The symbol's _x property represents pan values and its _y property represents volume values. A simple grid maps the *x*- and *y*-coordinates for the symbol; when you move the circle, dynamic text fields report the new volume and pan levels (**Figure 4.7**).

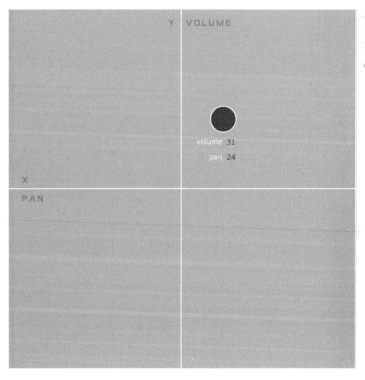

Figure 4.7 *Try moving the circle to hear how the sound's volume and pan values change.*

Open sndObj_beyond1.fla from the CD-ROM.

Note that the movie's Stage is set to 400 x 400 pixels. The following code is attached to the movie clip symbol:

```
onClipEvent (load) {
  sound1 = new sound(this);
  sound1.attachSound("mySound");
  sound1.start(0, 1000);
}
onClipEvent (mouseDown) {
if (this.hitTest(_root._xmouse, _root._ymouse, true)) {
  startDrag ("", true);
  }
}
onClipEvent (mouseUp) {
  stopDrag();
}
onClipEvent (enterFrame) {
  volume = Math.round(this._y/4);
  pan = Math.round(this._x/2-100);
  sound1.setPan(pan);
  sound1.setVolume(volume);
}
```

The formula used to establish pan values translates a 400-pixel range into an acceptable parameter range for the setPan() method: - 100 to 100. The volume formula similarly takes this 400-pixel range and divides it by 4 to allow a range between 0 and 100. These values are continuously read (based on fps) by an enterFrame clip event.

Spatial Relationships

Next, let's look at how the distance between two movie clip symbols can determine volume. This will allow us to create an unusual sonic experience.

 Open sndObj_beyond2.swf from the CD-ROM.

This example, "Web of Gossip," goes beyond using a coordinate system to feed values to the setVolume() method.

A white movie clip symbol, which represents you, is surrounded by five gray movie clip symbols, which represent other people (**Figure 4.8**). Each gray symbol has a sound attached to it, representing its own narrative of gossip and music. The volume of each gray symbol is based on its distance from the central symbol. Dragging the symbols simulates the effect of a person walking around in a crowded room: For example, as the white symbol approaches one of the gray symbols, the gray symbol's volume increases. As a bonus, you can record and play back via screen coordinates the movie clips' journeys through the room.

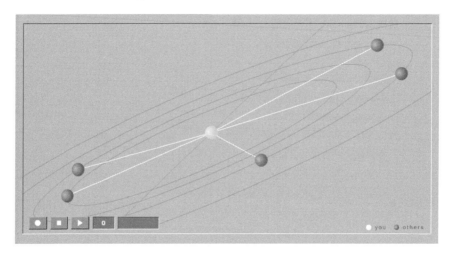

Figure 4.8 *Drag the white circle toward one of the gray circles and hear what happens.*

 Open sndObj_beyond2.fla from the CD-ROM.

Most of this file's functionality is executed through a series of functions on the main timeline. Each of the five gray movie clip symbols has three states: The symbol is either updating its volume levels based on its distance from the white symbol, recording its position, or playing back what has been recorded.

The following code is attached to the gray movie clip symbols:

```
onClipEvent (load) {
  root.initSound(this);
}
onClipEvent (enterFrame) {
  if (_root.recording) {
    _root.record(this);
  }
}
```

```
  if (_root.playing) {
   _root.playback(this);
  }
  root.update(this);
 }
```

Upon load, each movie clip symbol makes a single call to an initSound() function on the main timeline. During the enterFrame clip event, each symbol also calls three functions: two are contingent on Boolean values and the third, update(), is repeatedly executed.

The following function on the main timeline instantiates each Sound object at its appropriate nesting level after it's called by each individual movie clip symbol and passed this as a parameter value:

```
function initSound(mcRef) {
 mcRef.ball.swapDepths(2);
 mcRef.snd = new Sound(mcRef);
 mcRef.snd.attachSound(mcRef._name);
 mcRef.snd.start(0, 9999);
 mcRef.attachMovie("line", "line", 1);
 update(mcRef);
}
```

Let's examine the three main timeline functions called by the movie clip symbols. The first one, initSound(), is called by each symbol as it's loaded. The function instantiates the Sound object, attaches a sound from the Library based on the name of the symbol passed as a parameter value, and begins playback. It also attaches a movie clip symbol with the instance name *microphone*. This symbol—a line—is used to visually connect the gray symbols to the white symbol. When this is done, a call is made from within this function to the update() function.

```
function update(mcRef) {
 var dX = mcRef._x-_root.microphone._x;
 var dY = mcRef._y-_root.microphone._y;
 mcRef.line._xscale = -dX;
 mcRef.line._yscale = -dY;
 var distance = Math.round(Math.sqrt(dX*dX+dY*dY));
 vol = Math.round((50/distance)*100);
 if (vol>=110) {
  vol = 110;
 }
 mcRef.snd.setVolume(vol);
}
```

The update() function is not only immediately called from the initSound() function, but continuously throughout runtime by each movie clip symbol. It updates the sound volume associated with each gray symbol based on its distance from the white symbol. It also sets the _xscale and _yscale properties for the attached line. Because we don't have programmatic access to the anchor points of our vector objects in Flash, we have to use this scale trick to connect the symbols with the line. We then take this distance value, flip it, and mold it into an acceptable parameter range for the setVolume() method with a maximum value of 110.

Recording Sound Coordinates

To record our audio trek, we use a straightforward frame-based approach that records the coordinates of each movie clip symbol in an array. Because the volume of each symbol depends on the relative positions of the white and gray symbols, re-enacting the coordinates over time lets us reproduce the volume levels.

The Record button on the main timeline sets the record variable's Boolean value to true. This activates a call from each movie clip symbol to the record function. Additionally, the status movie clip symbol on the main timeline reacts to this change by incrementing the count variable scoped to its timeline.

The following code is attached to the status movie clip symbol on the main timeline:

```
onClipEvent (enterFrame) {
  if (_root.playing || _root.recording) {
    count++;
  }
}
```

Clicking the Record button sets the value of count to 0. When count first increments to 1, we delete any previously created arrays and create a new array representing each movie clip symbol's x- and y-coordinates over time.

```
function record(mcRef) {
if (status.count == 1) {
  delete mcRef.recordX;
  delete mcRef.recordY;
  mcRef.recordX = new Array();
  mcRef.recordY = new Array();
}
```

Let's look at how we can add elements to the array:

```
mcRef.recordX.push( mcRef._x );
mcRef.recordY.push( mcRef._y );
if (status.count > frameLimit) {
 recording = false;
 status.count = 0;
 status.gotoAndStop("quiet");
 }
}
```

We then use the push() method of the Array object to add *x*- and
y-coordinates to the end of the array, effectively recording each movie
clip symbol's coordinates during each passing frame. (If the frame rate
were higher, we would record more coordinates for each movie clip
symbol as each second passes.) We limit the size of the arrays so that
viewers' resources won't be overloaded. This is done by checking the
value of count relative to the frameLimit variable. If this conditional
statement returns true, recording is stopped and count is reset to 0.

After recording this information, we establish some playback functionality
via this function on the main timeline:

```
function playback(mcRef) {
 if (status.count > mcRef.recordX.length) {
  playing = false;
 } else {
 mcRef._x = mcRef.recordX[status.count];
 mcRef._y = mcRef.recordY[status.count];
 }
}
```

The playback() function works in a similar manner. If the Play button is
clicked, playing is set to true and each movie clip symbol makes a call to the
playback() function. The movie clip symbols use this function to retrieve
their respective *x*- and *y*-coordinates as elements from their arrays. (Each
movie clip symbol has two arrays: one each for its *x*- and *y*-coordinates.)
After each element is retrieved, it's used to set the current coordinate values
for each movie clip symbol. This continues until count has exceeded the
length of each array.

As you can see, this technique uses an innovative approach for feeding
values to the setVolume() method. It also offers a straightforward method
of recording in real-time the coordinates of practically anything in Flash.

Preloading Attached Sounds

Because multiple sound files can easily increase your project's file size, it's good practice to use some type of preload system. There are, however, a few problems associated with this. For example, Flash will download sounds exported via a linkage identifier before it renders the first frame of a movie. This means viewers won't see any graphics until all the sounds have downloaded, defeating the purpose of a preload system. In addition, attached sounds must be downloaded completely before they're instantiated and set to play. Consequently, it's a good idea to use a preload system that checks from one level and then loads the SWF with sounds set for forced export into a level above it or into a movie clip instance on the parent level.

In the following example, sound is loaded into a movie clip symbol in sndObj_preload.swf, from ext_sound.swf, which contains a sound set for export.

 Open sndObj_preload.swf and ext_sound.swf from the CD-ROM.

For accurate performance, these files must be tested on a server. Testing them on a local hard drive won't simulate the degree of limited bandwidth that viewers may encounter online. Flash's bandwidth profiler also won't help, as it simulates streaming playback only for the file currently being tested, not for the externally loaded file.

 Open sndObj_preload.fla from the CD-ROM.

The following code is attached to a movie clip symbol that contains a dynamic text field and progress bar. This is executed past frame 1 (preload tests executed on frame 1 aren't always 100 percent reliable).

```
onClipEvent (load) {
loadMovie ("ext_sound.swf", _root.sndContainer);
bar._width = 0;
var percent = 0;
}
```

When this movie clip loads, the loadMovie() function begins downloading the ext_sound.swf into a symbol named sndContainer on the main timeline. This symbol is used as a container for the sound. We also set the width of the progress bar inside the movie clip to 0 so it doesn't display at full length with slower connections. LoadMovie(), despite its order in this series of statements, is executed last.

The following code is on the status bar movie clip symbol:

```
onClipEvent (enterFrame) {
currentLoad = _root.sndContainer.getBytesLoaded();
totalLoad = _root.sndContainer.getBytesTotal();
if (currentLoad>0) {
 percent = Math.round(currentLoad/totalLoad*100);
 percentOutput = percent+" %";
 bar._width = percent*2;
if (percent>=100) {
 root.gotoAndStop(5);
  }
 }
}
```

On the enterFrame clip event we declare and initialize some variables to represent the current load and total load values (in bytes) of the data being transferred into the sndContainer symbol. We then check if any data has been received so that percent isn't set to NaN (not a number). (Although a data clip event might seem better suited for this system than an enterFrame clip event, problems have been reported with the former when tested over fast connections.)

If the currentLoad is greater than 0 (meaning that we have received some data), we divide currentLoad by totalLoad (giving us a range between 0 and 1). This is multiplied by 100 and rounded to the nearest integer for a percent value. The percent value is constantly updated and used for output into the dynamic text field and to control the length of the progress bar (its full length is 200 pixels). If all of ext_sound.swf has downloaded, we move to the next frame on the main timeline and begin playing back the sound in the sndContainer movie clip.

After everything has been preloaded, we move to the next frame on the main timeline:

```
testSound = new Sound (_root.sndContainer);
testsound.attachSound("loadSound");
testSound.start(0,3);
```

In this frame we instantiate the externally loaded sound with sndContainer as its target. The target is important here, as the sound is only available within the movie clip in which it's loaded.

Showcase Project

My showcase project is a modification of a visual sound mixer I developed at zinc Roe design. It uses Flash's global and local coordinate systems to rotate objects based on the coordinate system of another movie clip object. It also switches between local and global coordinates for pan and volume values.

 Open sndObj_showcase.swf from the CD-ROM.

This project lets you select up to six animated movie clips symbols, each representing a different sound, and drag them out from the center of the platter (**Figure 4.9**). This synchronizes them in a complex rhythmic exchange that creates an experimental music composition.

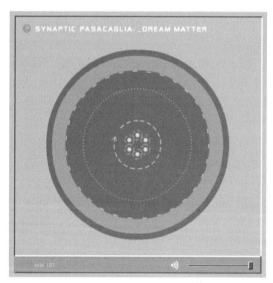

Figure 4.9 *Spatial relationships and rotation speed are used to mix sounds in an experimental musical composition.*

How is this a mixer? When you drag a symbol, its distance from the center of the platter determines its volume, scale value, and animation speed. These settings are updated in real-time as you drag the symbol. Symbols further from the center will be louder, larger, and animate more quickly. If you release a symbol outside of the platter area, it will return to its initial position and stop playing.

Once you reposition the symbols, you can grab the platter and give it a spin. As it rotates, individual sound volumes remain fixed but the pan levels change, making the sounds move between speakers.

Let's review the key programming techniques used in this example.

 Open sndObj_showcase.fla from the CD-ROM.

Attaching Symbols and Sound Objects

One of the features of this example is that it attaches Sound objects to dynamically attached movie clips. Let's look at the code in the actions layer's frame. When the file loads, it attaches six instances of a clip to the platter's timeline. The coordinates of these programmatically attached movie clip symbols are based on the platter's coordinate system. These symbols are used as containers for each Sound object. The temporary path reference generated for each symbol (root.platter.s1, _root.platter.s2, and so on) is stored as mcRef. Also, the _xscale and _yscale of each symbol at load time is set to 50 percent when they're attached to the platter.

```
for (var i=1; i<=soundNum; i++) {
platter.attachMovie("soundSprite", "s"+i, i);
mcRef = platter["s"+i];
mcRef._xscale = mcRef._yscale = 50;
```

Each movie clip symbol is dynamically positioned in a circular pattern around the platter's center based on the number of sounds required at runtime (determined by soundNum). The following code defines a radian value used to space the symbols by taking the circumference of a circle (2*Math.PI) and dividing it by the number of sounds in the mixer:

```
Var soundNum = 6;
var spacing = 2*Math.PI/soundNum;
mcRef._x = startDistance*Math.sin(spacing*i);
mcRef._y = startDistance*Math.cos(spacing*i);
mcRef.initX = mcRef._x;
mcRef.initY = mcRef._y;
```

This spacing value (after being multiplied by the index variable i) is used with the math object's sine and cosine methods to plot a circular path at a specific distance (startDistance or radius) from the platter's center. (The sine and cosine methods require a radian value, not a degree.) These initial positions are recorded with initX and initY; if you drag the symbols off the platter, this returns them to their original positions.

Next, we instantiate each sound object:

```
mcRef.sndObj = new Sound(mcRef);
mcRef.sndObj.attachSound(mcRef._name);
```

The Sound objects are instantiated with a parameter based on the nesting level of each attached movie clip symbol. This lets us individually control each Sound object. The sounds have been prepared for export in the linkage properties panel with the identifiers `s1`, `s2`, and so on.

Each of these also corresponds to the name of the symbol used as a container for the Sound object. This lets us use the `attachSound()` method based on the `_name` of `mcRef` (which resolves to `s1`, `s2`, and so on.). I find this technique useful when referring to Sound objects instantiated at different nesting levels within a document.

After each Sound object has been instantiated and associated with a movie clip symbol, we make a call to the `sync()` function with a list of Sound objects to be synchronized. The `sync()` function uses the arguments array. The following code gives us the flexibility of sending any number of Sound objects as arguments:

```
sync(platter.s1.sndobj,platter.s2.sndobj,platter.s3.sndobj,
→ platter.s4.sndobj,platter.s5.sndobj,platter.s6.sndobj);
function sync() {
for (var i=0;i<arguments.length;i++) {
 arguments[i].setVolume(0);
 arguments[i].start();
 arguments[i].stop();
 arguments[i].start(0, 9999);
 }
}
```

As mentioned earlier, this creates enough of a buffer for a limited number of sounds—three, in this case—to be synchronized at start. Based on my experience, I believe the synchronization order may be related to the order in which a sound ID is assigned to each Sound object at instantiation (check the list variables at runtime). I'm not aware of any documentation regarding this issue, however.

Now all the movie clip symbols are positioned on the platter and the Sound objects are instantiated. I placed the code that controls the file setup and most of the dynamic sounds aspects on the main timeline to centralize it.

Whenever you drag and drop a movie clip symbol, it calls the following functions:

```
function drag(mcRef) {
mcRef.startDrag(true);
mcRef.moving = true;
}
```

These functions are called by a hidden button inside each movie clip symbol. The drag function initiates a `startDrag()` on the movie clip symbol whose reference is passed to the function in `mcRef`. The Boolean variable moving is set to true, which lets the movie clip symbol call the `setVol()` method. Volume is updated only while a movie clip symbol is being moved.

Determining the Distance Between Symbols

To determine if a movie clip symbol has moved off the platter, we must find its distance from the center of the platter. If it's further from the platter's center than the platter's radius, it's off the platter. Because the coordinates of `mcRef` are based on the platter's coordinate system (remember that the attached movie clip symbols are nested inside the platter's timeline), we can modify a traditional distance formula to do the trick.

Usually a distance formula looks at the differences in x- and y-coordinates of two movie clip symbols. The code below represents a more traditional approach to determine distance (similar to what was used in the sndObj_beyond2.fla). I used `Math.abs()`, which gives you an absolute value based on a number's distance from 0, to avoid the problem of `Math.pow()` returning NaN. (In some early versions of the Flash Player, `Math.pow()` doesn't accept negative values and can return NaN.)

This is a more typical code example that compares two movie clip symbols:

```
dX = Math.abs(clip1._x - clip2._x);
dY = Math.abs(clip1._y - clip2._y);
distance = Math.sqrt(Math.pow(dX,2) + Math.pow(dY,2));
```

We don't need to look at two symbols in this case; we can just use the coordinates of mcRef. In other words, the local *x*- and *y*-coordinates of mcRef will determine the _x and _y difference in pixels between mcRef and the platter's registration point (simulating the distance between two objects). If we use the long form for this formula, we can avoid using Math.pow() and Math.abs():

```
function drop(mcRef) {

var distance =
Math.sqrt((mcRef._x*mcRef._x)+(mcRef._y*mcRef._y));
if (distance > platter.radius) {
  mcRef._x = mcRef.initX;
  mcRef._y = mcRef.initY;
  mcRef._xscale = mcRef._yscale = 50;
  mcRef.sndObj.setVolume(0);
  mcRef.activeState.gotoAndStop(1)
  mcRef.speed = 0;
}
stopDrag();
mcRef.moving = false;
}
```

If the distance from mcRef is greater than the platter's radius, we know the symbol has gone off the platter. At this point, the symbol is returned to its original position at load. The code stops the sound and animation, and sets moving to false, which disables the call to setVol().

Tracking Pan Values

The next two functions, located on the main timeline, are integral to the mixer. They determine pan and volume for each sound. Let's first examine the setPan() function:

```
function setPan(mcRef) {
var pan;
pt = new Object();
pt.x = mcRef._x;
pt.y = mcRef._y;
mcRef.localToGlobal(pt);
pt.x = platter._x-pt.x;
pt.y = platter._y-pt.y;
```

The `setPan()` function is called repeatedly from an enterFrame clip event (on the activeState movie clip symbol in the sound sprite). The pan values must be continuously updated as the movie clip symbol is dragged and while the platter is spinning. Because the symbols inside the platter's timeline are dependent and locked into its local coordinate system, we use the `localToGlobal()` method to get the position of the symbol relative to the main timeline's global coordinates. To use this method, we instantiate a generic object called `pt` and give it *x*- and *y*- properties to store `mcRef`'s current x- and y-coordinates. This method requires an object to translate `mcRef`'s coordinates to global coordinates.

We then subtract the global coordinates from each other and establish `mcRef`'s coordinates relative to the platter's center. This is needed to calculate the angle of the `mcRef` as the platter is spinning. The `Math.atan2()` method uses *y*- and *x*-coordinates (in that order) to perform an arc tangent calculation representing a radian measurement of the angle between the platter's center and the movie clip symbol. This radian value is then converted to an angle (`angle in degrees = radian/Math.PI*180`):

```
angle = Math.atan2(pt.y,pt.x)/Math.PI*180;
```

Because these angle values resolve outside normal `setPan()` parameter values (they resolve between - 180 and 180 based on a full circle), we must diminish its value range by dividing it by 1.8:

```
pan = angle/1.8;
mcRef.sndObj.setPan(pan);
```

Tracking Volume Values

The next function alters the volume only while the movie clip symbol is being dragged. Once again, we'll determine the movie clip symbol's distance from the platter's center based on a local coordinate system.

```
function setVol(mcRef) {
var distance =
Math.sqrt((mcRef._x*mcRef._x)+(mcRef._y*mcRef._y));
```

From this we create a value range for the volume. Volume will be set to 0 if it's dragged within a 10-pixel radius of the platter's center and volume levels will max out near the edge at about 110, adding a little boom power to each sound. We also use volume to determine the speed of the movie clip symbol's animation and its scale values. Speed actually controls how many frames the activeState movie clip symbol will skip during its animation sequence.

This code excerpt from the setVol() function on the main timeline gives a little more variety to the behavior of each movie clip symbol:

```
var vol = (distance-10)/(platter.radius/120);
if (vol < 0 || distance > platter.radius) {vol = 0;}
mcRef.sndObj.setVolume(vol);
mcRef.speed = Math.floor(vol/15);
mcRef._xscale = mcRef._yscale = 10 + vol;
```

Now we can determine the volume and pan of our Sound objects based on the spatial relationships between the movie clip symbols and the platter—whether they refer to local or global coordinate systems. Let's shake it up by spinning the platter and listening to the sounds as they pan through the left and right speakers.

Using Rotational Values

The spinning platter uses an old Flash developers' trick to track the speed of the symbols being dragged. Only in this case, it's tracking each symbol's rotational speed while it's being rotated. A button inside the platter movie clip symbol sets the dragging Boolean to true or false. If dragging is true, we determine the platter's rotation based on how many degrees the mouse has moved since the last enterFrame was read (newAngle-oldAngle). If it's false, we record this difference in angularSpeed and the platter continues to rotate at that speed. This is all executed on the platter movie clip's enterFrame clip event:

```
onClipEvent(enterFrame) {
oldAngle = newAngle;
newAngle = Math.atan2(_root._ymouse - _y, _root._xmouse -
  → x) /Math.PI*180;
if (dragging) {
//platter is being rotated by user
  this._rotation += newAngle-oldAngle;
} else {
  this._rotation += angularSpeed;
  }
}
```

Once again we use the ever useful `Math.atan2()` and a radian conversion formula to determine the angle between the mouse (based on its global coordinate) and the platter's center. Because this is tracked by an enterFrame clip event, the speed being updated depends on the fps set in Flash's Movie Properties.

One problem remains: We don't want viewers to spin the platter so fast that panning between speakers becomes a pointless effect. We solve this by limiting the rotation speed when the platter is released (to a positive or negative value, depending on its orientation).

The following code is attached to the button inside the platter movie clip's timeline:

```
on(release,releaseOutside) {
dragging = false;
angularSpeed = newAngle - oldAngle;
if (angularSpeed > 16) angularSpeed = 16;
if (angularSpeed < -16) angularSpeed = -16;
}
```

Global Volume Control

The last component to examine is the volume slider that controls all the sounds in the mixer. This code, attached to the thumb movie clip symbol in the slider's timeline, offers a simple way to control all the sounds in the player:

```
onClipEvent (load) {
globalSound = new Sound();
}
```

We achieve this global control by instantiating a global Sound object without attaching a sound to it. This still lets us control all the sounds in the player. Then we adjust the volume of this global Sound object in the following statements through the slider's local coordinate system, which in this case is 0 - 100:

```
onClipEvent (enterFrame) {
if (adjusting) {
 volume = this._x;
 globalSound.setVolume(volume);
```

This next section of code uses a timeline-based approach to update the volume meter's appearance on the main timeline:

```
if (volume == 0) {
root.volMeter.gotoAndStop(1);
} else if (volume<40) {
root.volMeter.gotoAndStop(2);
} else if (volume<80) {
root.volMeter.gotoAndStop(3);
} else {
root.volMeter.gotoAndStop(4);
  }
 }
}
```

That's it. I hope this inspires you to control the Sound object in new and innovative ways. There are an infinite number of techniques you can use to create new types of visual mixer interfaces, such as depth sorting, scale values, 3D interfaces, and speed of objects. I hope to see more of these types of applications in the future.

Tips for Using Sound in Flash

- Before importing a sound into Flash, begin with high-quality source files (16-bit resolution and 44.1 kHz sample rate).

- For optimal quality sound, import sound files with sample rates that are a multiple of 11 (such as 11.025 or 22.05 kHz); otherwise, Flash will resample the audio.

- Set individual compression levels for each sound within Flash. Be careful, however, to not decrease the original compression (from 32 kbps to 164 kbps, for example) of your MP3 file. This will only increase file size, not quality.

- To determine the best compression settings (bit rate) for an MP3 file, consider the bandwidth of your target audience. Flash offers bit rates between 8 kbps and 160 kbps. If you're targeting Web users with dial-up connections slower than 56 kbps, choose a low bit rate such as 16 or 24 kbps. For high-speed DSL or intranets, choose a higher bit rate, such as 128 or 160 kbps.

- If you're working with large sound files in Flash, increasing the amount of available RAM on your computer will help prevent freezes. You should have enough RAM to cover Flash's normal operations plus the size of the raw sound file(s) you're using. Mac users should allocate more RAM to Flash.

- Be careful when creating a global Sound object. Sometimes instantiating the Sound object in a movie clip just one nesting level above the main timeline will decrease headaches in the long run—especially if you plan to use attached sounds in loaded levels. The global Sound will not take over all the sound in your player.

- The Sound object can be mildly taxing on viewers' resources. Be sure to delete the variable that refers to the object once you no longer need it. This is especially important when using multiple sounds. Don't forget to stop a sound, however, before deleting it. If you don't, it will develop a mind of its own and behave unpredictably.

- Sometimes when you delete a sound that's no longer in use from the Library, the size of the authoring file remains the same. If this happens, resave the file with a different name.

- When testing a movie with a large number of sounds—or one long sound—you may want to temporarily override the default MP3 compression setting, as the MP3 encoding process can take substantially longer than other compression formats.

A Final Note

I hope this chapter has given you a solid understanding of how the Sound object works. You should now be able to apply this knowledge to situations requiring single sound usage as well as those requiring multiple sounds with individual controls.

An important aspect of this chapter was searching for unusual techniques to feed values to the setVolume() and setPan() methods for the Sound object. I hope you continue this sonic journey on your own.

5: Component System Architecture

Eric E. Dolecki is a Senior Interactive Designer and Interactive Technology Manager at Boston-based Directech eMerge. By day, he develops interactive projects for technology clients such as NCR Teradata, WorldCom, and Lotus. By monitor light at night, he works on his personal site, www.ericd.net, and creates Flash projects. His Flash work has been published in *Computer Arts* magazine, and he has received numerous Flash Kit awards. Eric finds inspiration in Flash peers Eric Jordan, Andries Odendaal, Vas Sloutchevsky, Yugo Nakamura, Guy Watson (a.k.a. FlashGuru), Manuel Clement, Joshua Davis, and the entire Super Samurai book team. When not working in Flash, Eric oil paints; develops 3D animations; creates original musical scores; and researches DHTML, WAP, ASP, CFML, XML, and database technologies.

There are many ways to develop and deploy complex projects in Flash 5, but that flexibility comes at a cost. Some complex Flash sites can take forever to load on a viewer's browser—and, from a developer's perspective, just about as long to create and edit. If you're working with huge source files and multiple instances of navigation, or if you have multiple developers working on the same files, you've got more complexity than you bargained for.

Choosing the right development method, therefore, can mean the difference between a project that's easy to update and easy to load, and one that's, well, a nightmare for everyone involved.

The solution? Component system architecture. This method lets you break complex projects into modules, or *components*, that can be developed and loaded individually. The result is easier updates for you and faster load times for your viewers.

In this chapter, you'll learn how to plan and build a component-based system, and how to prevent usability problems from hampering your project.

What Is Component System Architecture?

Component system architecture breaks a Flash project into a set of individual modules, or components, that load on an as-needed basis. This architecture offers three key advantages:

- Sites load more quickly because components load only when called.

- Sites are easier to create because you don't have to work on one large source file. A team of developers can work on a project simultaneously, each working on his or her own component. Later, all the components can be assembled into the final project.

- Sites are easier to update. You can quickly edit one aspect of a Web site—navigation, for example—without affecting every other area of the site.

Dividing a project into components does not mean breaking a Flash project into scenes, or breaking a movie into separate movie clips. Instead, think of dividing your project into *functional* components as they relate to your design. For instance, you might put your site's navigation system in one component, background images in another, text from variables in another, and so on. It also makes sense to put larger assets—such as audio files or certain graphics files—into components, so they'll load more quickly.

 Component system architecture doesn't work only on fully Flashed sites. You can also apply this method to HTML-based sites that have some Flash content.

Using component system architecture dramatically reduces load times and increases your productivity. It also promotes a collaborative environment. By divvying up the development work, you can let programmers with special talents work on specific project areas, designers perform their magic on others, and get the best work out of everybody. And component-based sites offer greater design freedom, letting you optimize your screen real estate without resorting to pop-up windows, frames, or other clutter.

Of course, anything that sounds this good has to have some drawbacks, and there are a few. If you're on a tight deadline, or if you're the sole developer working on a project, another approach may be better, as component-based systems do require more planning and development up front. They also need a longer quality control period because bugs and usability errors can crop up in more places—and finding them can be harder. It's best to save component-based design for larger projects, as breaking smaller projects into components may prove to be more trouble than it's worth.

 If you haven't seen Eric Jordan's site, www.2Advanced.com, check it out (**Figure 5.1**). It's an excellent showcase for component system architecture.

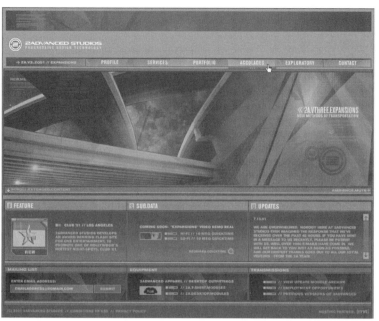

Figure 5.1
www.2Advanced.com
is a great example of
component system
architecture.

Ready to learn more about component system architecture? Let's take a look at the technology behind it.

loadMovieNum(): The Core Technology

The key Flash 5 technology behind component system architecture is the loadMovieNum() action. This lets you communicate with external Flash movies (SWFs) and combine them with the original, or root, movie. The root movie sets the frame rate, the Stage size, and the background color.

Loaded movies give you a whole new level of control: For instance, a movie in one level can set variables in another movie on another level, control the timeline of another loaded movie, or even control a series of nested movie clips in multiple loaded movies.

When you load an external SWF into another Flash movie, you use levels to keep track of their locations. The original Flash movie is always at Level 0 (known in ActionScript as _level0); subsequent movies load at higher levels.

For example, this action:

```
loadMovieNum ("xyz.swf", 1);
```

loads the SWF file named xyz into Level 1, which is the level directly above the root movie.

 To create a level, just specify the level number you want to use and load a movie into it. (Although I wouldn't recommend it, you can load as many as 16,384 levels into a Flash movie.)

Loaded movies have transparent Stages by default; this lets the movies on the levels beneath them show through. If you want a loaded movie to hide the movies beneath it, cover its entire Stage with an opaque rectangle or graphic. This chapter's sample site takes advantage of transparent areas in loaded movies.

Relative vs. Absolute Paths

To load a movie, Flash must first know where to find it. You can use either a relative or absolute path to direct Flash to the movie. Which method works better when creating component-based systems? First, let's review the two types of paths. To do so, we'll revisit the action from the previous section:

```
loadMovieNum ("xyz.swf", 1);
```

This action uses a relative path. It's relative to the Flash file calling the new movie. The root movie will look within the directory it resides in to locate the SWF.

Likewise, the following action uses a relative path:

```
loadMovieNum ("../old_flash/xyz.swf", 1);
```

Conversely, an absolute path has no particular frame of reference; instead, it's an exact direction that works from anywhere:

```
loadMovieNum ("http://www.domain.com/flash/xyz.swf", 1);
```

Although absolute paths may seem like a clearer construction, I recommend using relative paths with component-based systems because they give you far more flexibility. You can move entire directories of components around on a server, and as long as the relationships between the components stay the same, the paths will remain intact. With absolute paths, if you move a component to a different directory, you risk breaking communication between that component and others.

The Two loadMovieNum Techniques

There are two techniques for using the `loadMovieNum()` action. Each technique positions the loaded movie differently.

Loading a SWF into a Level

This is the standard technique. When you load a movie of any size into a level, Flash places it into the specified level at the upper left corner of the root movie. Depending on the size of the loaded movie's Stage, one of three things can happen (**Figure 5.2**):

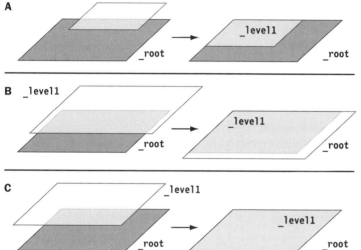

Figure 5.2 *How loaded movies relate to the root movie.*

If the Stage of a loaded movie (Level 1) is smaller than the Stage of the root movie (Level 0), the loaded movie will show any objects at the bottom and right-hand boundaries of its Stage (**A**). You'll need to create a mask to block objects that you don't want viewers to see, or recreate the SWF to match the Stage dimensions of the root movie.

If a loaded movie's Stage is larger than the root movie's Stage, it will be cropped at the bottom and right-hand boundaries (**B**).

For best results, the loaded movie's Stage size should be identical to the root movie's Stage size (**C**). This requires a little more planning, but it's worth it.

Loading a SWF into a Container Movie Clip

You can also load movies into empty movie clips, or container movie clips, on the root movie's Stage. This method places the upper left corner of the loaded movie at the registration point of the container clip (**Figure 5.3**). Because you can place container clips anywhere on the Stage, this method lets you place your loaded movie wherever you want.

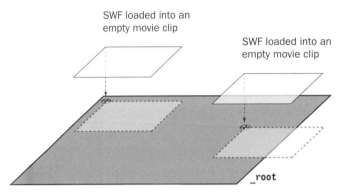

SWF loaded into an
empty movie clip

SWF loaded into an
empty movie clip

_root

Figure 5.3 *How movies loaded into container movie clips behave.*

The advantage of this method is that you can manipulate container clips like any other movie clip, using alpha channels, movement, rotation, and scaling. This is helpful if you're developing games or draggable navigational elements, for instance. You can use separate movies as site components that you can affect with ActionScript.

Movie clips require instance names so they can be targeted by the loadMovieNum() action. For example, to load a movie into a movie clip with the instance name *targetclip* on Level 4, your code would look like this:

```
loadMovie ("xyz.swf", "_root.level4.targetclip");
```

Loaded movies inherit the movie clip's properties from those already applied to the container clip. To remove the loaded movie, you simply delete the clip.

Although you can attach movie clips to a loaded movie, there are a few restrictions:

- You can only attach movie clips from a SWF's own library.

- You can't attach movie clips across levels. For instance, you can't attach Level 0 movie clips to Level 5.

- You can't duplicate a movie clip after loading a SWF into it.

I prefer the standard loadMovieNum() technique because it helps me organize my components and lets me see my design elements laid out in their respective layers. I also prefer having the registration point in the upper left corner: Designing a SWF that will be loaded into a movie clip can be a real pain when you have to center the graphics around the corner of the Stage. Plus, I don't load many movies into levels that I need to manipulate.

For more information on this topic, see page 98 of the Flash 5 ActionScript Reference Guide, or visit one of the many Flash forums on the Internet. These are among my favorites: http://board.flashkit.com/board/index.php, www.ultrashock.com/ff.htm?http://209.132.201.125/forums/index.php, and www.flazoom.com/flashboard/index.shtml.

To see examples of how loaded movies work, go to www.macromedia.com/support/flash/ts/documents/loading_movie_clips.htm.

Targeting with Multiple Levels

Targeting can get complicated when you're working with multiple levels. For instance, this code:

```
_root.foo = "bar";
```

targets the variable foo on the main timeline of the movie in which the script resides, and sets it to equal the string bar.

If you want to target the variable foo on the main timeline in another loaded movie (let's say Level 5), you need to specify its level, like this:

```
_level5.foo = "bar";
```

To target the variable foo on the main timeline in another loaded movie (Level 5 again), which is inside a movie clip with the instance name *target*, your code would look like this:

```
_level5.target.foo = "bar";
```

It can be easy to forget that using _root alone targets an object or variable on the movie's own main timeline. To target a timeline, movie clip, or variable in any other level, be sure to specify the level.

Planning Your Components

Good planning is the key to a successful component-based project. Planning your levels carefully will allow your components to fit together seamlessly, creating the illusion of one unified site.

First, you must break your project into logical components—based on functions, file size, and anything else that makes sense for your project. Then, you must decide at which level each component will reside. Because loaded movies in higher levels overlap those in lower levels, the placement of each component affects its display. Considering how components relate to each other will help you decide how to arrange your levels.

Put It on Paper

All of these components and levels can get pretty confusing, which is why I recommend creating a level map and tacking it onto your wall. The map can be as simple as a list of the movie names and their corresponding levels:

Level 4: sample_one.swf
Level 3: audio (audio_1.swf, audio_2.swf)
Level 2: audio_controls.swf
Level 1: main areas (xyz.swf, pdq.swf, asdf.swf)
Level 0: main.swf

I prefer a more graphical approach, however. **Figure 5.4** shows the level map I used to create the sample Flash site for this chapter.

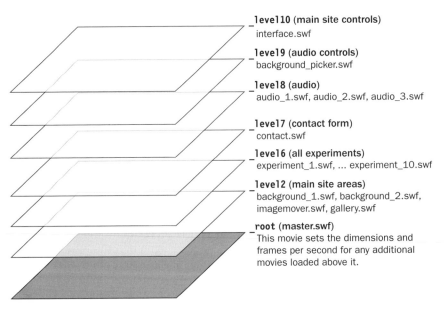

Figure 5.4 *The level map that I prepared for my sample site helped me visualize my components.*

As you can see, this map forces you to visualize how your components are positioned on their respective levels. For some developers, this approach is enough. They can imagine—in their heads—where components are placed, and how they will interact with each other.

 Note that I'm not loading any information into levels 1, 3, 4, or 5 on the level map in Figure 5.4. You don't have to load movies in sequential order— you can load movies into levels 5, 10, and 15 if you like.

Other developers need to map their projects out further on paper. One way to do this is to create thumbnails of each level on separate sheets of tracing paper. Each thumbnail should show where a loaded component would display on its respective layer. Use guide layers with rules to section off visible and invisible areas. Once you do this, stack your levels to simulate various loading scenarios. This will quickly help you spot potential problems. For instance, you might discover that a graphic in one component is inadvertently overlapping a graphic in another component in a lower level. If the two components load simultaneously, one may need to communicate to the other one—to unload it, perhaps, or hide it. Whenever you imagine a situation like this, write down how you'll deal with it.

Whether you're working alone or with a team of developers, planning everything on paper will prevent you from making costly changes to your architecture once scripting has begun. Although every project will have a few bumps in the road, the more you plan, the better you'll be able to handle those bumps.

Showcase Site

Throughout the rest of this chapter, we'll examine the key areas of my sample project, which is a fully functional component-based Flash site. I'll take you through various components and explain how I put it all together.

You'll find all of the source files on the accompanying CD-ROM as FLA and SWF files. Feel free to follow along in Flash and inspect the code. Don't worry if the individual SWFs appear to be broken or incomplete—they're not. Remember, the site is built of components, and most of them depend on others to function properly.

Open either master.swf or index.html from the CD-ROM to see the completed site (**Figure 5.5**).

Figure 5.5 *The completed site.*

Earlier, I showed you the level map I created for this site. Before we begin examining the site, I'd like to explain why I chose to put the components where I did.

Level 10—I placed the main navigation component on the highest level in the site because the navigation needs to sit above the other components; to have another component ever load above this one would greatly affect usability. The navigation component masks the tops and bottoms of the stages of movies loaded beneath it (**Figure 5.6**). This level also contains a draggable Feature window with scrolling text.

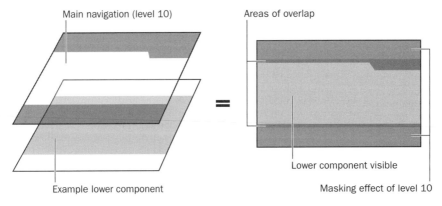

Figure 5.6 *Loading the navigation component into Level 10 lets it mask movies beneath it.*

Level 9—I placed the audio controls in Level 9 (**Figure 5.7.**) When this component is loaded, only the controls at the bottom left are visible; the rest of the file is masked by Level 10 artwork (**Figure 5.8**).

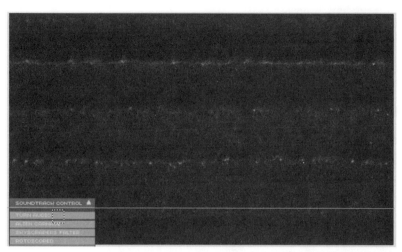

Figure 5.7 The audio control component is loaded into Level 9.

Figure 5.8 Level 10's artwork masks Level 9's Stage, exposing only the audio control tab.

Level 8—The audio files called from the audio controls in Level 9 are loaded into Level 8. Although these files contain no visible elements, they must still load into a level so they can played and unload.

Level 7—I placed the contact form in Level 7. When loaded, only the form's Open and Close buttons are visible; the rest of the component sits off the Stage to the right (**Figure 5.9**). Clicking the Open button brings the form onto the Stage, where it becomes fully visible (**Figure 5.10**).

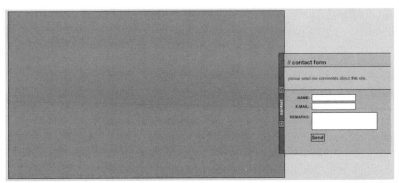

Figure 5.9
Only the Open and Close buttons are visible on the Stage in contact.fla.

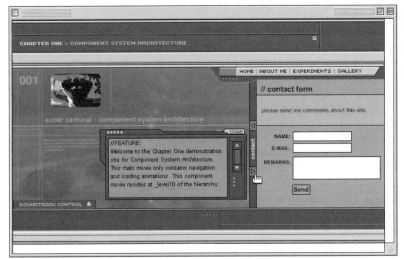

Figure 5.10
Clicking the Open button activates the contact form component.

Level 6—I placed experimental Flash movies in Level 6. When loaded, they are partially covered by the audio controls and contact form, which must always be visible.

Level 2—I placed the four main site areas—Home, About Me, Experiments, and Gallery—into Level 2. When loaded, these components are also partially covered by the audio controls and contact form.

As we make our way through the sample site, I'll discuss in more detail the communication between various components in different levels.

Creating master.swf: The Root Movie

My first task was to create master.swf, the root movie of the Flash site (Level 0). This movie loads interface.swf, the main navigation component (which also provides the initial visuals) into Level 10. Therefore, it contains no artwork, just some ActionScript.

I created a new file in Flash at 600 x 350 pixels and a frame rate of 32 fps, and saved it as master.fla. On the first frame, I placed this code:

```
loadMovie ("interface.swf", 10);
stop();
```

 Open master.swf from the CD-ROM. You'll notice that interface.swf immediately loads into Level 10 and the site experience begins.

Creating interface.swf: The Navigation and Main Site Component

Next, I created interface.swf. This component, which contains navigational buttons, a preloader, and masking artwork for the top and bottom of the Stage, acts as the site's nerve center, communicating with all the other components. Because of this, it was the most complicated to author—and the most crucial to keep bug-free.

 Open interface.fla from the CD-ROM (**Figure 5.11**).

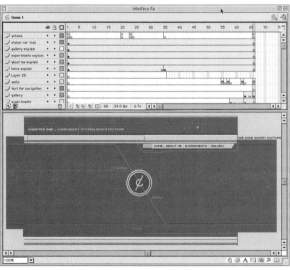

Figure 5.11 interface.fla from within the Flash authoring environment.

TIP Because this component has several conditional statements and multiple levels of communication, it's hard to step through it in chronological order. Opening the components in Flash and following along will help you see the associations in the system.

The Preloading Sequence

Preloading is a technique that prevents Flash movies from playing back in an unexpected or choppy manner. Because developers can't know every viewer's connection speed, they use preloaders to make sure a movie's entire contents are loaded before playback begins.

Most preloading sequences, however, are pretty boring. Anything you can do to make yours different from the 43 million text-styled "loading" animations you see everywhere would be most welcome. My preloading method features a set of doors that, in effect, close the interface while a component loads. Once the component is fully loaded, the doors open to reveal it. This system makes the wait pretty cool.

Here's how I planned the preloading sequence for the site's four major components: Home (background_1.swf), About Me (background_2.swf), Experiments (imagemover.swf), and Gallery (gallery.swf).

1. A viewer requests a major component, such as Gallery, from interface.swf.

2. The central area of interface.swf, which will display loaded movies, is empty (**Figure 5.12**).

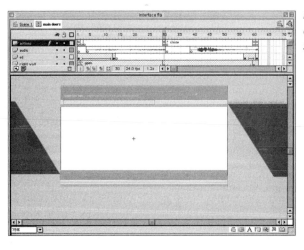

Figure 5.12 interface.fla with its doors open. The central area of the Stage is transparent by default.

Preloading Actions:
New Advances Since ifFrameLoaded()

Because any component can have only one, or just a few keyframes in its timeline, the `ifFramesLoaded()` action is no longer the best preloading method. Since Flash 4, Macromedia has added better actions for doing this, such as the `getBytesLoaded()` action, which gives you more control and lets you abstract your code from being tied to frame labels or numbers.

You've most likely seen preloaders that display the percentage of the movie loaded. This technique offers great feedback. Here's the routine I use:

Place a `stop()` action on the first frame of your movie's main timeline.

Following that `stop()` action, enter code that checks to see if all the bytes in the movie have been loaded. Place an empty movie clip on the Stage and place this script on it:

```
OnClipEvent (load) {
    total= int (_root.getBytesTotal());
}

onClipEvent (enterFrame) {
    loaded = Math.ceil(_root.getBytesLoaded());
    percent = Math.ceil(loaded/total*100);
    if (percent >= 100) {
      _root.play();
    }
}
```

`Math.ceil()`, which replaces the deprecated `int` function in Flash 4, rounds the number to an integer. This avoids a percentage value of something like 18.277% or a value of 0. Although `math.ceil()` is an accurate way to calculate the amount of file loaded, it doesn't display the percentage figure. For that, the variable itself needs to be displayed via a dynamic text field. You can do this by adding:

```
_root.percent = percent + " %";
```

before the `if` statement. Make sure a dynamic text field on the Stage is set to the variable percent. You'll see the percentage grow until it reaches 100; then, it will begin playing the main timeline inside the movie. This technique ensures that all the bytes in the movie are loaded before proceeding.

3. A set of doors in interface.swf closes the empty area, hiding the loading component (**Figure 5.13**). A small movie clip animation plays in the center of the doors to show that loading is taking place.

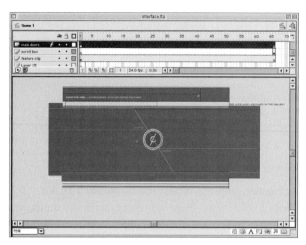

Figure 5.13 *Behind closed doors, the component loads.*

4. While the component is loading behind the scene, it also sends the value of a variable to a dynamic text field in interface.swf. This displays the text "loading interface," followed by a percentage figure.

5. When the component has finished loading, a preloader within it tells interface.swf that it's done and that it's OK to open the doors to display the loaded component. It also resets the loading variable in interface.swf to stop displaying the "loading interface" text.

6. The doors in interface.swf open to display the newly loaded component.

Examining the Preloading Sequence's Code

Notice that interface.fla is split into two scenes: Preloader and Scene1. Preloader works as I've described above, but I included some graphical feedback in a form of a thin orange progress bar. Feel free to peruse the preloader's code in the Flash Movie Explorer.

After the preloader loads the movie contents, the playhead jumps to Scene1. This code is on the first frame:

```
goget = "background_1.swf";
```

This initiates the variable goget, which we'll use to call the doors to close and load various main area movies into the site. The component interface.fla uses this variable in the Doors movie clip (**Figure 5.14**):

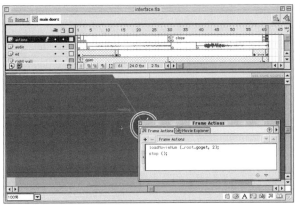

Figure 5.14 *The variable* goget *called from within the Doors movie clip in interface.fla. This is how all main areas are loaded into Level 2.*

On frame 20 you'll find this code:

```
loadMovieNum (goget, 2);
```

Because the doors are closed in the site, we load the Home component, background_1.swf, into Level 2.

After background_1.swf loads, the first frame of Scene1 tells the Doors movie clip (instance name: *doors*) in Level 10 that it's now safe to open the doors to reveal the component. The code for this is shown below:

```
_level10.doors.gotoAndPlay(2);
```

We will use this key communication throughout the site.

In addition to the preloader ActionScript in background_1.fla, I added the following line of code:

```
stop();
_level10.load = "loading the home area";
```

This sets the variable in Level 10 (interface.fla). During preloading, it will display the text "loading the home area." Because this variable value is set in Level 10, it's displayed in the corresponding dynamic text field with the variable value of load.

After the Home component loads into Level 2, I need to tell the doors in Level 10 to open to display it. Here's what the code looks like:

```
_level10.doors.gotoAndPlay(2);
_level10.load = "";
stop();
```

Setting the load variable in Level 10 to "" sets it to nothing. This makes the "loading the home area" text disappear once the component finishes loading.

By now, you can see it's easy to control a movie from another level: Just designate the proper level in which to communicate, and target the variable or instance in that level. It's a powerful aspect of Flash authoring that should not be overlooked.

Setting Up the Navigation

After the site loads, the navigation buttons slide in from the right side of the window. These buttons contain several actions that ensure usability and help load sections into the site. Let's look at how they work.

Back to the timeline in interface.fla: On frame 23, I placed the following code:

```
loadMovieNum ("contact.swf", 7);
loadMovieNum ("background_picker", 9);
```

Move the playhead to the end of Scene1 and select the Home button on the Stage. Now, look at the code for the Home button in the Object Actions panel:

```
on (rollOver) {
    home.gotoAndPlay(2);
}

on (rollOut) {
    home.gotoAndPlay(7);
}

on (release) {
    // Make sure to kill any experiments not closed
    unloadMovieNum (6);
    goget = "background_1.swf";
    doors.gotoAndPlay("close");
    _root.news = "yes";
}

on (release) {
    _root.news = "yes";
      if (_level7.status == "open") {
      _level7.contact.gotoAndPlay(16);
      _level7.status = "closed";
    }
}
```

The Home button displays text when you roll over it. This script tells the movie clip with the instance name *home* to, upon rollover, go to the frame that begins the tween for the display. Rolling off the button tells the movie clip to proceed and hide the text. The script also closes any experiments left open in the Experiments area by unloading any movie in Level 6. In addition, it sets the variable goget to background_1.swf inside the Doors movie clip. This variable loads the correct file into Level 2 and tells the movie clip to close. If the contact form is open, clicking the Home button also tells it to close.

The remaining buttons have almost identical code. For example, here's the code for the About Me button:

```
on (rollOver) {
    _root.about.gotoAndPlay(2);
}

on (rollOut) {
    _root.about.gotoAndPlay(7);
}

// start things on selection

on (release) {
    // doors closing calls the proper .swf
    goget = "background_2.swf";
    _root.news = "no";
    // hide the feature container from view
    _root.feature._visible = false;
    _root.feat._visible = false;
    _root.doors.gotoAndPlay("close");

}

on (release) {
    // Make sure to kill any experiments not closed
    unloadMovieNum (6);
    if (_level7.status == "open") {
      _level7.contact.gotoAndPlay(16);
      _level7.status = "closed";
    }
}
```

This code works like the Home button's does, but it also manipulates the Feature window on the home page. Rolling off the About Me button affects the Feature window and the Feature button. (In this code, I made them both invisible to get them out of the way.)

The Feature Window

The home page includes a draggable Feature window with scrollable text. Here's how it looks in its open position (**Figure 5.15**):

Figure 5.15 *The Feature window in its default open position.*

If a viewer clicks the window's Close button, the window is replaced by a small Feature button that reopens it (**Figure 5.16**).

Figure 5.16 *The Feature window in its button form.*

When a viewer goes to another site area, the Feature window is hidden. To handle this, the window's two states—open position and button form—are broken into two separate movie clips. While the window is hidden, any buttons within its respective movie clip won't work.

What's cool about this window is that it appears to have a memory of its own. Try this: Drag the window to a different position on the home page, then click the Close button. This hides the window and brings up the Feature button. Now, click the Feature button to make the window visible again. It appeared where you last dragged it—not in its default position.

Using ActionScript to control the window's visibility gives you much more flexibility than using a frame-based system for displaying and hiding elements. Although it appears as if the clip's coordinates for the Feature window have been stored, the clip hasn't moved at all—its visibility properties are merely toggled.

The Feature window's text is loaded from a text file named news.txt (you can find this on the CD-ROM). The dynamic text box displays the variable daTextBox set to word wrap, HTML, and selectable. After the contents of the text file are loaded, the variable can be displayed.

The code on the Feature window movie clip (instance name: *feature*) looks like this:

```
onClipEvent (load) {
    loadVariables ("news.txt", _root.feature);
    scrolling = 0;
    frameCounter = 1;
    speedFactor = 3;
}

onClipEvent (enterFrame) {
    if (frameCounter%speedFactor == 0) {
      if (scrolling == "up" && daTextBox.scroll>1) {
        daTextBox.scroll--;
      } else if (scrolling == "down" &&
        daTextBox.scroll<daTextBox.maxscroll) {
        daTextBox.scroll++;
      }
      frameCounter = 0;
    }
    frameCounter++;
}
```

The content for news.txt looks like this:

```
daTextBox=//FEATURE:<br>Welcome to the Chapter One
→ demonstration site for Component System
→ Architecture.<br>This main movie only contains navigation
→ and loading animations. This component movie resides at
→ level10 of the hierarchy.<br><br>This should allow for
→ plenty of space to load components underneath. Many sites
→ have a news section not unlike this one right on their
→ home page. This serves that purpose. A link to macromedia
→ can look like <u><a href='http://www.macromedia.com'><font
→  color='#ff3300'>this</font></a></u>.<br><br>Also note
→ that this information is being driven by a text file with
→ supported HTML tags within it. Cool. You could back-end
→ this information with a database!
```

I won't get into how the scrolling text box works as it's not the focus this chapter, but feel free to investigate its code, along with the code for the Feature window and the buttons.

Creating contact.swf: The Contact Form

 Open contact.fla from the CD-ROM.

The contact form lets site viewers email me via their default email program. It's a pretty standard component and was fairly simple to create.

Figure 5.17 The contact form in its closed position.

When the form is closed, only the Open and Close buttons are visible (**Figure 5.17**). When the form is open, the Open button won't work; when the form is closed, the Close button won't work. This is handled by conditional button controls that read the form state as either opened or closed.

Look inside contact.fla. On the first frame in Scene1, I placed this code, which sets up some variables:

```
// Put your email address here.
email = "testing@test.com";
name = "Your Name Here";
mailto = "mailto:" + name + "<" + email + ">";
subject = "Your Subject Here";
status = "closed";
```

Here's how the conditional button controls work. On the top button (the Open button) sits this code:

```
on (release) {
    if (_root.status == "closed") {
      _root.contact.gotoAndPlay(2);
      _root.status = "open";
    }
}
```

The button is conditional. If the variable status is set to open, the button does nothing. The code also sets the conditional variable if it does function. This lets the component track the condition of the form. On the bottom button (the Close button) I placed this code:

```
on (release) {
    if (_root.status == "open") {
      _root.contact.gotoAndPlay(10);
      _root.status = "closed";
    }
}
```

When the form is open, the Open button won't work, but it will close the form if it's open. The variable, again, is set to maintain tracking.

Here's how I set up the form to send email. On the contact form's Send button, I placed this code:

```
on (press) {
    getURL ("mailto:test@test.com" + "?subject=" +
    → root.subject + newline + "&body=" + "Name : " +
    → name + newline + "E-mail : " + email + newline +
    → "Remarks : " + remarks);
    root.contact.gotoAndPlay(16);
}
```

The getURL() action calls the viewer's default email application. Change the mailto: address to wherever you would like the email to be sent. If you don't, your incoming email will be sent to never-never land and you'll think no one has been using your form. If you have ASPMail at your disposal, you can set this system to call your ASP page with the same getURL() function (just change the way your variables are set up first).

Creating background_picker.swf: The Audio Control Component

 Open background_picker.fla from the CD-ROM.

The audio control component lets site visitors listen to one of four audio tracks or toggle the sound off. In its default position, it displays only a title bar and button (**Figure 5.18**).

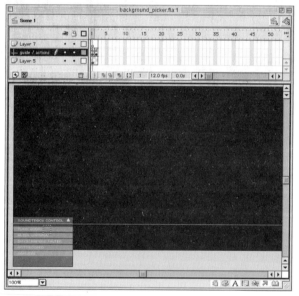

Figure 5.18 The audio control component in its FLA file, in its default position.

Clicking the button opens the component. When a visitor selects an audio track, a dot next to the selected track's name provides visual feedback (**Figure 5.19**).

Figure 5.19 *The audio control's interface makes it easy to select tracks.*

If a visitor doesn't choose an audio track within eight seconds, the component closes. This prevents it from possibly obscuring site elements below it.

On the first frame of background_picker.fla, I placed this code:

```
audio = "off";
default = "audio_1.swf";
```

This initiates the variable for audio and sets the default audio to a chosen SWF file. Audio is set to off because, by default, audio_1.swf plays when the site is launched. The button that turns off the audio has a dynamic text field set to _root.audio. So, at the outset, this will display as turn audio <"off">. We'll replace the variable with "- -" when no audio is playing. You'll see this come together in a second.

On the second frame I placed the following code:

```
stop ();
loadMovieNum (default, 8);
_root.picker.marker.gotoAndStop(2);
```

This loads the default audio file. It also targets a movie clip inside the component to place a marker next to the audio button called Alien Carnage (which is the title of the default audio).

Let's dig into the guts of the component now.

The movie clip Picker MC (located in the Library) controls the opening of the component. The small triangular button has a large hit area that covers the entire tab area. Clicking the button starts the opening tween sequence (**Figure 5.20**).

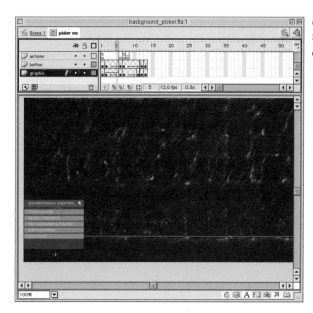

Figure 5.20 *The component's timeline, showing the opening and closing tweens.*

On frame 7 inside Picker MC is a stop() action and a movie clip with the instance name *timer_clip*. This is the engine that times the component's open position. On the first frame in the timer clip, you'll see this code:

```
pauseTime = "8000";
movieTime = 0;
```

On the second frame (with a frame label of go_timer), resides this code:

```
movieTime = Number(getTimer ());
```

On the third frame (with the If statement all on one line):

```
if
(Number(getTimer())>Number(Number(pauseTime)+Number(movieTim
e))) {
    _root.picker.gotoAndPlay(8);
    gotoAndStop (1);
}
```

On the fourth frame:

```
gotoAndPlay (_currentframe-1);
```

This counts down eight seconds and then targets the Picker movie clip to play at frame 8, which initiates the closing tween. But wait—whenever someone opens the component, they have only eight seconds to choose a song or turn off the audio? That wouldn't be very nice. Instead, the timer is reset whenever a viewer selects an audio button. To see this work, and to see how the rest of the audio control system works, let's look at the code on one of those buttons.

Double-click the main component on the Stage (instance name: *picker*). This opens Picker MC (as it appears in the Library.) Double-click this movie clip to open picker_graphic (also as it appears in the Library.) The buttons reside in this graphic symbol. Select the button above the text "Alien Carnage."

Here's what the code on this button looks like:

```
on (release) {
    loadMovieNum ("audio_1.swf", 8);
    _root.audio = "off";
    song = 1;
    marker.gotoAndStop(2);
    _root.picker.timer_clip.gotoAndPlay(1);
}
```

The selected audio—in this case, audio_1.swf—is loaded into Level 8. We set the variable audio to off, set the song to 1, mark the chosen audio label, and tell the timer clip to go to frame 1 and play. This resets the timer clip to the eight-second countdown.

The code on the Skyscrapers Falter button looks like this:

```
on (release) {
    loadMovieNum ("audio_2.swf", 8);
    _root.audio = "off";
    song = 2;
    marker.gotoAndStop(3);
    _root.picker.timer_clip.gotoAndPlay(1);
}
```

I think you can see a pattern developing. We load all audio clips into Level 8. If a movie is already there, the new movie replaces the old one, and each button resets the timer.

In case you want to run conditional statements that prevent the current audio file from reloading, I've set the variable song. My audio clips aren't that long, so I didn't need to use this. If you want to loop longer clips, however, running conditionals in the selection would help prevent odd audio events, such as a clip starting over again mid-loop. Have fun with this.

TIP When the audio component is closed, the arrow graphic points up; when it's open, the arrow graphic points down. It was easy to add this usability: I just edited the instance of the button on several keyframes.

Creating background_2.swf: The About Me Component

Open background_2.fla from the CD-ROM.

Three rollover buttons—Home, Pers, and Wrk—in the About Me component provide textual and audio feedback. (That's me doing the voiceover around 3 am.) Each button has a marker to show which area is being displayed (**Figure 5.21**).

Figure 5.21 The About Me component loaded within the site.

The code on the Home button (Button 1 in the Library) looks like this:

```
on (rollOver) {
    _root.about.flash.gotoAndPlay(2);
    about.gotoAndStop(2);
    home.gotoAndStop(2);
    heart.gotoAndStop(1);
    work.gotoAndStop(1);
}
```

This code is simple. It's targeting several movie clips with the instance names *home*, *heart*, and *work*. These movie clips serve as button markers. The idea of marking buttons is the same as that of radio buttons. Targeting the movie clip with the instance name *about* displays the requested content—in this case, information about my home life. Each button functions in the same way; only its targeting and target frame calls differ slightly.

To spice up this component, I've added some random drifting boxes. On the first frame keyframe, I placed this code:

```
objects = 5;
_level10.load = "";
loop = 1;
while (loop<=objects) {
    duplicateMovieClip ("bar", "bar" add loop, loop);
    loop = loop+1;
}
```

This code removes the loading display of the variable load in Level 10. It also limits to five the number of objects (boxes) that can be on the Stage at once. It duplicates the movie four times, and the boxes are animated with code on the movie clip itself.

On the movie clip of a simple white box with the instance name *bar* (which sits on the stage), I placed this code:

```
onClipEvent(load){
    _x = Math.random()*300;
    speed = Math.random()*5 + 1;
    _y = Math.random()*300 - (_height/2);
    _xscale = Math.random()*150;
    yscale = Math.random()*150;
    alpha = Math.random()*30;
}

onClipEvent(enterFrame){
    _x += speed;
    if(_x >= 300){
        _xscale = Math.random()*150;
        _yscale = Math.random()*150;
        speed = Math.random()*5 + 1;
        _y = Math.random()*300 - (_height/2);
        _x = _width*-1;
        _alpha = Math.random()*30;
    }
}
```

Beyond this, I decided to have a little fun. Check out the invisible button on my nose. And no, I don't like bananas on my cereal, thank you very much.

Creating imagemover.swf:
The Experiments Component

 Open imagemover.fla from the CD-ROM.

Geoff Stearns, who wrote Chapter 1, Breathing Life into Flash, created the six experimental Flash movies in this section. Viewers can launch an experiment by clicking a button (a box marker follows the cursor as it rolls over the buttons), or by clicking the preview image's launch button (**Figure 5.22**). All of the source files reside on the CD-ROM—comb through them and enjoy.

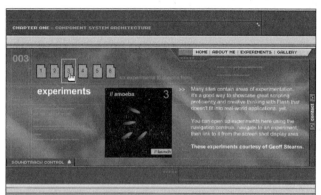

Figure 5.22 *The Experiments section loaded within the site.*

I don't want to get too caught up into the engine that provides this functionality, but I'll go through the code quickly so you can see how it works.

A movie clip with the instance name *control* sits to the left of the Stage. It contains the following ActionScript.

On frame 1:

```
stop();
```

On frame 2:

```
Xsquare = _root.blue._x;
Xdiff = _root.Xpos2-Xsquare;
Xmove = Xdiff/5;
_root.blue._x = Xsquare+Xmove;
```

And on frame 3:

```
gotoAndPlay (2);
```

This provides physics to the movement in the box marker's scrolling system. When you see the code on one of the buttons, you'll see how this works. The outlined box marker has the instance name *blue*.

First, however, let's look at the code for the movie clip with the instance name *control2*, which controls the preview images' movement. The preview images sit inside the movie clip with the instance name *large*.

On frame 1:

```
stop();
```

On frame 2:

```
Xsquare = _root.large._x;
Xdiff = _root.Xpos-Xsquare;
Xmove = Xdiff/3;
_root.large._x = Xsquare+Xmove;
```

And on frame 3:

```
gotoAndPlay (2);
```

To see the system come together, we need to activate the scripts in the above clips by targeting them with buttons. The buttons in this system sit inside a movie clip with the instance name *navi*. I'll show you the code in buttons one and two so you can put it all together.

Button 1 (// butterfly) code:

```
on (release, rollOver) {
    _root.xpos = 1062;
    _root.xpos2 = 67;
    _root.control2.gotoAndPlay(2);
    _root.control.gotoAndPlay(2);
}

on (release) {
    loadMovieNum ("experiment_1.swf", 6);
}
```

Button 2 (// colorfade):

```
on (release, rollOver) {
    _root.xpos = 882.5;
    _root.xpos2 = 95;
    _root.control2.gotoAndPlay(2);
    _root.control.gotoAndPlay(2);
}
```

```
on (release) {
    loadMovieNum ("experiment_2.swf", 6);
}
```

Notice that each button's variables are different. This controls the movement of both the outlined box marker and the preview movies. It's a cool way to let viewers to choose the component they want to see.

The buttons load each respective experiment into Level 6 for viewing. This creates a serious usability problem, however: Although the buttons are hidden beneath each experiment, they're still active. Remember how we handled the Feature window in interface.fla earlier in the chapter? Here, I applied the same technique, but in a slightly different way. After each experiment loads, you'll see the following code on frame 1 of Scene1 (sometimes accompanied with experiment-specific code):

```
fscommand ("allowscale", false);
_level2.navi._visible = false;
stop ();
```

Aha! We simply tell the navigation buttons in Level 2 (in imagemover.swf) to disappear. It's a perfect solution, as viewers can't see them anyway. And because it's not a frame-based solution, it's less work for you.

The Close button for each experiment contains this code:

```
on (release) {
    _level2.navi._visible = true;
    unloadMovieNum (6);
}
```

This makes the navigation buttons reappear and unloads the experiment currently in Level 6.

 Remember that the main buttons in interface.fla also unload any movie in Level 6. Why did I decide to do this? What happens if a viewer in the Experiments section goes to the Gallery without first closing an open experiment? The experiment would remain in Level 6, covering a section of the Gallery—and there'd be no way to close it until the viewer returned to the Experiments section. The result: a terrible usability problem. Therefore, we've built logic into our system to prevent such a situation. It's a simple solution, but an invaluable one.

Creating gallery.swf: The Gallery Component

Open gallery.fla from the CD-ROM.

The Gallery component displays some strange photographs and an even stranger animation. The 10 images scroll horizontally; when the cursor rolls over an image, the image gets larger (**Figure 5.23**). When the cursor rolls off, the image scales back to its original size. It's an interactive and interesting way to present images.

Figure 5.23 *The Gallery component loaded within the site.*

While it's beyond the scope of this chapter to describe how this works, I'll display the code so you might have an easier time going through it.

The gallery images sit inside a movie clip (called Gallery Display in the Library) with the instance name *gallery*. Here's the code for the first frame of the main timeline of Scene1:

```
// number of pictures in Gallery
pics = "10";
gallery.pics = "10";
```

Inside the gallery clip on the first frame sits this code:

```
sizeratio = 1.7;
// change the above to change the enlargement ratio
spacing = 1.5;
speed = -18;
// speed is the speed of motion; make it negative to
reverse direction; lower number higher speed
stopgap = 20;
picsize = 100;
pics = 10;
```

```
p = 1;
while (Number(p)<=Number(pics)) {
    set ("pic" + p + "/:p", p);
    setProperty ("pic" + p, _x, p*(spacing*picsize));
    p = Number(p)+1;
}
topscale = 100*sizeratio;
lowscale = ((pics*100)-topscale)/(pics-1);
wide = getProperty(border, _width);
```

On the second frame of the gallery movie clip:

```
M = getProperty("point", _x);
// following includes stop gap size, and get mouse position
if (Number(M)<Number(stopgap)) {
    if (Number(M)>Number(-stopgap)) {
      I = M;
      } else {
          I = -stopgap;
      }
    } else {
    I = stopgap;
}
rate = (M-I)/speed;
```

On the third frame of the gallery movie clip:

```
gotoAndPlay (_currentframe-1);
```

Inside the gallery movie clip on the Stage (called Gallery Resizer in the Library) resides another movie clip with the instance name *actions*. It contains the resizing ActionScript. On its first frame:

```
if (_root.Number.ok != 0) {
    if (Number(_root.ok) == Number(p)) {
      newxscale = _root.topscale;
      } else {
      newxscale = _root.lowscale;
    }
    if (Number(_root.ok) != Number(p)) {
      newxscale = 100;
    }
}
xstep = (newxscale-xscale)/5;
```

On its second frame:

```
if (Number(xscale)<>Number(newxscale)) {
    xscale = Number(xscale)+Number(xstep);
    } else {
    xstep = "0";
}
_xscale = xscale;
_yscale = xscale;
gotoAndPlay (_currentframe-1);
```

This code lets viewers directly manipulate the images, each in its own movie clip (which lets us change their _xscale and _yscale properties.) The code also allows for scrolling and duplication. Code in the individual movie clips helps control the scaling and position of the elements.

I've left this code with its original Flash 4 syntax. Although I converted it to Flash 5 for this book, I had enough fun doing so that I thought you might enjoy the challenge as well. It's not that difficult, although some of the actions are quite long—but that's where the fun is, anyway.

 The Bonus_Stuff folder on the CD-ROM includes some extra sample files. Feel free to play around with these.

Last Notes

I hope this chapter has given you a glimpse into the power of component system architecture. We've covered the key Flash 5 technologies that are used, and we've seen that you don't need to rely on heavy ActionScripting to get the job done. And that's the beauty of this approach: It lets you focus your coding and developmental energies on the components themselves—not on implementing the completed system.

Almost any medium- to large-scale Flash project that you become involved with will benefit from the use of component system architecture. Why? Because it works. And it works really well.

6: Creating Dynamic Flash Pages

Max Oshman is president of WebWork, LLC (www.Webwork.tv) and co-founder of XYPNO Interactive (www.xypno.com), based in Montclair, New Jersey. As lead programmer at both companies, he specializes in creating data-driven Flash sites and is fluent in server-side scripting languages such as ColdFusion, ASP and PHP. Among the many companies he has worked for are Perception Inc., BoogieTV, LLC (www.boogie.tv), and The Exit Proms Event. He also contributes to resource Web sites such as www.flashcfm.com and www.virtual-fx.net.

One of the biggest trends in the Flash development community is dynamic Flash. Dynamic Flash sites, which pull information from external sources such as databases, text files, or XML documents, are faster and easier to update than regular Flash sites. Now you can create dynamic Flash sites by using a server-side scripting language such as ColdFusion, ASP, or PHP in conjunction with ActionScript. This chapter will explain these coding techniques and then show them in action in three real-world applications that you can easily adapt to any Web site.

The three projects—a message board, hit counter, and chat room—all use Flash as the front end (to a database, text file, and server, respectively), but each uses a different scripting language to connect Flash to the back end. The message board is coded with ColdFusion, the hit counter uses PHP, and the chat room uses ASP. To better understand how and why the server-side scripts work, I'll give you a line-by-line explanation of each one.

Once you've completed this chapter, you'll have an advanced working knowledge of back end integration with Flash and a solid understanding of ColdFusion, PHP, ASP, and SQL.

Dynamic Flash Pages: The Basics

If your Web site's content needs to be frequently updated, a dynamic Web site may be just what you need. Dynamic Web sites pull information from external sources such as databases, text files, or XML documents. For example, news sites like CNN.com or large e-commerce sites like amazon.com would be nearly impossible to update without the use of a database.

For viewers, dynamic Web sites mean fresh, up-to-the-minute content; for developers, they mean fast and easy site maintenance. Because updating a database is as simple as editing text, anyone can do it, including those with no programming experience. This means your project's most significant overhead will be site creation, not maintenance. Two popular dynamic Flash sites are ShockFusion (www.shockfusion.com) and Flashroots (www.flashroots.com/alt).

Server-Side Scripting Languages

Although Flash can read from and write to text files on a hard drive, it can't read from or write to text files on a server, nor can it connect directly to a database. This is where server-side scripting languages come in. To create dynamic Flash sites, you need to use a server-side scripting language such as ColdFusion, Hypertext Preprocessor (PHP), Active Server Pages (ASP), Perl, or Java Server Pages (JSP). These languages let you integrate Internet, intranet, and extranet applications with backend and Internet technologies such as databases and XML.

In this chapter we'll discuss ColdFusion, PHP, and ASP. All three have their strengths and weaknesses. For example, it's easy to connect to databases with ColdFusion, but it's expensive, so it may be impractical for many free-lance developers. PHP is fast, multi-platform compatible, and free, but beginners may find its syntax hard to understand. ASP is easy to learn and free, but it's supported only on Windows-based servers. Although I prefer ColdFusion, check out all three languages and decide which one works best for your project.

ColdFusion

ColdFusion, which was created by Allaire and is now owned by Macromedia, is coded using ColdFusion Markup Language (CFML), an extension of Hypertext Markup Language (HTML). A CFML document looks like a standard HTML document, so it's easy to understand and implement. CFML documents, however, have more functions, conditional operators, and database commands, including more than 70 tags and 200 custom functions. Sites created with ColdFusion include Half (www.half.com) and Amazon (www.amazon.com).

Although, like HTML, you can write ColdFusion code in a basic text editor (be sure to save the file with a .cfm extension), I strongly recommend using the optional ColdFusion Studio. This CFML editor helps you create ColdFusion scripts more quickly, as well as debug them.

PHP

PHP is a robust, open-source server-side scripting language. You can write PHP code in a text editor and save the file with a .php extension. PHP's syntax is closely related to that of C/C++, which may make it difficult for beginners. Unlike C and C++, however, you don't have to compile PHP in order for your applications to work. Sites created with PHP include PHP (www.php.net) and We're Here Forums (www.were-here.com).

ASP

ASP is Microsoft's server-side scripting language. You can write ASP code in a text editor and save the file with an .asp extension, or use a program like Microsoft VisualInterDev, which makes scripting easier. Although server applications such as ChiliSoft ASP let you run ASP on non-Windows environments like Solaris and UNIX, installing such software is a long and tedious process. Sites created with ASP include Microsoft (www.microsoft.com) and Barnes & Noble (www.barnesandnoble.com).

Key Concepts and Terms

Before we begin examining our showcase projects, let's review a few concepts and terms that you'll need to know to use the featured technologies.

ODBC and SQL

Open Database Connectivity (ODBC) is a database interface that lets server-side scripting language talk to a database. It eliminates a database's discrepancies so your script can work with it. For example, some databases have extra security features like a login name and password. ODBC can eliminate this if you don't want your database to be password-protected.

ODBC uses Standard Query Language (SQL) to extract and manipulate data in a database. The beauty of SQL is that it's based upon four main statements that can be combined in different ways to produce an infinite number of results. Here are the four main statements and their purposes:

STATEMENT	EXPLANATION
Select	Query a table for data.
Insert	Add new data to a table.
Update	Update existing data in a table.
Delete	Delete data from a table.

Whether you're programming with ColdFusion, PHP, or ASP, you need a thorough knowledge of SQL—you can't access a database without it. You'll see SQL in action in the ColdFusion section of the message board.

Microsoft Access

Microsoft Access is one of the most popular database applications. Although it's easy to use, it allows only a small number of concurrent users, so it's not the best choice for Web sites that expect a large number of simultaneous hits. For such sites, either Oracle8i or Microsoft SQL Server is a better choice, but both programs are more difficult to learn.

URL-Encode Format

Flash uses the URL-encode format to encode special characters. Flash will turn an URL-encoded string created by a server-side scripting language into a list of variables within its own memory. The following string is in URL-encode format:

```
Macromedia=Flash&Allaire=ColdFusion&Combined-An+awesome+combo
```

Flash will recognize and decode this string. Upon import, you'll have three variables: `Macromedia`, `Allaire`, and `combined`. These variables will be loaded along with the values assigned to them in the string:

VARIABLE	VALUE
Macromedia	Flash
Allaire	ColdFusion
Combined	An awesome combo

Notice that the +'s translate into spaces. The chart below shows most of the symbols that Flash will recognize and translate into their corresponding characters.

SYMBOL	CHARACTER
+	Space
%21	!
%22	"
%23	#
%24	$
%25	%
%26	&
%27	'
%28	(
%29	)
%2[Aa]	*
%2[Bb]	+
%2[Cc]	,
%2[Dd]	-
%2[Ee]	.
%2[Ff]	/
%3[Aa]	:
%3[Bb]	;
%3[Cc]	<
%3[Dd]	=
%3[Ee]	>
%3[Ff]	?
%5[Bb]	[
%5[Cc]	\
%5[Dd]	]
%5[Ee]	^
%5[Ff]	_
%7[Bb]	{
%7[Cc]	|
%7[Dd]	}
%7[Ee]	~
%60	`

GET and POST

There are two main ways to send information from page to page: GET and POST.

GET. Using GET to transfer information from one page to the next appends the information to the end of an URL string in a var=val&var=val syntax. Flash will automatically decode the query string. The main problem with using GET is that its size is limited to the maximum length of a request string (approximately 1,024 characters).

POST. Using POST to transfer information from one page to the next embeds the information in an HTTP header in a var:val var:val syntax. You can send large amounts of data using this method. In fact, the size limit is so large—if a limit exists—than it's unknown.

Showcase 1: Message Board

My first showcase project is a multi-forum, multi-threaded message board with features such as registration, user-login, email responding, and user preferences. (You can customize this project to fit the topic of your site.) The back end is a Microsoft Access database; it's connected to Flash by ColdFusion. We'll discuss how to take data out of and insert data into a database using Flash as a front end.

 To see the completed project, open message_board.fla from the CD-ROM. It's in the ColdFusion sub-folder in the Chapter 6 folder. The rest of the source files for this showcase are also in this sub-folder.

Creating the Database

The database is the foundation of the message board application. Let's discuss its key points.

Open message_board97.mdb from the CD-ROM. (If you don't have a copy of Microsoft Access, download a demo version from www.microsoft.com.)

You'll see four tables: Forums, Replies, Security, and Threads (**Figure 6.1**). Each table has a different purpose; together, they make the message board work.

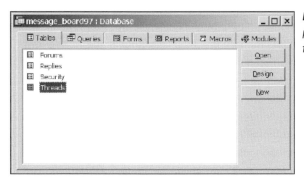

Figure 6.1 The database that powers the message board has four tables.

A *primary key* is the term used for column(s) that must possess unique values. For example, if you set a column to be the primary key, no two rows in that column can contain the same value. In fact, most databases that have the primary key function, such as Access, will give you an error message if you try to enter the same value twice.

Let's look at the four tables in the database:

Forums

The Forums table is where we specify the names of the message board's forums. You can have as many forums as you want and name them whatever you want. To customize the message board, just modify the tables.

Replies

The Replies table stores all of the replied messages (but not the original messages). Unlike the Forums table, nothing is predefined except for the column names. When a user responds to a post, the content is dynamically updated.

Security

User login information is stored in this table. When a user signs up, the Security table is dynamically updated.

Threads

When a user posts a new message, the information is stored in this table. If you combine the Thread and Replies tables, the database will still work, but I don't recommend this. New posts require a subject line, but replies do not, and this can affect database performance. (Speed is one of the biggest issues when working with databases and Flash.)

 If your Web hosting company supports ColdFusion and supplies you with ODBC connection(s), follow the instructions on the company's FAQ to add the DataSource Name (DSN) to the server. If you don't want to use your hosting company, or it doesn't support one of the technologies used in the chapter, sign up for free hosting services at www.freecfm.com and refer to its FAQ to add the DSN. Regardless of which hosting service you use, the DSN that you give the database must remain constant. The database's DSN for this project is message_board.

Creating the Server-Side Scripts

Now that we've seen how the foundation of the application was created, let's look at how I created the brains. The following ColdFusion scripts serve as the middleman between Flash and the database: Flash loads a ColdFusion script, ColdFusion makes a request to the database, and then ColdFusion outputs everything into Flash. These scripts, therefore, are extremely important for the success of the message board. If anything needs to be bug-free, it's them. That's true not only for this application, but for any application that uses a server-side scripting language to communicate between Flash and an external source.

Setting the DSN: application.cfm

 Open application.cfm from the CD-ROM.

 If your DSN doesn't correspond to the DSN specified in the ColdFusion scripts, your application won't work. It's important, therefore, to set the DSN early. In this script we'll set the DSN for the message board.

Let's review the code:

```
<cfset dsn="message_board">
```

The <cfset> tag is used to set values to variables. In this case, we're setting the variable dsn to the value of message_board.

An application.cfm file—a header that you don't have to call—is automatically included at the top of every ColdFusion script located in the same directory. In addition, a footer called onrequestend.cfm is automatically included at the end of every ColdFusion script located in the same directory. If these files don't exist on the server, nothing will malfunction. If they do exist, however, ColdFusion will handle the information inside of them.

Signing Up: signup.cfm

 Open signup.cfm from the CD-ROM.

Users must sign up to use the message board. This script takes the user-specified name and password and adds it to the database.

Let's look at the code:

```
<cfquery datasource="#dsn#" name="threads">
```

The `<cfquery>` tag is used to send SQL statements to an ODBC driver. The datasource attribute specifies the DSN we want to use. Because we've already created application.cfm, which automatically sets the variable `dsn` to `message_board`, we can simply refer to the variable `#dsn#` as the value for the datasource attribute.

 Note the # symbols that surround the variable `dsn`. Whenever you reference variables in ColdFusion, you must place the variable name between these symbols. If you don't, the variable names will output as plain text.

```
Insert into
Security (username,password,notify)
```

The Insert statement, one of the four main SQL statements, adds information into a table. The `into` keyword specifies into which table you want to add information (in this case, the Security table). The three words in parentheses are the names of columns that have been created.

```
Values ('#form.username#','#form.password#',#form.notify#)
```

The `values` keyword is the third part of the Insert statement. The order in which the values are listed must correspond correctly with the column names or else you'll get data in the wrong columns. The first value listed will be entered into the first column name listed. The word "form" means that the value should be taken from a form. The form name comes after the `form` keyword. Note that single quotes denote a string data type; no quotes denote a numeric, or a bit data type.

```
</cfquery>
```

Just as in HTML, you must close your tags. This code closes the `<cfquery>` tag. It tells ColdFusion Server there will be no more SQL statements and closes the connection with the ODBC driver. You can have more than one `<cfquery>` tag in a script; just be sure to close all tags or your script won't work.

Protecting the Message Board: security.cfm

 Open security.cfm from the CD-ROM.

This script protects the message board from unregistered users by telling Flash whether a user is registered.

Let's go over the code:

```
<cfparam name="form.username" default="none">
<cfparam name="form.password" default="none">
```

The `<cfparam>` tag lets you specify default values for parameters. The name attribute is required, and a variable name must be passed to it. When a default value is specified, the value is used whenever the variable is used. In this example, we're setting `form.username` and `form.password` to none.

```
<cfcontent type="application/x-www-urlform-encoded">
```

The `<cfcontent>` tag sets the content of the page in URL-encoded format, which makes the data more readable by Flash.

```
<cfquery datasource="#dsn#" name="login_check">
```

Just as in the past scripts, this line of code lets you send SQL statements to an ODBC driver. The datasource name is the value of the variable `dsn`; `message_board`. The name of this query is `login_check`. Unlike the previous script, however, the results of this query will be referenced by other parts of the script. Therefore, the value of the name attribute is important. We have named this query `login_check`.

```
select id,username
from security
```

The Select statement, the most commonly used SQL statement, queries a table for data. The statement has two necessary components: tables and columns. In this code we'll select information from the Security table's id and username columns.

```
where username='#form.username#' and password='#form.password#'
```

The Where statement filters data retrieved by the Select statement. When the Select statement is processed, the data in the database is compared to the restrictions set forth by the Where statement, and only the data that meets the restriction(s) is retrieved. In this case, the data is compared to the values of two variables from the Flash movie: username and password. The data will only be retrieved if the username and password entered into the specified textboxes are equal to the information entered into one of the rows in the database.

```
</cfquery>
<cfif login_check.recordcount eq 1>
```

The <cfif> tag lets you create conditional code. It's comparable to an If statement in Flash. The variable login_check.recordcount tells you how many results were found from the query named login_check. (Now you can see why it's important to name your queries.) The operator eq means *equal to*; therefore, eq 1 means *equals 1*.

The chart below lists the conditional operators you can use in a <cfif> tag.

OPERATOR	EXPLANATION
IS, EQUAL, EQ	Checks if the two values are equal
IS NOT, NOT EQUAL, NEQ	Checks if the two values are not equal
CONTAINS	Checks that the first value is contained within the second value
DOES NOT CONTAIN	Checks that the first value is not contained within the second value
GREATER THAN, GT	Checks that the first value is greater than the second value
LESS THAN, LT	Checks that the first value is less than the second value
GREATER THAN OR EQUAL, GTE	Checks that the first value is greater than or equal to the second value
LESS THAN OR EQUAL, LTE	Checks that the first value is less than or equal to the second value

```
<cfoutput query="login_check">
```

The <cfoutput> tag is used to output ColdFusion variables, including results from a <cfquery>. Because there can be more than one <cfquery> in a script, it's important to always tell the server which query you're referencing—even if you only have one query in your script. There are two ways to do this:

1. When opening the <cfoutput> tag, include query= "name_of_query".

2. Write name_of_query.variable before the name of every variable that's returned from the query.

The first method is faster and easier to program, but the second method gives better results and is easier to debug.

Note that `<cfoutput>` sets up a loop. Therefore, if more than one record is retrieved, ColdFusion will output more than one row.

```
&user_id=#id#&password=#password#&loaded=1&
```

This line of code looks complicated, but it isn't. The & symbol eliminates extra spaces that ColdFusion outputs. Next to the & symbols are names of variables from the Flash movie.

 I recommend putting an & symbol at the beginning and end of entire URL string. Although it's not necessary, it's a safe thing to do because Flash may ignore the variable if it has white space around it. Surrounding the URL string with the & symbol makes sure that ColdFusion doesn't add any extra white space.

Following the equal sign are the values to which you are setting the variables. We set the Flash variables to the assigned values. You can set variables in Flash to anything you want: numbers, text, and/or variables from ColdFusion. Note that when you set a Flash variable to a value from within a ColdFusion script, you don't have to use the `<cfset>` tag, only the & and = symbols. The total syntax is: &flash_var_name=value.

```
</cfoutput>
<cfelse>
```

The `<cfelse>` tag is comparable to the `else` statement in Flash. `<cfelseif>` also exists and it is comparable to an `elseif` statement in Flash.

```
&loaded=0&
</cfif>
```

Here we close the `<cfif>` tag. The `<cfelse>` and `<cfelseif>` tags don't need matching `</cfelse>` or `</cfelseif>` tags.

This script gives you a good opportunity to recognize programming logic. Obviously, ColdFusion doesn't offer a function that determines if a user has registered, so you must figure it out yourself. It's easy: Just compare the entered information with data in a database. If results are returned from the check, the user has registered. Remember, just because a programming language doesn't provide a function doesn't mean something can't be done. All you need is a little logic!

Displaying the Forums: forums.cfm

 Open forums.cfm from the CD-ROM.

This script will display the forums that users can chose from. The forum names are taken from the Forums table and then output into Flash.

Let's look at the code:

```
<CFHEADER NAME="Cache-Control" VALUE="no-cache">
```

The <CFHEADER> tag lets you mediate the contents of the HTTP header. Cache-Control tells the header to either cache the loaded content or not cache it. In this example we don't want the content to be cached, so we set the VALUE to "no-cache".

```
<cfquery datasource="#dsn#" name="get_forums">
<cfcontent type="application/x-www-urlform-encoded">
select id,forums
from forums
</cfquery>
<cfset id_list="">
<cfset forum_list="">
<cfloop query="get_forums">
```

The <cfloop> tag lets you loop through parts of your code until a condition is met. ColdFusion offers five types of loops. Here, we're using the Query loop, which loops once for every row returned from a <cfquery>. (ColdFusion's other loops are For, List, Collection, and While.)

```
<cfset id_list=ListAppend(id_list,id,"|")>
```

The ListAppend function adds an element to a list. In this case, we're adding the value of the variable id (which came from the <cfquery> named get_forums) and the character | to the list id_list (the | character is known as a delimeter). Because there are five rows under the id column in the database, the result of this code is:

```
id_list = 1| 2| 3| 4| 5|
<cfset forum_list=ListAppend(forum_list,forums,"|")>
```

This line of code acts like as the previous one, except we're adding the variable forums instead of id to a list. Here's the result of the code:

```
forum_list = Macromedia| Allaire| ColdFusion| Flash|
→ ActionScripting|.
</cfloop>
```

This tells ColdFusion to stop looping through the code. You can also use the <cfbreak> tag to terminate a loop. The <cfbreak> tag, however, is more commonly used in conditional code, and the </cfloop> tag is more commonly used to end loops that aren't nested within conditional code.

```
<cfoutput>
&forum_id=#id_list#&forum_title=#forum_list#&forums_loaded=1
→ & </cfoutput>
```

This sets the Flash variable forum_id to the ColdFusion variable id_list, the Flash variable forum_title to the ColdFusion variable forum_list, and the Flash variable forums_loaded to 1.

Creating a Post: post_thread.cfm

Open post_thread.cfm from the CD-ROM.

This script puts a subject and message from a registered user into the database. This lets users post questions or comments for others to read and respond to.

Let's review the code:

```
<cfquery datasource="#dsn#" name="get_original">
insert into
threads(subject,message,username,forum_id)
values('#form.new_thread_subject#','#form.new_thread_message
→ #','#form.username#',#form.forum_id#)
</cfquery>
```

This script doesn't contain any new coding concepts. It inserts information into the specified database columns.

Displaying All the Threads: threads.cfm

 Open threads.cfm from the CD-ROM.

This script outputs all of the threads from a specified forum into Flash.

Let's review the code:

```
<CFHEADER NAME="Cache-Control" VALUE="no-cache">
<cfcontent type="application/x-www-urlform-encoded">
<cfparam name="form.forum_id" default="1">
<cfquery datasource="#dsn#" name="threads">
select id,subject,username
from threads
where forum_id=#form.forum_id#
</cfquery>
<cfset id_list="">
<cfset subject_list="">
<cfset username_list="">
<cfloop query="threads">
<cfset id_list=ListAppend(id_list,id,"|")>
```

This code appends the value of id to id_list with a delimiter of |.

```
<cfset subject_list=ListAppend(subject_list,subject,"|")>
```

This appends the value of subject to subject_list with a delimiter of |.

```
<cfset username_list=ListAppend(username_list,username,"|")>
```

This code appends the value of username to username_list with a delimiter of |.

```
</cfloop>
<cfoutput>&thread_id=#id_list#&thread_subject=#subject_list#
 ↱ &thread_username=#username_list#&threads_loaded=1&</cfoutpu>
```

This sets the Flash variable thread_id to the ColdFusion variable id_list, the Flash variable thread_subject to the ColdFusion variable subject_list, the Flash variable thread_username to the ColdFusion variable username_list, and the Flash variable threads_loaded to 1.

Displaying a Thread: thread_detail.cfm

Open thread_detail.cfm from the CD-ROM.

This script outputs the original post and all of the replies to the selected thread.

Let's review the code:

```
<CFHEADER NAME="Cache-Control" VALUE="no-cache">
<cfcontent type="application/x-www-urlform-encoded">
<cfparam name="form.thread_id" default="1">
<cfquery datasource="#dsn#" name="get_original">
select username,message
from threads
where thread_id=#form.thread_id#
</cfquery>
<cfquery datasource="#dsn#" name="get_replies">
select username,message
from replies
where thread_id=#form.thread_id#
</cfquery>
<cfset username_list="none">
<cfset message_list="#get_original.message#">
```

This code sets the variable username_list to none and the variable message list to #get_original.message# (the message variable that came from the query named get_original).

```
<cfloop query="get_replies">
<cfset username_list=ListAppend(username_list,username,"|")>
```

This code appends the value of username to username_list with a delimiter of |.

```
<cfset message_list=ListAppend(message_list,message,"|")>
```

And this appends the value of message to message_list with a delimiter of |.

```
</cfloop>
<cfoutput>&message=#message_list#&username=#username_list#&
 → thread_details_loaded=1&</cfoutput>
```

Finally, this sets the Flash variables to the assigned values.

Message Reply and Email Notification: post_reply.cfm

 Open post_reply.cfm from the CD-ROM.

This is the most complicated script in the entire application. First, it adds a user's reply to a specified thread into the database. Then, it gathers the email addresses of everyone who posted a message to the thread and sends an email to tell them that there has been a response to the thread.

Let's carefully review the code:

```
<CFHEADER NAME="Cache-Control" VALUE="no-cache">
<cfcontent type="application/x-www-urlform-encoded">
<cfquery datasource="#dsn#" name="get_original">
insert into
replies(username,message,thread_id)
values('#form.username#','#form.reply_message#',#form.thread
→ _id#)
</cfquery>
<cfquery datasource="#dsn#" name="get_poster_email">
select username
from threads
where id=#form.thread_id# and notify=1
</cfquery>
<cfset email_list="#get_poster_email.username#">
<cfquery datasource="#dsn#" name="get_reply_email">
select username
from replies
where thread_id=#form.thread_id# and notify=1
</cfquery>
<cfloop query="get_reply_email">
<cfset email_list=ListAppend(email_list,username)>
```

This code appends the value of username to the variable email_list. This creates a list of all the post-makers, both the original poster and the users who replied to the post.

```
</cfloop>
<cfset loop_length=Len(email_list)>
```

This code sets the variable loop_length to the length of the value of the variable email_list.

```
<cfloop from="1" to="#loop_length#" index="loop_index">
```

This type of loop is called a `for` loop. The `from` attribute is the start position in a `for` loop and the `to` attribute is the end position. This loop will loop from 1 until it reaches the length of the list. The `index` attribute contains the name of the variable that holds the current element that's being looped through. All three of these attributes are required in a `for` loop.

```
<cfmail to="#ListGetAt(email_list,loop_index)#"
from="you@yourdomain.com" subject="FlashCFM message board
→ post">
```

The `<cfmail>` tag sends mail from a ColdFusion template. The ListGetAt function returns an element of a list at a specified position. In this example, the ListGetAt function returns an element from the `email_list` at the position specified by the loop. By doing this, everyone in the list will get this email and the loop won't end until the length is reached. The `from` attribute is the email address that sends the email; the `subject` attribute is the subject of the email. These are the three required attributes for the `<cfmail>` tag.

```
Message Board Post
```

This is the message body of the email. Everything between the `<cfmail>` and `</cfmail>` tags is the message body, and can include anything from HTML tags to embedded SWF files to ColdFusion variables.

```
</cfmail>
```

This tells ColdFusion to close the mail application.

```
</cfloop>
```

Creating the Front End in Flash

Here it is: The final piece of the puzzle. Think of a front end as the skin that covers all the ugly code we just reviewed. In this section we'll examine the key areas of the message board's front end and see how it works in conjunction with the ColdFusion scripts we just reviewed. In a nutshell, it works like this: ActionScript calls a ColdFusion script to communicate with the database, and then ColdFusion sends the information back to Flash, which displays it.

Open message_board.fla from the CD-ROM. You'll find this section easier to understand if you follow along in Flash and inspect the code.

As you can tell by the number of ColdFusion scripts created for this project, the application has multiple sections. Here are the seven scenes I created for the Flash movie: login, sign up, forums, threads, new thread, thread details, reply.

As we discuss each scene, please go to the specific scene in message_board.fla and follow along.

The Login Scene

This scene lets registered users log into the message board (**Figure 6.2**). If they're not registered, they may click on a link to go to the sign up scene.

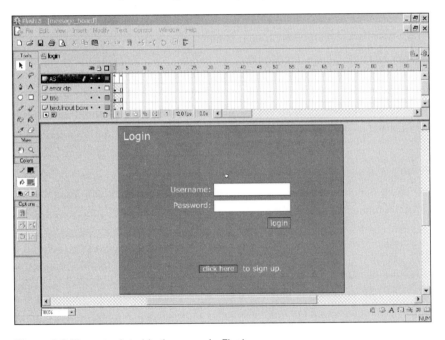

Figure 6.2 *The completed login scene in Flash.*

I created two textboxes—username and password—that people can use to enter their username and password, respectively. Then I created a login button and assigned it the following actions:

```
on (release) {
 if (username eq "" || password eq "") {
  with (error) {
   gotoAndPlay ("fields");
  }
 } else {
  loadVariablesNum ("security.cfm", 0, "POST");
  gotoAndPlay (2);
 }
}
```

! Flash will load an external file only if it resides on the same server as the Flash movie itself. For example, if the Flash file is located on www.yourdomain.com and the external file is located on www.mydomain.com, you can't load the file into Flash. You can, however, trick Flash into loading files that reside on other servers. For instance, you can have a ColdFusion script (or any other server-side script) take data from another site and then output it into Flash, as if the file did, in fact, reside on the same server.

The above code is just simple form validation. It checks if either the username or password textboxes have been left empty (the operator || means *or*). If they're empty, with the movie clip with an instance name *error* (the with function performs the same job as the tellTarget() function), the Flash movie goes to the frame labeled *fields*. If none of the textboxes are empty, the code loads security.cfm into level 0 and send the variables using POST. Finally, it goes to and plays frame 2.

Here's the code on the first keyframe of the AS layer:

```
user_id=0;
forum_id=0;
stop ();
```

These three lines of code are easy to understand. All they do is initialize the variables user_id and forum_id, then make sure the scene stops so Flash doesn't get stuck in an infinite loop through all the scenes.

I assigned the following actions to the third keyframe of the AS layer:

```
if (loaded == "1") {
  gotoAndPlay ("forums", 1);
} else if (loaded == "0") {
  with (error) {
    gotoAndPlay ("incorrect_login");
  }
  gotoAndStop (1);
} else {
  gotoAndPlay (2);
}
```

This simple script is what we've all been waiting for: your first encounter with ColdFusion and Flash integration. We've loaded the ColdFusion variables into Flash; now it's time to use the loaded data.

If loaded is equal to 1, the Flash movie will go to and play frame 1 of the forums scene. If ColdFusion returned a value of 0 for the loaded variable (no results from the query), then the movie clip named error will go to and play the frame named incorrect_login to tell the user that the entered information was wrong. Then it will go to and stop on frame 1 of the main timeline. If loaded was not set yet to 1 or 0, the Flash movie will go to and play frame 2.

This sets up a loop to check if the entire ColdFusion script has loaded. Due to a variety of factors, such as a large database or a slow modem, it can take a while for the database to send results back into Flash. Therefore, we send the scene back to frame 2 until it loads rather than let it play to the next scene or go back to frame 1. If we put a stop (); action instead of the gotoAndPlay() action, once the variables have completely loaded into Flash, nothing will happen—Flash won't run through the If statements again.

 This important concept is used not only throughout this project, but also in almost any project involving a database and Flash.

The Sign Up Scene

This scene lets unregistered users sign up to access the message board (**Figure 6.3**). After they sign up, they're returned to the login screen to sign in.

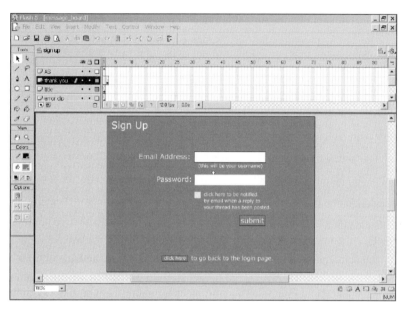

Figure 6.3 The completed sign up scene in Flash.

I assigned the following actions to the first keyframe of the AS layer:

```
stop ();
notify = 0;
```

This script stops the Flash movie from looping through all the scenes and sets the variable notify to 0. We'll use this variable shortly.

I created two textboxes, username and password; their utility is self-explanatory.

Next, I created a check box for users to mark if they want to be notified via email when someone has replied to their post. I created a movie clip, and on its first frame, I created a button and assigned the following actions to it:

```
on (release) {
  root.notify = 1;
  gotoAndStop (2);
}
```

This chunk of code sets the notify variable on the main timeline to 1, then goes to and stops on the second frame of the movie clip.

I inserted a keyframe on the second frame of the movie clip and assigned the button the following actions:

```
on (release) {
  root.notify = 0;
 gotoAndStop (1);
}
```

This code does the same thing as the last chunk of code, except it changes the notify variable back to 0, then goes to and stops on the first frame of the movie clip.

I then created on the main timeline another button for users to submit their login information. The button has the following actions:

```
on (release) {
 if (username eq "" || password eq "" ) {
  with (error) {
   gotoAndPlay ("fields");
  }
 } else {
  loadVariablesNum ("signup.cfm", 0, "POST");
  username = "";
  password = "";
  gotoAndStop (2);
  }
 }
```

Once again, this is simple form validation. The code checks to see if either the username or password textboxes are empty. If they are, with the movie clip with the instance name *error*, it goes to and plays the frame labeled fields. If both textboxes are not blank (Else), then it loads signup.cfm into level 0 with POST. Then it sets the username and password variables to null and goes to and stops on frame 2 of the main timeline.

Next I added a keyframe on frame 2 of the Thank You layer. I created a button so the user can return to the login scene to log into the message board:

```
on (release) {
 gotoAndStop ("login", 1);
}
```

This tells Flash to go to and stop on the first frame of the scene named login.

The Forums Scene

This scene presents users with a list of all the forums they can browse (**Figure 6.4**).

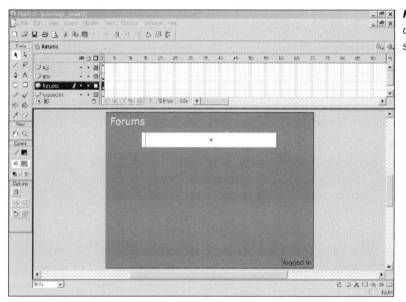

Figure 6.4 The completed forums scene in Flash.

One of the reasons this is such a great application to customize is that everything is automatic; you need to manually predefine only the forum names.

The database can have an infinite number of forums, so Flash must be able to handle this. To do this, I duplicated a movie clip once for every forum listed in the Forums table. I created a movie clip and named it forum_clip. Inside that clip I created another one named forum, which consists of a textbox (to display the forum's name) and a button (so users can access the forum). In the forum_clip movie clip, I assigned the following actions to the first frame of the AS layer:

```
loadVariables ("forums.cfm", this);
forum._visible = 0;
```

This script loads forums.cfm into the current location and sets the visible property of the forum movie clip to 0.

Next, I added the following actions to frame 3 of the AS layer:

```
if (forums_loaded == "1") {
  stop ();
  forum_title = forum_title.split("|");
  forum_id = forum_id.split("|");
  loop_length = forum_title.length;
  ystart = getProperty("forum", _y);
  for (i=0; i<loop_length; i++) {
    duplicateMovieClip ("forum", "forum"+i, i);
    setProperty ("forum"+i, _y, ystart+40*i);
    set ("forum"+i+".title", forum_title[i]);
    set ("forum"+i+".forum_id", forum_id[i]);
  }
} else {
  gotoAndPlay (2);
}
```

Although you've already seen how Flash and ColdFusion work well together, this script shows the power of the combination.

If forums_loaded equals 1, the Flash movie will stop. (All the variables are loaded, so there's no need to loop—that's why it stops.) Next we split the variable named forum_title into substrings wherever | occurs and put the results into an array. We used the list append function in our ColdFusion scripts, and | as the delimiter so we could split the list up in Flash. We do the same thing with the variable forum_id: Split it up wherever the | character appears.

Next, we set the variable loop_length to the length of the variable forum_title. Now it's time to duplicate the forum movie clip, once for each forum. To do this, we set up a for loop. The loop begins with i being equal to 0. Every time the loop goes back to the beginning, Flash checks to see if i is greater than loop_length. If it is, the loop will stop; if it isn't, then i will be incremented by 1. We duplicate the movie clip and name it *forum*+i. Because there are five forums in our message board, the movie clip will be duplicated five times and named forum1, forum2, and so on.

We then set the *y* position of the movie clips so they don't duplicate on top of each other, which would cause usability problems. We then set the title and forum_id properties of the duplicated movie clips. If loaded does not equal 1, then we go to and play frame 2, once again sending Flash into a two-frame loop until loaded is equal to 1.

241

On the button in the forum movie clip (located within the forum_clip movie clip) I assigned the following actions:

```
on (release) {
  root.forum_id = this.forum_id;
  root.forum_title = this.title;
 tellTarget ("_root") {
  play ();
 }
}
```

This code sets the `forum_id` of the main timeline equal to the `forum_id` of the movie clip (the `forum_id` was assigned to the movie clip during the duplications). It also sets the `forum_title` of the main timeline equal to the title of the movie clip (the title was assigned to the movie clip during the duplications). Next, we tell the main timeline to play on, which brings us to the threads scene.

The Threads Scene

When a user selects a forum, he's sent to this scene, which displays all the subject lines of the threads from the selected forum (**Figure 6.5**).

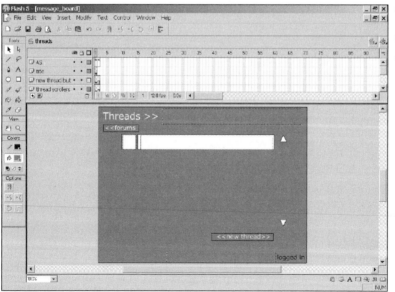

Figure 6.5
The completed threads scene in Flash.

I set up the movie clip that would be duplicated in order to display all the subject lines. First, I created a movie clip called thread_clip, which contains another movie clip named thread. The thread movie clip consists of two buttons and two textboxes: thread_id (to display the thread's id) and subject (to display the thread's subject). In the thread_clip movie clip I added the following actions to the first frame of the AS layer:

```
forum_id = _root.forum_id;
loadVariables ("threads.cfm", this, "POST");
thread._visible = 0;
```

This sets the variable forum_id to the value of forum_id that's located on the main timeline. Then we load threads.cfm into the current location using POST. Finally, we set the visibility of the movie clip with the instance name *thread* to 0.

Here are the actions on the third frame of the AS layer:

```
if (threads_loaded == "1") {
  stop ();
  thread_id = thread_id.split("|");
  thread_subject = thread_subject.split("|");
  thread_username = thread_username.split("|");
  loop_length = thread_id.length;
  ystart = getProperty("thread", _y);
  for (i=0; i<loop_length; i++) {
    duplicateMovieClip ("thread", "thread"+i, i);
    setProperty ("thread"+i, _y, ystart+40*i);
    set ("thread"+i+".subject", thread_subject[i]);
    set ("thread"+i+".thread_id", thread_id[i]);
      → set ("thread"+i+".thread_username",
      → thread_username[i]);
  }
} else {
  gotoAndPlay (2);
}
```

If forums_loaded equals 1, the code stops the movie. Next the code splits the variables named thread_id, thread_subject, and thread_username into substrings wherever | occurs and puts the results into arrays (one array for each variable that was split). Then the code sets loop_length to the length of the thread_id.

Before we start the duplications, we need to get the *y* position of the thread movie clip so we know where to place the duplicated movie clips. We set `ystart` to the *y* position of thread. (If you don't want to use the `getProperty()` function, you can write `thread._y` instead.)

To duplicate the movie clip we use a `for` loop. The loop starts with `i` being equal to 0. Every time the loop returns to the beginning, Flash checks to see if `i` is greater than `loop_length`. If it is, the loop will stop; if not, then `i` will be incremented by 1. We duplicate the thread movie clip and set the *y* position to `ystart+40*i`. (The variable `i` can be any number from 0 to as many threads as there are. It's multiplied by `i` so none of the movie clips are duplicated on top of one another. No movie clip will have the same value for `i`, so it's a unique value.)

We then set three more properties for each movie clip: `subject`, `thread_id`, and `thread_username`. To do so we access an element of the array. How do we know that we don't assign two movie clips the same property? Once again, by using the variable `i` to access an element of the array, we're sure that no other movie clip will have that element because `i` will never be the same in any two movie clips (because we increment it every time the loop begins again). If `threads_loaded` doesn't equal 1, Flash goes to and plays frame 2, once again setting up a two-frame loop until all the variables are loaded in.

Here are the actions on the two buttons inside the thread movie clip:

```
on (release) {
  root.thread_id = this.thread_id;
  root.subject = this.subject;
  root.author = this.thread_username;
  tellTarget ("_root") {
    play ();
  }
}
```

This code sets the `thread_id` variable on the main timeline to the `thread_id` variable in the movie clip. It also sets the `subject` variable on the main timeline to the `subject` variable in the movie clip, and sets the `author` variable on the main timeline to the `thread_username` variable in the movie clip. Finally, it tells Flash to play the main timeline.

As you can see, there are other objects on the Stage other than the forum_clip movie clip. What happens when there are lots of duplications and the duplicated movie clips cover the other objects on the Stage? To solve this problem, I masked the threads layer. This way, users will only see the movie clips under the mask.

Unfortunately, I ran into another problem. What happens if there are so many thread duplications that they don't all fit on the Stage, and some threads are no longer visible to users? To solve this problem, I created two scrollers. I assigned the following actions to the up scroller:

```
on (release) {
 if(thread._y < 89.95){
 thread._y = thread._y+40;
 }
}
```

I assigned the following actions to the down scroller:

```
on (release) {
 if (thread._y+thread._height > 300){
 thread._y = thread._y-40;
 }
}
```

This block of code states that if the y position of the thread movie clip plus the height of the movie clip is greater than 300, then set the y position to the current position minus 40 pixels.

Finally, I inserted the following actions to the second keyframe of the AS layer:

```
gotoAndStop ("thread details", 1);
```

This code brings users to the thread details scene where they can view all the messages in the selected thread.

The New Thread Scene

This scene lets users post a new thread into one of the forums (**Figure 6.6**).

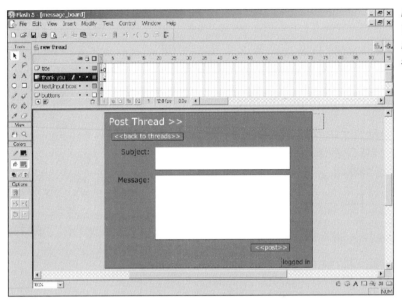

I created two textboxes: new_thread_subject and new_thread_message. Then I created a button that will post the new thread and assigned it the following actions:

```
on (release) {
loadVariablesNum ("post_thread.cfm", 0, "POST");
gotoAndStop (2);
new_thread_subject = "";
new_thread_message = "";
}
```

This tells Flash to load post_thread.cfm into level 0 using POST. It will then go to and stop on frame 2. It sets the variables new_thread_subject and new_thread_message to null.

The Thread Details Scene

When users click on a thread's subject line they are brought to this scene, which displays the thread's original message and its responses (**Figure 6.7**).

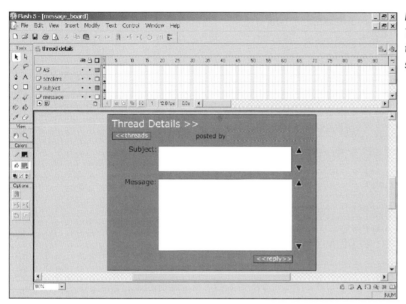

Figure 6.7

The completed thread details scene in Flash.

In this scene, Flash has to display both the thread's subject and all of its messages. I created a textbox and gave it a variable name of subject. This took care of displaying the thread's subject.

I then created a movie clip named message_clip. Inside it I created a textbox with the variable name thread_message. I assigned the following actions to the first frame of the AS layer:

```
thread_id = _root.thread_id;
loadVariables ("thread_detail.cfm", this, "POST");
```

This sets the variable thread_id to the value of the variable thread_id on the main timeline. Finally we load thread_detail.cfm into the current location using POST.

I assigned the third keyframe of the AS layer the following actions:

```
if (thread_details_loaded == "1") {
 new_message = message.split("|");
 new_username = username.split("|");
 loop_length = new_username.length;
 thread_message = "";
 for (i=0; i<loop_length; i++) {
  if (i==0) {
    thread_message = thread_message+new_message[i]+"<br><br>";
    } else {
    thread_message = thread_message+new_username[i]+":
    → "+new_message[i]+"<br><br>";
   }
  }
 stop ();
 } else {
 gotoAndPlay (2);
 }
```

If thread_details_loaded is equal to 1, then the code splits the variable
new_message into substrings wherever | occurs and puts the results into an
array. Next it splits the variable new_username into substrings wherever |
occurs and puts the results into an array. The loop_length variable is then
set to the length of the new_username variable and the thread_message
variable is set to null.

To put all the responses and their posters in one textbox, we set up a for
loop. The loop begins with i being equal to 0. Every time the loop returns
to the beginning, Flash checks to see if i is greater than loop_length. If it
is, the loop will stop; if not, then i will be incremented by 1. If i equals 0
(this can only happen on the first loop; after that it can't be 0 because it's
being incremented), the code sets the variable thread_message to itself plus
the first element of the array new_message. (We know it's the first element
of the array because if i didn't equal 0, Flash would be processing the Else
statement. How do we contact the first element of an array again?
Array_name[0]).

At this point, we add some HTML tags to create space between responses. You can't use every HTML tag in Flash, but you can use a few. Flash can recognize the following HTML tags:

HTML TAG	OPTIONAL ATTRIBUTES
<A HREF = "URL">	None
<B>	None
<Font>	Color = "#xxxxxx", Face= "Type Face", Size= "##"
<I>	None
<P ALIGN = "">	Right, Left, Center
<U>	None

If i doesn't equal 0, then the code sets the variable thread_message equal to itself plus an element of the new_username array (this unknown element can't be the first element of the array) plus ":", plus an element of the new_message array. (We will refer to the same element number in the new_username and new_message arrays.) It also adds some HTML tags to create spacing between entries. When the loop is complete the Flash movie will stop. If thread_details_loaded doesn't equal 1, then the movie goes to and plays frame 2, once again creating a two-frame loop until all the variables have been loaded in.

I created up and down scrollers for both the subject and thread_message textboxes. I assigned the following actions to the up scroller of the subject textbox:

```
on (release) {
  subject.scroll = subject.scroll-1;
}
```

This code tells the subject textbox to scroll up.

I assigned the following actions to the down scroller of the subject textbox:

```
on (release) {
  subject.scroll = subject.scroll+1;
}
```

This tells the subject textbox to scroll down.

I assigned the following actions to the up scroller of the thread_message textbox:

```
on (release) {
  message_clip.thread_message.scroll =
  ⇢ message_clip.thread_message.scroll-1;
}
```

This tells the thread_message textbox, which is located within the movie clip with the instance name *message_clip*, to scroll up.

Finally, I assigned the following actions to the down scroller of the thread_message textbox:

```
on (release) {
 message_clip.thread_message.scroll =
  → message_clip.thread_message.scroll+1;
}
```

This tells the thread_message textbox, which is located within the movie clip with the instance name *message_clip*, to scroll down.

The Reply Scene

This scene lets users reply to a post (**Figure 6.8**).

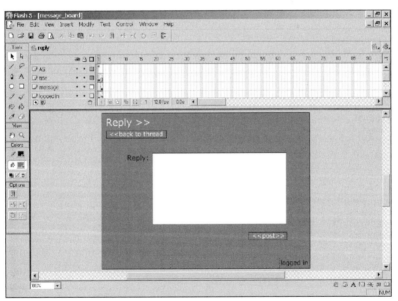

Figure 6.8 *The completed reply scene in Flash.*

I created a textbox with the variable name reply_message. This is where users enter a reply to the specified thread.

I then create a Post button for users to click; this loads the ColdFusion script that puts the specified information into the database:

```
on (release) {
 loadVariablesNum ("post_reply.cfm", 0, "POST");
 gotoAndStop (2);
}
```

This code loads post_reply.cfm into level 0 using POST. It then goes to the second frame of the scene and stops.

Finally, I added a second keyframe to numerous layers and created a button that returns users to the thread. Here's the code on the button:

```
on (release) {
  gotoAndStop ("thread details", 1);
}
```

This returns users to the Thread Details scene where they will see their post.

Showcase 2: Counter

Tracking Users

This project shows you how to create a counter, one of the easiest ways to track Web site traffic. The counter's back end is PHP and the front end is Flash.

 Open counter.fla from the CD-ROM to see the completed project (**Figure 6.9**). You'll find the sources files for this showcase in the PHP sub-folder in the Chapter 6 folder.

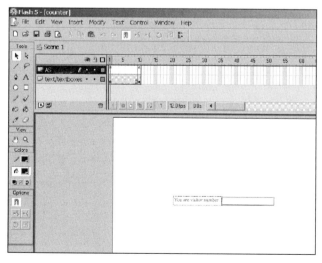

Figure 6.9 The completed counter in Flash.

count.php

 Open count.php from the CD-ROM.

This is an excellent example of how PHP works well with text files. It gets information from the file, manipulates it, and then sends it into Flash.

Let's go over the PHP code before we create the front end:

```
<?
```

If you save an .html file as a .php file, it will still work. So how do you tell the server to handle the code as if it is a PHP script? You must use the <? tag. This is called short tags because it is written <? instead of <?php. The server must be configured in a certain way to use short tags. Most servers are; if not, use <?php instead.

```
$counterloc = "count.txt";
```

Variables, which are case-sensitive in PHP, are represented by the $ sign. The count.txt is a .txt file that we'll soon discuss. You must write the full system path to this file for the counter to work.

```
$counterloc_array = file($counterloc);
```

This sets the variable counterloc_array to file($counterloc). The file function opens the $counterloc (count.txt) and returns the file in an array. Each line of the file is made into an element of the array.

$counterloc_array[0] - This is the first line of the text file.

$counterloc_array[1] - This is the second line of the text file.

$counterloc_array[2] - This is the third line of the text file.

```
$counterloc_array[0]++;
```

This line of code takes the first element of the array (line one of the text file) and adds 1 to it. It's the same in Flash: To increment a number by 1 you can use ++ and to decrement a number by 1 you can use --. The above code does the same thing as $counterloc_array [0] = $counterloc_array[0] + 1; would.

```
$cl = fopen($counterloc, "w");
```

The fopen function opens a file or URL. *w* is the mode in which the file will be open. This mode means that it will open the file and erase its contents. Below are the other modes:

MODE	EXPLANATION
r	Reading. Pointer starts at the beginning of the file.
r+	Reading and writing. Pointer starts at the beginning of the file.
w	Writing. Erase all of the content. Pointer starts at the beginning of the file.
w+	Reading and writing. Erase all of the content. Pointer starts at the beginning of the file.
a	Writing. Pointer starts at the end of the file.
a+	Reading and writing. Pointer starts at the end of the file.

```
fputs($cl, "$counterloc_array[0]");
```

The fputs function writes to a file. The file is $cl, and $counterloc_array[0] is the content to write. The $counterloc_array[0] was increased by 1 before it was rewritten to a text file; therefore, when it is rewritten, the number is 1 greater than it was before the user accessed the site. That's how the counter works.

```
fclose($cl);
```

This closes an open file ($cl) using the fclose function.

```
echo "hitnum=$counterloc_array[0]";
```

Echo is a language construct used to output a string. Because it's not a function, you're not required to put the string in parentheses. We're assigning the hitnum variable within Flash a value of $counterloc_array[0]. Some people prefer to use Print() instead of echo because it's easier to remember; they are interchangeable.

 Open count.txt from the CD-ROM. Note that this is only a blank document. The PHP script writes the number of hits into this document; that number is then output into Flash. The beauty of this technique is that it produces very small files, which increase your application's speed. For example, a text file can have 10 digits (a billion hits), but the file size will be a mere 1KB.

The Flash Front End

Let's look at how I created the Flash front end that displays the number of hits.

 Open counter.fla from the CD-ROM.

I created two textboxes, one name hitnum and one named visitor_num. The first displays the number of hits. Inside the second textbox I typed "you are visitor number", so when the number of hits is displayed (let's assume there are 927 hits), it says, "You are visitor number 927".

Next I assigned the following code to frame 1 of the AS layer:

```
if (time_around == "1") {
  stop ();
} else {
  loadVariablesNum ("count.php", 0, "POST");
}
```

This code states that if the variable time_around equals 1, then stop the movie, but if it doesn't equal 1 then load count.php on level 0 using POST.

Finally, I assigned the following code to frame 10 of the AS layer:

```
time_around = time_around + 1;
```

This code simply adds one to the time_around variable.

What's the purpose of the time_around variable? If you put only a load-variables() action on the first keyframe, the counter won't work. If you put a keyframe on the tenth frame (like we did) and let Flash loop, the counter will not only add 1, it won't stop adding numbers. The time_around variable establishes when Flash has gone through all the frames once. This gives Flash enough time to load all the variables from the PHP script without having the counter loop.

If you don't understand completely, try it for yourself. Get rid of the time_around variable and let Flash loop—you'll see what I'm talking about. Wasn't that easy? Enjoy the counter!

Showcase 3: Chat Room

This final project shows you how to create a chat room, an excellent way to communicate over the Internet and a way to draw visitors back to your site. The chat room's back end is ASP and the front end is Flash.

 Open chatv01asp.fla from the CD-ROM to see the completed project (**Figure 6.10**). You'll find the source files for this showcase in the ASP sub-folder in the Chapter 6 folder.

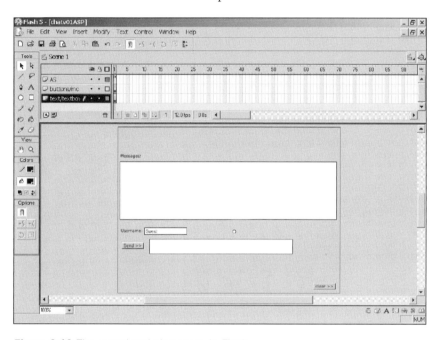

Figure 6.10 *The completed chat room in Flash.*

chatserver.asp

 Open ChatServer.asp from the CD-ROM.

This script is the brains of the operation. It handles everything from clearing to updating the chat. This is a good example to study because it takes information from Flash, manipulates it, and then sends it back into Flash—everything you need to know to create complex applications.

Let's go over the ASP code before we create the front end:

`<%`

All ASP code must be situated in between <% and %> or it will print as regular text.

```
Function HexChar(ByVal i)
 If i < 10 Then
  HexChar = Chr(i+Asc("0"))
 Else
 HexChar = Chr(i-10+Asc("A"))
 End If
End Function
```

This creates a function named HexChar that encodes a number from 0 to 15 to a single hex digit.

```
Function URLEncode(ByVal s)
 Dim result, ch
 Do While Len(s) > 0
  ch = Asc(s)
  s = Right(s, Len(s)-1)
  If (ch >= Asc("a") And ch <= Asc("z")) Or (ch >= Asc("A")
  → And ch <= Asc("Z")) Then
   result = result & Chr(ch)
  ElseIf ch = Asc(" ") Then
   result = result & "+"
  Else
   'result = result & "*" & ch
   'result = result & "!" & (ch/16) & (ch mod 16)
   result = result & "%" & HexChar(Int(ch/16)) & HexChar
   → (ch Mod 16)
  End If
 Loop
 URLEncode = result
End Function
```

This creates a function named URLEncode that encodes the control and punctuation characters in a string to %xx hex values. This ensures special characters are rendered properly within the chat.

```
Response.Expires = 0
```

This code makes sure the chat session is never cached. This ensures that new variable values will be represented.

```
action = Request.QueryString("action")
```

This sets the variable `action` to the value of the string "action" that exists within the Flash movie. The Request Object retrieves submitted information. The information can come from an HTML form, QueryString, cookie, or environment variables.

```
msg = Request.form("data1")
user = Request.form("user")
id = Request.form("server")
```

Here we set the variable `msg` to the value of the variable `"data1"` that exists in the Flash movie. We also set the variable `user` to the variable `"user"` that exists within the Flash movie. Finally we set the variable `id` to the value of the variable `"server"` that exists within the Flash movie.

```
If Len(id) = 0 Then
 id = "default"
End If
```

This checks if the length of the variable `id` equals 0. If it does, then the code sets `id` to "default".

```
Application.Lock
```

This protects access to the chat session.

```
If action = "send" Then
 list = Application(id)
 list = list + user + ": " + msg + chr(13)
 → +"================="+ chr(13)
 Application(id) = list
```

This checks if `action` equals "send". If it does, this adds the string to the chat session and sets `list` to the value of the sender, the message and the separator line.

```
ElseIf action = "clear" Then
 list = ""
 Application(id) = list
```

This checks if `action` equals "clear". If it does, then this clears the chat session by setting the variable list to an empty string.

```
Else'If action = "update" Then
 list = Application(id)
End If
```

This checks if `action` equals "update". If it does, then it returns the updated information to the chat session.

```
Application.Unlock
```

This permits access to the chat session in order to output the variables back into Flash.

```
response.write("list="+URLEncode(list))
```

The Response Object is much like the Response Object in JavaScript. It sends information to the browser, sends cookies to the browser, and redirects the browser to another URL. In this case, we're sending information to the browser. We set the Flash variable `list` to the value of "list", in URL-encode format.

The Flash Front End

This Flash front end is more complicated than the PHP one. In that project, we only had to receive data; here, we must send and receive data.

 Open chatv01asp.fla from the CD-ROM.

I assigned the following actions to the first keyframe of the AS layer:

```
id = "Xypno";
function updateit () {
loadVariables("http://www.yourdomain.com/ChatServer.asp?acti
→ on=update", "", "POST");
}
```

This sets the variable `id` to Xypno. Next, I created a function called `updateit()`, which loads chatserver.asp and sets the string action to update. The variables will be loaded into the current location (Target) using POST.

I created three textboxes: list, user, and data1. The first textbox displays the entered information; the second lets users specify a username; and the third lets users type messages.

I assigned the following actions to the send button:

```
on (press, keyPress "<Enter>") {
 loadVariables("http://www.yourdomain.com/ChatServer.asp?
 → action=send", "", "POST");
 data1 = "";
}
```

If the user presses the button or presses the Enter key, this code loads chat-server.asp and sets the string action to send. The variables will be loaded into the current location (Target) using POST. Then the code sets the variable data1 to null to clear the textbox.

Here's the code on the clear button:

```
on (release) {
 loadVariables("http://www.yourdomain.com/ChatServer.asp?
 → action=clear", "", "POST");
}
```

This loads chatserver.asp and sets the string action to clear. The variables will be loaded into the current location (Target) using POST. The reason for having this is because if the chat log becomes too long, it may slow down. Instead of having the chat automatically delete parts of the log, this gives the user the choice of doing so.

I then created a movie clip named serverscroller. The following actions were assigned to the first keyframe of the AS layer:

```
root.updateit();
root.list.scroll = _root.list.maxscroll;
```

This calls upon the function updateit() on the first keyframe of the main timeline. If the chat loads new text into the list textbox it needs to scroll; this scrolls the list textbox up (if no text is loaded, the textbox won't scroll).

Frame 15 of the AS layer has the following actions:

```
gotoAndPlay (1);
```

This simply sends the movie clip back to frame one, so the chat log keeps updating.

Finally, I dragged the serverscroller movie clip onto the main stage. That's it—a chat room in Flash!

CREATING DYNAMIC FLASH PAGES : SHOWCASE 3: CHAT ROOM

Extra Help

Here are some Web sites that specialize in dynamic Flash:

FlashCFM (www.FlashCFM.com) Run by Zap Designs, a top-of-the-line Web design company, FlashCFM is by far the best Internet resource for ColdFusion and Flash integration, offering source code for beginners and advanced programmers alike. If you're having trouble with the source code or you want to create your own application, you can post questions on the message board and get in-depth responses from the experts. This should be the first place you go for help.

EasyRew (www.freecfm.com/e/easyrew/research) Follow along the educational explorations of noted programmer Richard S. Rew. Read through his ColdFusion and Flash integration tutorials to advance your knowledge level from beginner to intermediate.

NVI Media (www.nvimedia.com/xtras) This site offers some good sample files for those new to ColdFusion and Flash integration.

FlashWave (www.flashwave.co.uk) This site has a wealth of information, especially on ASP, but also on PHP and Perl. Unfortunately, it's rarely updated and most of the files are in Flash 4 format, not Flash 5.

CFM-Resources (www.cfm-resources.com) The best free ColdFusion hosting company on the Internet. If your hosting company doesn't support the technologies that this chapter discusses (ODBC, ASP, PHP, and ColdFusion), I strongly recommend signing up for the service of CFM-Resources.

Quiz

 Think you know it all? Find out by taking the following quiz—no peeking at the chapter text! You'll find the answers in a PDF file on the CD-ROM.

1. Why is a dynamic Flash site better than any other type of Web site, whether it's static or dynamic?

2. How is a primary key useful?

3. What's the purpose of the URL-encode format?

4. If you need to pass a large amount of data from one page to another, what method would you use and why?

5. What's the purpose of ODBC?

6. What's the difference between an application.cfm and an onrequestend.cfm?

7. What are the three parts of an Insert statement?

8. What are the complete syntaxes for outputting variables into Flash from a ColdFusion, PHP, and ASP script?

9. In PHP, what does the file () function do?

10. How can you trick Flash into loading variables from a file that exists on a different server?

7: Flash Interface Design

Til Mauder studied industrial design at Art Center College of Design in Pasadena, California, and now works as an interface design consultant in Berkeley, California. His work includes interfaces for Sun Microsystems; interactive advertising for Macy's; and online educational tools for San Francisco State University, NYU, and Pearson. He designs both Flash-based consumer Web sites and traditional corporate sites. He particularly enjoys interaction design and the process of crafting an experience for the audience.

Oliver Shaw is a London-based Flash designer. He was captivated by Flash from the start because it was radically different from the HTML Web sites he was developing and surfing. While earning a degree in multimedia design at Staffordshire University in northern England, he experimented with ActionScript and joined the rapidly growing Flash community. He then applied his Flash skills in a commercial environment and is now a Senior Flash Designer at AMX Network. He is focused on the challenges of usability, information architecture, and experience design. You can see Oli's latest Flash experiments at www.disfunktional.com.

One of the interesting things about Flash Web sites is that they can mimic traditional desktop applications. Site visitors can drag and drop, select, and copy and paste objects, and alert boxes can pop up to ask them questions or offer information. On most HTML-based Web sites, none of this happens. Flash's ActionScript beats HTML hands down when it comes to creating engaging and effective Web interfaces, especially those that provide user-response mechanisms—paths for communication between the viewer and the Web site.

There are many ways to refine the interaction, speed, and consistency of your Flash user interfaces. In this chapter, we'll show you how to make what we call *widgets*—symbols with a twist. Developers have traditionally used symbols in Flash for content elements that are used multiple times—fish in an aquarium, for example. The twist is that you can create custom *interface* components and reuse them throughout your site.

What's a Widget?

You may have seen the term *widget* used in different ways. We define it as a movie clip containing ActionScript that controls another movie clip—in most cases, its container movie clip or the main timeline.

In Flash 4, designers in need of a more object-oriented approach to scripting would store an often-used script in a frame and just keep calling that frame whenever they needed that script. But it's hard to keep track of frames. Flash 5 lets you store movie clip symbols in the Library. Sure, you could program everything into your main timeline and it would work. But wouldn't it be nicer to have a collection of widgets that you could simply drop into a movie clip instance—without any additional coding? When you use widgets for frequently used interface elements such as pull-down menus and hyperlinks, you offer viewers a more consistent Flash Web site experience. Of course, reusing content also improves your site's performance.

The widget examples in this chapter are subtle interface effects that can create a memorable experience for your viewers. Our two projects demonstrate different design approaches and programming techniques. The first is a Flash-based photo album that's designed to keep the visitor focused on the pictures. Its navigational elements at the bottom of the screen become more animated and interactive only when the viewer moves the pointer over the navigation links. The ActionScript widgets used in this project comprise little movie clips that contain specific instructions that affect the parent timeline.

The second project, an experimental interface, uses an interactive tool palette that opens only when it's dragged into the main screen area. This project shows you how to develop widgets using `onClipEvent()` and `function()` to create interface elements that respond with different behaviors, depending on where the viewer drags them.

Creating a Photo Album

The interface for the photo album focuses viewers' attention on the photography. The rest of the screen remains static and uses low-contrast color combinations so it doesn't distract viewers' attention from the content. When viewers direct their pointers to the menu system, the interface springs to life with subtle animated effects that don't compete with the imagery. Rollover menu items also scale up to become clearer and easier to read.

Make your projects stand out by carefully considering the way you implement small, commonly used elements such as hyperlinks. The photo album site may not strike you as advanced in terms of its overall visual design; what's innovative is the subtle behavior of the links.

Figure 7.1 *Subtle hyperlink enhancements work behind the scenes to make for more elegant interaction with the viewer.*

Figure 7.2 *The rollover effect of the link scaling up in size and changing colors uses two widgets: scale and fade.*

Creating a Hyperlink that Scales and Fades

We use four widgets in this example: scale, fade, inertia, and masking. Scale and fade are located in movie clip symbols in the Library because they were originally developed for a different project (**Figure 7.3**). The other two, inertia and masking, were not really intended as widgets during project development. Once we finished, though, we realized that these behaviors are widgets indeed.

 Open album.swf from the CD-ROM and roll your pointer over the text navigation at the bottom of the screen. Note how the text becomes larger and bright yellow as you roll the pointer over it, and it recedes more slowly into the background on mouseOut. When you click the text, it changes color and remains that way to indicate it as being visited, just as you'd expect from a regular hyperlink. Here's how it's done.

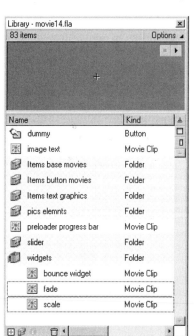

Figure 7.3 *The scale and fade widgets have been copied from a different project and pasted into this project's Library.*

 First, open album.fla from the CD-ROM.

We created two widgets, scale and fade, that can be called by any movie clip. In this example, we applied these effects to text links, but you could use any movie clip anywhere in your site to achieve the same effect.

Creating the Scale Widget

The scale widget is a multiple-frame loop, which was commonly used in Flash 4 development. It needs to sit inside the movie clip that it's supposed to affect. All you need to do is drag it into the movie clip you want to control and call the instance *scale* (**Figures 7.4** and **7.5**).

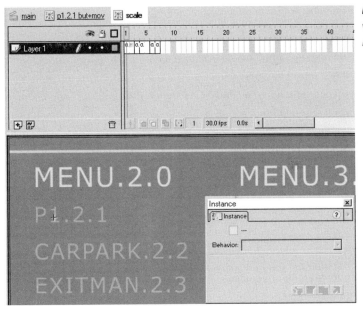

Figure 7.4 *The scale widget is a multi-frame loop.*

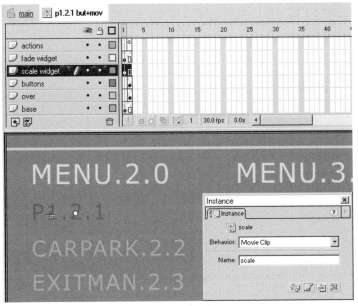

Figure 7.5 *The scale widget sits inside the movie clip.*

In the first frame, labeled *init*, the local variables are initiated. These are the maximum scale factor allowed and the minimum scale factor. Because the symbol is designed to function without needing its own instance name, we're not initiating any variables in an onLoad() frame action. We don't want the movie clip to continue playing, so we'll put a stop() action at the end.

```
maxScale = 125;
minScale = 100;
stop ();
```

The scaleUP frame is called from the parent movie clip's mouseOver event, which we'll examine later. Here, the widget scales its parent movie clip and then moves to the following frame, which just goes back to the scaleUP frame to repeat the process.

```
if (maxScale>_parent._xscale) {
 _parent._xscale = _parent._xscale+((maxScale-_
 → parent._xscale)/1.7);
 _parent._yscale = _parent._xscale;
} else {
gotoAndStop (1);
}
```

The scaleDOWN frame is identical to scaleUP, except it decreases the scale. Note the different scale factor at the end of line 2 to make the effect slow and smooth. Again, the next frame simply returns the playback head to this frame.

```
if (_parent._xscale>minScale) {
_parent._xscale = _parent._xscale+((minScale-_
 → parent._xscale)/14);
_parent._yscale = _parent._xscale;
} else {
gotoAndStop (1);
}
```

Calling the Scale Widget

Open one of the link movie clips on the main timeline; you'll see a two-frame movie clip. The sub actions layer contains the widgets, and the second frame has a plain vanilla button with the ActionScript telling the scale widget what to do.

```
scale.gotoAndPlay ("scaleUP");
```

The second part of the script is also self-explanatory. In the third part, the on(press) event, the color is set to yellow, because this link is now considered visited. *Base* refers to the instance sitting in the base layer switching the colors.

```
base.gotoAndStop ("set");
```

Of course, there's more going on here, namely the communication with the fade widget. We'll now look at the sub actions layer and locate the fade widget.

Creating the Fade Widget

Again, we're talking about a straightforward three-frame loop. In the first frame, the variables are initiated. The al variable is used by the parent's movie clip base (in layer base) and the fade_speed1 and fade_speed2 variables control the speed at which the fade up and fade down will occur. For this project, we chose a fast fade up, so the viewer sees an instantaneous fade up of color on rollover, and then a gradual fade away on roll off.

```
al = 0;
fade_speed1=20;
fade_speed2=3;
```

In the second frame, the parent's text clip "over" is being called. Initially it's 0, because the pointer hasn't rolled over it yet.

```
parent.over._alpha= al;
```

In the third frame, the script checks if the local condition active is true or false and executes the appropriate statements for increasing or decreasing the alpha of the base movie clip.

```
if (active == 1 and al<100) {
al = al+fade_speed1;
} else if (active == 0) {
if (al>0) {
al = al-fade_speed2;
} else {
al = 0;
}
}
gotoAndPlay (2);
```

Creating the Inertia Widget

Do you see what else is happening in this interface? There's an inertia effect applied to the sliding yellow bar that highlights which menu column you're in, following the `_root._xmouse` and slowing down as it approaches the pointer's location.

Such effects can be distracting when you're looking at the navigation, so the script also checks to see if the slider is over a menu list (one of the four column headers), and if it is, the slider rests and the title of the menu column is highlighted.

Figure 7.6 *Here the slider bar follows* _xmouse *with inertia.*

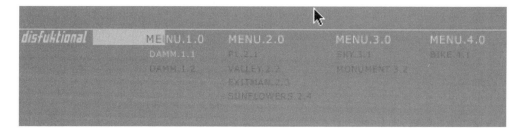

Figure 7.7 *The slider bar moves back to its start position.*

Look at the slider movie clip that we've so aptly named *slider*. It's the yellow box on the left. As always, we're first loading our variables in the `onClipEvent(load)` and initializing the slider's start position, home_x. An intriguing part is the `friction` variable. Play around with it and give it different values to see the effect. You can make the slider slip around like a hockey puck, or have it grind its way across the screen like a Firestone tire.

```
onClipEvent (load) {
home_x = _root.slider._x;
slider_w = _root.slider.box1._width/2;
friction = 1.9;
gap = 25;
count=3;
inZone = 328;
m1=_root.m1._x;
m2=_root.m2._x;
m3=_root.m3._x;
m4=_root.m4._x;
}
```

The last four lines specify variables we'll use to address the menu columns and their widths. We'll use them in the function that stops the slider from moving while the mouse is over a link.

Alternatively, you could have used an array, like so:

```
mx = new Array(_root.m1._x, _root.m2._x, _root.m3._x, _
→ root.m4._x);
```

But that seems a bit complicated for just four elements.

The variable inZone is the vertical location of the yellow horizontal line, which we've just looked up via the rulers view.

The next function, follow(), is initiated below in the (enterFrame) event as soon as the pointer is below the yellow line. It makes the slider move, with goto_x = ((slider_x-_root._xmouse)/friction)+_root._xmouse as the inertia algorithm.

```
function follow () {
slider_x = _root.slider._x;
goto_x = ((slider_x-_root._xmouse)/friction)+_root._xmouse;
_root.slider._x = goto_x;
}
```

Now onto the action in the (enterFrame) (**Figure 7.8**).

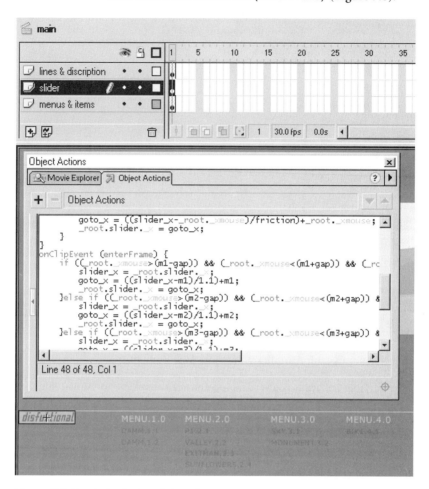

Figure 7.8 *The ActionScript of the slider on the main timeline.*

When we developed this, we thought we could save a few lines of code by employing a `for()` loop going through calculations for each of the four menu columns. It proved to be buggy with this design, however. Sometimes a design can be more stable when you code things a bit less efficiently.

TIP If you find that something isn't working right, even though the syntax and everything else looks OK, try a less complex code. It might not do all the things you intended, but you'll be able to track down the problem. When we created an array for our links navigation so it would be built dynamically, the inertia widget suddenly stopped working. There was no clear reason for this, so we had to go back to the code you see on these pages.

Now look at the first `if()` statement and notice the use of our previously setup variable mx. This `if()` statement causes the slider to stop if the `_root._xmouse` is over a menu column as well as below the yellow line.

```
onClipEvent (enterFrame) {
if ((_root._xmouse>(m1-gap)) && (_root._xmouse<(m1+gap)) &&
→ (_root._ymouse>inZone)) {
slider_x = _root.slider._x;
goto_x = ((slider_x-m1)/1.1)+m1;
_root.slider._x = goto_x;
}else if ((_root._xmouse>(m2-gap)) &&
→ (_root._xmouse<(m2+gap)) && (_root._ymouse>inZone)) {
slider_x = _root.slider._x;
goto_x = ((slider_x-m2)/1.1)+m2;
_root.slider._x = goto_x;
}else if ((_root._xmouse>(m3-gap)) &&
→ (_root._xmouse<(m3+gap)) && (_root._ymouse>inZone)) {
slider_x = _root.slider._x;
goto_x = ((slider_x-m3)/1.1)+m3;
_root.slider._x = goto_x;
}else if ((_root._xmouse>(m4-gap)) &&
→ (_root._xmouse<(m4+gap)) && (_root._ymouse>inZone)) {
slider_x = _root.slider._x;
goto_x = ((slider_x-m4)/1.1)+m4;
_root.slider._x = goto_x;
}else if (_root._ymouse<inZone ||
→ (_root._xmouse<(home_x+slider_w))) {
goHome();
}else {
follow();
}
}
```

Creating the Masking Widget

By now you have an idea of how widgets are set up and the various ways they can be applied. The previous example of the widgets used in the photo album shows that the scale widget is applied to both the mask layer and the layer containing the bitmaps, since the two elements are scaling at different speeds. We're doing this because scaling bitmap animation in Flash is always a bit choppy. Therefore, we'll create the thumbnail effect by displaying only a part of the bitmap in the thumbnail view (**Figure 7.9**).

273

Figure 7.9 *You see only a cropped version of the bitmap.*

As your pointer moves over the thumbnail image, the scale effect is applied to two elements: the bitmap itself and the mask that builds its frame. The scaling takes place so quickly that you might have to play with this a few times to see it in the SWF file. If you look closely, you can see what's happening (**Figures 7.9**, **7.10** and **7.11**).

Figures 7.10 and 7.11 *As the pointer rolls over the thumbnail, the bitmap and the mask that builds its frame scale at different rates.*

Open the pics movie clip in the main timeline, and then the mask movie clip. This is the starting setup of the pictures in the album, where the scale of the mask is set to 100 percent with the frame action s=100.

Locate the invisible, unnamed mask-scaling widget sitting in the middle layer of the pics movie clip you're looking at (**Figure 7.12**). The first frame sets variables for use in the following frame.

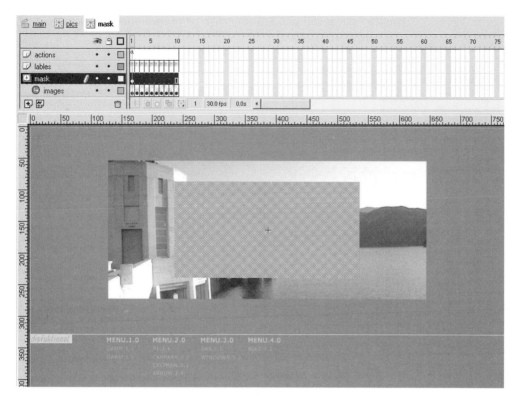

Figure 7.12 The mask-scaling widget.

```
friction = 0.45;
velocity = 0.27;
```

The next frame scales the mask and the bitmap accordingly.

```
a = _parent.mask;
a.xscale = a.xscale*friction+(a.s-a._xscale)*velocity;
a.yscale = a.yscale*friction+(a.s-a._yscale)*velocity;
a._xscale += a.xscale;
a._yscale += a.yscale;

b = _parent.mask.image;
b.xscale = b.xscale*friction+(b.sb-b._xscale)*velocity;
b.yscale = b.yscale*friction+(b.sb-b._yscale)*velocity;
b._xscale += b.xscale;
b._yscale += b.yscale;
```

From the parent clip pics, look at the script of the button that activates the zoom-in effect (**Figure 7.13**).

Figure 7.13 *Activating the zoom effect.*

The rollover event sets the variables sb of the bitmap inside the mask movie clip to 50. That's half of 100, so the bitmap should grow twice as big on rollover. The rollout event reverses things by resetting the variables for the mask and the bitmap to their original values.

```
on (rollOver) {
this.mask.image.sb = 50;
this.mask.s = 300;
}
on (rollOut) {
this.mask.image.sb = 100;
this.mask.s = 100;
}
```

Widgets control their host movie clips essentially the same way a tellTarget() event controls inline movies, except they talk in reverse direction. This is important difference because tellTarget() needs to know the names of movie clip instances. Widgets rely on telling their host movie clips via the generic _parent property. Just as you would reference relative URLs in HTML tags, you can go up multiple layers like this: _parent._parent._parent._yscale. This would control the _yscale property of a clip sitting three layers up in the nesting hierarchy. For more about this type of programming, check out www.behaviorclips.com. This site, which was still in progress at press time, shows there is a growing interest in developing Flash movies this way.

Creating Tool Palettes

This project shows how to develop interface elements using `onClipEvent()` in combination with functions to create more complex interface elements. A hyperlink is a pretty straightforward piece of functionality. A tool palette, though, can be more interesting and useful. We kept the examples in this showcase simple so you could readily see the structure, but you'll see that you can program quite a lot of complexity into each palette element. With this project, we explore how some fairly established interface standards could be turned into something that appears perhaps less utilitarian but entertaining. When it comes to experimental approaches to Web design, it's easy to go overboard, and the result is often frustrating for your site visitors. The idea in this project is to invite the visitor to do some exploration, something often required by advertising agencies and entertainment-oriented sites, which are more inclined to employ Flash exactly because of these aspects.

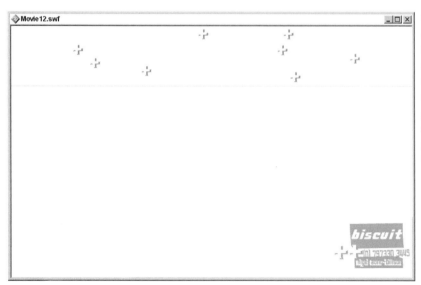

Figure 7.14
Although you don't see much here at first, there are about five pages worth of graphics packed into this screen.

Open palettes.swf from the CD-ROM and watch the little icons randomly move across the top of the screen, almost as if they're floating down a stream. Rolling over an icon displays a tool tip, which reuses the fade widget from the previous project. Clicking the icon doesn't do anything, but try dragging it. The palette opens and displays its contents, and you can place it anywhere on screen. Closing the palette returns the icon to the top of the screen. You can also drag the palette back to the top of the screen and it will close itself.

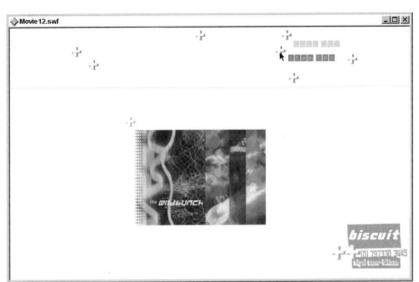

Figure 7.15
When you drag an icon down, the palette opens.

 Now open palettes.fla from the CD-ROM.

Using function() and onClipEvent()

To create the icon's flowing effect, you call two functions: one to randomize animations and one to move the elements. The motion stops when the pointer moves above a certain point. Because we want to be able to easily add additional elements, component-style, to the main timeline, we'll check if the opposite is true, then invoke our action. Is the pointer outside the river, and is the palette element swimming? If so, let's move it.

```
if (_root._ymouse>=112.0 && this._y<=112.0) {
this.randomMove();
this.moveMe();
}
```

Fading Tool Tip

We use the fade widget to let viewers know there is functionality or content behind the flowing icons. Look for the invisible movie clip instance fade inside the item's tool tip movie clip (**Figure 7.16**).

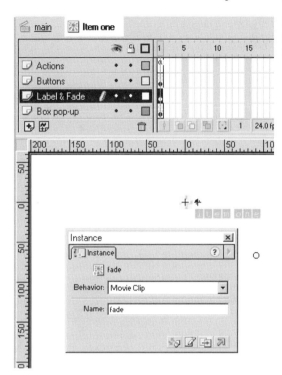

Figure 7.16 *The fade widget from the previous project is reused here in a different context.*

We're loading variables in the movie clip event (load) mainly to save processing time. Even at today's blistering processor speeds, it's better to have the processor chunk away at screen updates rather than reloading variables every time the playback head enters a frame.

```
al = 0;
fade_speed1=20;
fade_speed2=3;
```

First we need to check if the tool tip should be active so that this event doesn't occur if the palette is open.

```
if (active == 1 and al<100)
```

The condition `active` equals 1 for as long as the movie clip is in its collapsed mode, and floating across the top of the screen.

```
on (rollOver) {
if (this._y<=129) {
this.fade.active = 1;
}
cross.gotoAndStop(2);
}
```

Don't worry about this part yet—it's just a heads up. We'll get to it later when we look at what happens once the viewer drags a palette into the main area of the screen.

Now back to the tool tip script. We've checked to see that the fade effect should indeed occur, and then increased opacity by a factor we set via the variable `speed1`. The remaining code fades the tool tip out if `active` is set to false.

```
if (active == 1 and al<100) {
al = al+fade_speed1;
} else if (active == 0) {
if (al>0) {
al = al-fade_speed2;
} else {
al = 0;
}
}
gotoAndPlay (2);
```

Compare this code with the code from the photo album hyperlink fade widget. Notice a difference? Neither do we. That's the beauty of reusable components!

This showcase used only the fade widget. We could have also used widgets to move the icons across the top of the screen, but we don't want to focus

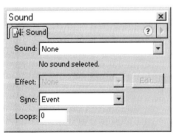

Figure 7.17
Programming a palette like this with widgets could become unwieldy and difficult to update.

on widgets in this example. Instead, we'll show you a different approach for setting up interactivity with ActionScript. Imagine programming a palette with lots of different functionality; for example, a sound palette (**Figure 7.17**). By using functions to point to specific interactive features, you can keep your code clean and located in a place where you can easily find it.

Let's get into the code and look at the functions we're using.

Creating Random Movement

Because we want the icons to move at random speeds as well as random durations of time, we set up a timer that will randomize both. The movieClipEvent(onLoad) initializes the variables we'll be using.

```
dragging = 0;
initialTime = 100;
friction = 0.62;
speedX = 0;
currentX = this._x;
```

Next, also inside the (onLoad), are our two movement functions, randomMove() and moveMe() (**Figure 7.18**).

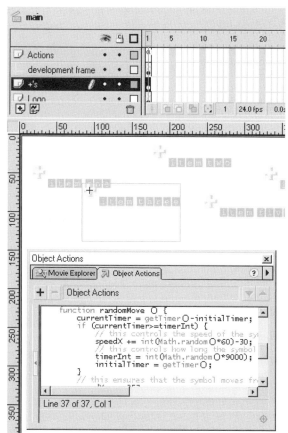

Figure 7.18 The randomMove() function of a menu item.

The names pretty much explain their purpose.

```
function randomMove () {
  currentTimer = getTimer()-initialTimer;
  if (currentTimer>=timerInt) {
    speedX += int(Math.random()*60)-30;
    timerInt = int(Math.random()*9000);
    initialTimer = getTimer();
  }
  speedX += .253;
}
```

In this function, two things are being randomized. First, we're setting a time interval at which the speed of movement is being changed. This setting occasionally can be negative, too, effectively moving an element backwards.

```
speedX += int(Math.random()*60)-30;
```

Second, we're setting a random duration of the movement itself to make the whole thing less predictable.

```
timerInt = int(Math.random()*9000);
```

The last line outside the if() statement ensures that the icon moves from left to right on the screen continually in a gradual motion.

Ensuring Continuity

Next, we're going to let the icons scroll across the entire width of the movie, but only if the icon isn't being dragged into the main area of the screen and is still inside the top area.

```
function moveMe () {
  currentX = this._x;
  if ((dragging == 0) and (this._x>778)) {
    this._x = 0;
  }
  speedX = speedX*friction;
  this._x += speedX;
}
```

At some point, the moving elements will hit the right side of the screen, so we have to make sure they get back on track at the leftmost side.

```
if (this._x>778) {
this._x = 0;
}
```

The Stage is only 773 pixels wide, but we wanted to make sure the icon is off the screen before it moves back to the left side.

Now that all our ducks are in a row, we can go onto the actual tool palette.

Checking Variable Conditions

When you drag an icon into the main area of the Stage, the palette opens. Let's look at how the palette symbol is set up.

The first element of interest is the invisible movie clip instance box in the box pop-up layer. The box pop-up movie clip contains an animation revealing the palette's contents.

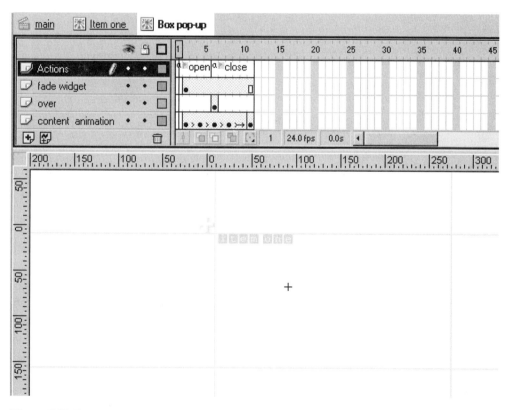

Figure 7.19 *Even while visibility is true (because you can't see any of the palette elements yet), the animation is not affected. Flash 5 is smart enough to know that invisible elements don't need to be calculated.*

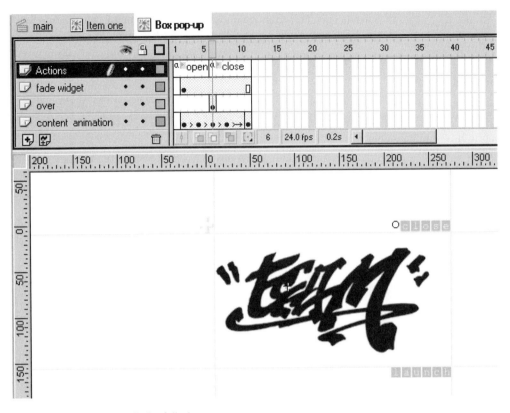

Figure 7.20 *The palette in its full glory.*

The second element is the button used to drag the palette around the screen and to display the tool tip.

We're looking at a standard scenario for button functionality with its four states: rollover, rollout, press, and release.

On rollover, the icon's color changes and the tool tip is displayed. The fade widget applies only if the cursor is in the top area of the Stage.

```
on (rollOver) {
if (this._y<=129) {
this.fade.active = 1;
}
cross.gotoAndStop(2);
}
```

On rollout, the fade widget is deactivated. You could also use the keyframes in the button itself instead of the cross movie clip. But this way gives you room for future expansion—hence, the `if` statement telling the movie clip cross to go back to frame 1.

```
on (rollOut) {
fade.active = 0;
if (cross != 1) {
cross.gotoAndStop(1);
}
}
```

This script closes the palette and returns it to the top of the screen, placing it randomly on the vertical axis. It remains in its original position, however, on the horizontal axis.

```
on (press) {
_parent._y = random(47)+10;
  gotoAndPlay("close");
}
```

Most of the action here happens only if the palette is in the main area of the Stage. If so, it'll see where the playback head of the box pop-up movie clip is and play the open or close sequence.

```
on (release) {
if ((this._y>=112.0) and (this.box._currentframe != 6)) {
fade.active = 0;
this.box.gotoAndPlay("open");
} else if ((this._y<=112.0) and (this.box._currentframe !=
→ 1)) {
fade.active = 0;
this.box.gotoAndPlay("close");
}
_parent.dragging = 0;
stopDrag ();
}
```

Unlike the examples about components in Chapter 5, the right-hand button in the close frame of the box pop-up movie clip returns the entire palette back to the top of the screen.

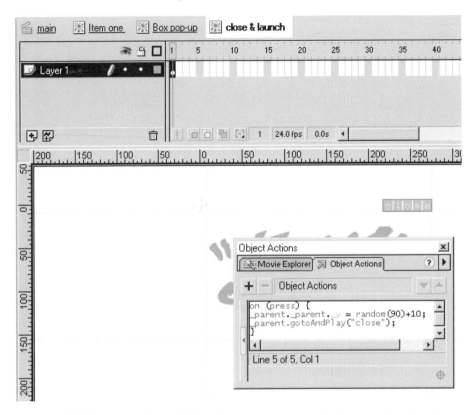

Figure 7.21 *This unassuming script has larger repercussions for its parent movie clips.*

```
on (press) {
_parent._y = random(47)+10;
gotoAndPlay("close");
}
```

Because the release event sets a property of its parent movie clip to a new value, what happens to the now closed palette is the same as if nothing had happened in the first place. This is because the script in the parent clip keeps checking its screen position and executes statements if these conditions change. The functions in the main timeline will place the icon in a random spot in the top of the screen and resume animating it—as if you had thrown it back into the river, so to speak.

That's a Wrap

These two interfaces represent different extremes in interface design. The photo album is designed to be functional and easy-to-use, while the palette interface is designed to be engaging and not necessarily intuitive. Not everything has to be designed with a usability bible beside you; likewise, not everything has to be designed to shock and astound. Flash is a renaissance of interaction design. It can be graceful and elegant, and still leave the viewer in awe.

Web sites, as well as Web-based utility applications, have just a few interface elements, or *modules*, that are used again and again. By developing a widget for each module, you can spend less time redoing work and more time creating response mechanisms that make the user experience fluid.

Some Useful Guidelines

Here are some tips for designing interface widgets that you can use for almost any Web site project. You'll find these tips easy to implement once you start developing a library of commonly used interface widgets.

Create back-button functionality. Most Flash-based sites don't let visitors retrace their steps as they click through the site. You should ensure that every possible step is accessible from the main navigation or implement an FSCommand into the containing HTML page. For more information on this, see Chapter 9, JavaScript-Flash Interactions.

Fine-tune your user-response mechanisms. Because widgets and SmartClips let you program once and deploy anywhere, you can invest more time creating smooth mouse-tracking and programmatic animation.

Orient the visitor. Many things that come automatically with HTML are not inherent in Flash. Visited link colors or other elements like the hierarchical trail often found running across the top of Web sites need to be incorporated into your site. Flash widgets and SmartClips can help.

Provide status feedback when loading movie clips. Develop a standard progress bar widget that gives viewers download feedback. The `getBytesLoaded()` and `getTotalBytes()` features in Flash make this quite easy and accurate.

Display text content immediately. While some rich-media elements like sound and bitmaps download, let your visitors at least start reading some text. There's no reason why today's complex features should prevent designers from optimizing the download experience. Reading about a site's content is more engaging than waiting for a loading animation.

Use interface elements consistently. Visitors have to learn an interface every time they go to a new site. Shorten this learning curve by keeping every interface element and your overall screen layout consistent throughout the site.

Use keyboard commands. People are accustomed using keyboard commands in software applications. By giving your site visitors alternative ways of navigating, you'll greatly enhance the experience. Imagine, for example, pressing Ctrl+M to display the site map.

Usability and Innovation

Flash designers face a dilemma: The technology lets them develop interfaces that mimic desktop software, but that can confuse site visitors, who expect a certain experience on the Web. Create an interface that's too different from other Web environments, and you risk losing visitors. So don't burden them with a long learning curve. Flash allows for some very effective innovation that's subtle enough to be overlooked. "Oh, I didn't even realize this site was in Flash!" That might be the best compliment you could get from a visitor.

8: XML and Flash

Michael Grundvig is co-founder of Electrotank, Inc. (www.electrotank.com) where he serves as Senior Application Developer and Secretary on the Board of Directors. He also works for Hallmark Cards, Inc. as a Web University Technical Lead, training employees so they may use current Web technologies in the ever-changing Internet environment. He specializes in developing server-side applications using various languages. He is based in Kansas.

XML is going to revolutionize our world. It will make better cars, end corruption, bring world peace, and help you get to sleep at night.

That is, if you believe the hype.

While it might not be quite as amazing as that, it's a very big deal in the IT world. In fact, XML has become such a huge success that you'd be hard pressed to find an enterprise-level application that doesn't use it in some way. What the hype doesn't tell you is how XML accomplishes this and how you can leverage XML in your own applications.

This chapter will cover what XML can and cannot do. We'll provide you with a strong grounding in the principles behind XML, as well as a working knowledge of the language and syntax. We'll discuss the various ways you can use XML in your applications, and show you how to avoid many of the common pitfalls people encounter when developing XML-based applications. To reinforce and finalize this discussion, we'll finish the chapter by developing a working shopping cart using Flash and XML.

What Is XML?

XML is a new markup language that solves many problems that application developers encounter on a regular basis. Before we dig into XML's capabilities and specifics, it's important to understand what problems it addresses and how it solves them. This will give you a better understanding of where you can use XML in your application development.

The Problem

Software applications have been evolving for a long time. As they've become larger and more capable, they've also become more sophisticated and specialized. This is due to growing business needs and increasingly more complicated business logic. I think Grady Booch expressed this sophistication best in his book *Object Oriented Analysis and Design with Applications*.

The distinguishing characteristic of industrial-strength software is that it's difficult, if not impossible, for individual developers to comprehend all subtleties of its design. Stated bluntly, the complexity of such systems exceeds the human intellectual capacity. Alas, this complexity we speak of seems to be an essential property of all large software systems. By *essential*, we mean that we may master this complexity, but we can never make it go away.

The Big Picture

Why are we talking about enterprise applications? XML was developed as a tool for application development. Flash may be a small subset of application development, but the two have common grounds. To become a good XML developer, it's crucial that you understand the bigger picture. If we covered only the mechanics of Flash/XML integration, you'd end up with a narrow view of the capabilities of XML and limited understanding of how to use it in your own applications.

The specialization and consequent sophistication in applications has come about from the understanding that it's simpler and more effective to be an expert in a single field than in all fields. Without getting into specific products, if you look at any enterprise application market, you'll find that there are many sub-areas of that market with only a few clear leaders in each. You'll notice, however, that the tools become more and more specific to a given industry or business, and the market gets smaller and smaller. Why is this? Because it's easier to be very good at one thing than to be good at everything. While that rather obvious statement often applies in general situations, it's a hard and fast rule in programming. You can't make it all yourself. With that in mind, the need for integration between these stand-alone products has become paramount.

For example, say that company XYZ makes an excellent tax system. This product would take an address and a dollar figure and return the appropriate amount of tax for that geographical area. (This is a smallish example to avoid making the explanation more complicated than it needs to be.) This product by itself is of limited functionality but quite useful overall. How does someone get the address and price into the system? This is where the integration comes in. The tax system would have to define a method for receiving and sending data. It would also have to define what the data needs to look like. Methods for passing data back and forth vary greatly based on the application and use. Traditionally, an application would define a proprietary format for the data that it received. As the software developer, you would then need to modify your application to support this data format.

Sound complicated enough? Now imagine you have 30 of these components and you must integrate them together. This becomes a software maintenance nightmare. Support costs rise, and not only that—now everyone needs to understand the multitude of code and data definitions involved.

The Solution

This is where XML enters the picture. XML provides a simple, flexible, language-independent, platform-independent, human-readable format for sending data. Whew, that's a mouthful! Let's break this down into its pieces.

Simple. XML is text-based markup so it's relatively simple to understand and use.

Flexible. XML offers almost limitless flexibility because you can create your *own* definitions and tags (more on this in a bit).

Language-independent. This is a real Holy Grail in software development. It means you can use many different programming languages and as long as they all speak XML, they can easily communicate with each other.

Platform-independent. This goes hand-in-hand with language independence. XML is not tied to any single operating system or platform. It's superb at crossing the various application tiers.

Human-readable. XML is just plain text, so you can read it without any sort of interpreter or viewing application.

It may help to think of XML as the glue between system components or applications.

Application Tiers

Throughout this chapter, I'll refer to various application tiers. This is a commonly used term in enterprise application development. Over the years, developers have learned that the easiest way to develop and maintain enterprise applications is to break them down into discrete pieces. The advent of newer languages facilitates this to an even higher degree. In the beginning of large-scale business application development, there was one tier. All aspects of the application ran on the same machine within the same program. This means that no distinction was made between the different aspects of the program, from business logic to data.

The '80s and early '90s saw a large push into client-server development. This push was partially caused by the explosion of affordable and more capable desktop computers. In client-server programming, applications are broken into two components. A server runs the shared pieces of the system: database access, legacy system integration, and so on. The client runs all the code necessary to take this data, massage it, and redisplay it back to the user. The client typically runs on the user's machine; the server runs on a remote machine. While this approach makes for less load on the server than in single-tier development, it's difficult to maintain in the long term due to its tight binding of data and business logic. It also creates the problem that all client machines must be updated with the newest software.

The next step in the evolution of enterprise applications is commonly referred to as three-tier or *n*-tier. This methodology advocates separating all layers of an application into discrete and logical components. A data tier would contain and access the database. The data tier and the business logic tier would communicate together, each handling their own tasks. The display tier is used to display the data to the user. The biggest thing to note is that each tier does *not* overlap with the other tiers. This allows the data and logic to be separated, thus making pieces of your application more responsive to change and more reusable between applications. This is the most commonly used software architecture in enterprise applications today.

The Showcase Project

As I mentioned in the introduction, the showcase project for this chapter is a functional Flash/XML shopping cart. Building this project will reinforce all the concepts discussed in this chapter, as well as require you to gain a better understanding of how to integrate XML with Flash.

The shopping cart application will feature an admin interface for viewing submitted orders, order history, and the ability for a user to place new orders. The Flash portion of this application will be written using object-oriented programming techniques. This might be new to some, but as we're developing a real-world application, it's important to use the most appropriate techniques available.

Tools for Viewing and Creating XML Documents

As we go through the phases of making and using XML documents, it will speed your learning process if you already know how to view and create the documents. As with all programming, a good tool can make the entire XML development cycle shorter and more pleasant. Here are the basic tools I use in XML creation.

The first and foremost tool is, of course, Flash. You use Flash to build and test your code directly. The Actions panel provides everything you need to load and parse XML documents easily and quickly. The two weaknesses of Flash are that you can't use it to create external documents (meaning you can't create an XML document and save it from within Flash) and it doesn't display the raw XML document easily. You can use `trace()`, but this often returns the data in a hard-to-read format.

To view XML documents, I use Microsoft's Internet Explorer 5 (or later). It contains an XML parser and some default style sheets that display XML documents in a friendly format. It also shows errors that may exist in your document. To use it, just save your XML document with an .xml extension and open it within Internet Explorer. It will automatically parse the document and display it for you (**Figure 8.1**).

To create XML documents, I use Macromedia's HomeSite, a superb text editor that lets you preview a Web page in the same window. This preview capability uses Internet Explorer, so you can preview your XML documents as you make them simply by pressing the Browse tab. If you don't have HomeSite, you can download a free trial version from www.macromedia.com, or use any other good text editor—even Notepad, SimpleText, or Microsoft Word will work.

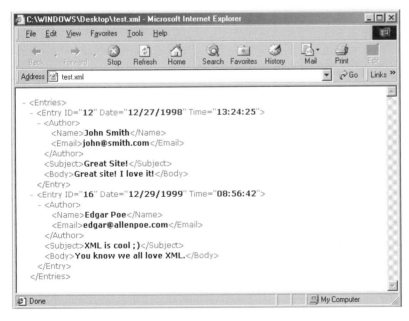

Figure 8.1 *This is how Internet Explorer 5.5 views an XML document. It shows you if there are errors with your document, and color-codes and formats it for you.*

While this application will be a functionally complete shopping cart, it won't contain an order processing system or secured login and credit card authentication. It's also missing many of the amenities of commercial shopping carts, specifically input validation of everything but credit card information, a confirmation screen, and product images. These features are beyond the scope of this chapter, and you'd need to customize them to your business needs, anyway.

 This book is not about server-side application development. Therefore, the CD-ROM includes the necessary server-side applications (written in ASP) to run this demo.

XML Basics

Without any further preliminaries, let's start building our first XML document!

Write Your Own

XML is a tag-based language like HTML. Unlike HTML, XML lets you define your own tags, thus making it extensible and more flexible. The best way to illustrate how XML works is to show you:

```
<MyXMLSample>My Data</MyXMLSample>
```

That's it. Not very impressive for something that has taken the world by storm, is it? XML documents contain arbitrary tags and attributes. You use the tag and attribute names that make sense for your application. By simply nesting the tags, we can end up with something a lot more useful:

```
<Address>
    <Street>1234 Lexington Ave.</Street>
    <City>Burbank</City>
    <State>Kansas</State>
    <PostalCode>66232</PostalCode>
    <Country>United States of America</Country>
</Address>
```

As you can see, XML is simple to read and does not require any interpretation: This XML document contains an address. The document could have been generated from a server-side application for Flash, or from Flash and about to be sent to the server. Any application that understands XML would be able to read the data in this document. XML tags look just like HTML, but the name and content are arbitrary. In the above example, I chose to use common English words for the tag names. This is important, as XML is designed to be as comprehensible as possible. Below is another simple example:

```
<User ID="12">
    <Username>Joe</Username>
    <Password>joespassword</Password>
</User>
```

Our first XML example didn't include any attributes, but this latest one includes 'ID' as an attribute in the 'User' tag. Attributes are another way to express data and relationships with XML. Don't worry; we'll discuss them in more detail later.

What's In a Name?

As we explore XML, more and more new words and terms will be introduced. Let's cover the most crucial ones now so we can start using them. Below is a simple XML document:

```
<Name>
    <First>John</First>
    <Last>Smith</Last>
</Name>
```

As this book assumes some familiarity with HTML, you already know that <First> is a start tag and </First> is an end tag. The combination of <First>John</First> is called an *element* or *node*. An element is the start tag, end tag, and everything in between. Elements can contain other elements as well as text. This is called *nesting*. The text between two tags is called PCDATA (Parsed Character Data).

Another important concept to discuss is *well formed.* This means an XML document follows all the necessary rules. It's important to note that *well formed* is not the same as *valid*. A valid XML document is one that matches the requirements put forth by its DTD (Document Type Definition). Flash's XML parser does not validate XML documents, so we won't cover validation or its related technologies.

XML Rules

In the coming pages, we'll cover the various XML rules you need to follow to make a valid XML document. By following these rules, you'll be able to make your own well-formed XML documents without any trouble.

- XML naming requirements must be met.

- XML tags must nest properly.

- XML tags must be closed.

- XML is case-sensitive.

- All attributes must be quoted.

- Inappropriate characters must be escaped.

- Only one root element.

Naming Requirements

Before you create all the tag names for your next project, it's important to realize that you can't use just any old name. There are some specific rules you have to follow.

- Tag names must start with a letter or a hyphen (-).

- Tags can't contain spaces.

- Tags can't start with the letters "xml" regardless of case. This means you can't use the letters "xml" in any form as the starting characters in your tag. For example, `<xmlNode>` or `<XMLNode>` is not valid, but `<myXMLNode>` is. Flash seems to let you get by this one, but it's not a good practice to get into.

- The first character of a tag must follow the "<" immediately.

These naming conventions apply to both attributes and tags. If you fail to follow these conventions, your document will not parse properly. At times, you won't notice any errors, but often you won't be able to retrieve data from the parsed document. When this occurs, you can use the "status" property of the XML object to determine the problem. We'll provide examples and discuss how this works later in the chapter.

Nesting Tags

HTML is sloppy and forgiving of syntax errors; XML is not. For example, XML tags *must* nest properly. In other words, you must open and close your tags in the correct order. This can be most easily seen with an example:

```
<First>
 <Second>
  <Third>
   <Fourth />
  </Third>
 </Second>
</First>
```

As you can see, all of the tags close after the tags they contain have been closed. If you don't nest your tags properly, the Flash XML parser will give you all sorts of errors to correct. Most commonly, it will just fail to parse the document and you'll need to find the error on your own. So if you're into inflicting extreme levels of pain on yourself or your co-workers, go ahead and mismatch your tags.

Closing Tags

You probably noticed something a bit strange in the last example. The 'Fourth' tag doesn't have an ending tag, only an odd placement of the '/' character. This brings me to my next point: All XML tags must be closed. This doesn't mean all XML tags must contain data. An empty tag is considered perfectly acceptable and you'll see it quite often.

There are two different ways to close XML tags. The first is to use a separate closing tag: `<tag>data</tag>` or `<tag></tag>`. The second method involves creating a single tag and using the forward slash: `<tag />`. The latter is commonly seen in Flash, because its built-in XML parser will automatically change `<tag></tag>` to `<tag />` for you. If you use the second method, remember that while `</tag>` is correct, neither `< /tag>` nor `<tag/ >` is (note the extra spaces).

Case

Another difference between XML and HTML is that XML is case sensitive. You can make your tags any case you choose, but the closing tag *must* be the same case. If the tags are not matched by case, then the XML parser won't parse properly and some odd results will occur. For example, <tag>my data</TAG> uses mismatched case, whereas <tag>my data</tag> is correct.

Note that if you do this: <tag>data</tag> and then this: <TAG>data</TAG>, you won't notice any errors in Flash, but you will on the server side. This is because XML sees those two tags as two different tags, even if you meant for them to be the same. When the server-side application attempts to validate the document with a supporting XML technology like DTD, it won't understand they're the same tag.

Flash and Validation

You won't see anything in Flash because Flash doesn't validate XML documents at this level. Flash only makes sure that your XML document doesn't break any syntax rules. As far as it's is concerned, it's valid to have two separate tags. We won't cover validation in this chapter, as Flash does not support it. If you're interested in learning more about validating XML documents, check your favorite technical bookstore for a dedicated XML book.

Quoting Attributes

This requirement is another difference between HTML and XML. HTML often allows for behavior (that is, punctuation) like this:

```
<font face=arial>The font is arial</font>
```

XML doesn't allow this behavior; this syntax would result in your document not parsing properly. You can use either single or double quotes, but don't mix them in a single attribute. For example:

```
<user id="12">Joe</user> or <user id='12'>John</user>
```

Either of those examples are valid. But the following would result in a parsing error:

```
<user id='12">Joe</user>
```

The original erroneous example is corrected below:

```
<font face="arial">The font is arial</font>
```

Escaping Characters

So far, we've discussed how tags and attributes are made. Now let's talk about what goes inside of them. XML documents contain only textual data. Because the XML tags themselves are just text, it's important to note that certain characters must be either avoided or escaped in your data to avoid a parsing error. Fortunately, there are only a few characters that can cause this problem—specifically, '<', '>' , and '&' . Using too many double quotes or apostrophes can foul up attributes as well. To avoid this problem, you can escape the offending characters or use CDATA (Character Data) sections. The escape codes are listed below.

ORIGINAL CHARACTER	ESCAPED CHARACTER
<	&lt;
>	&gt;
&	&amp;
'	&apos;
"	&quot;

Let's illustrate this with an example.

```
<Document>
 <Message abrev='this isn't as long'>This is my <b>test</b>
 → string & I hope you like it!</Message>
</Document>
```

Attempting to parse this will give you errors. The attribute "abrev" uses apostrophes to delineate the string, but the string itself also contains an apostrophe. This causes the XML parser to close the string at an inappropriate place. It then sees text that's not inside of an attribute, and fails in the parse. A second problem is that some HTML has crept into our data. You may have a valid reason to use the "bold" tag, but as HTML also uses "<" and ">" to surround tags, we now have a second parsing error.

There are two possible solutions. The first is shown below.

```
<Document>
 <Message abrev='this isn&apos;t as long'>This is my
 → &lt;b&gt;test&lt;/b&gt; string &amp; I hope you like
 → it!</Message>
</Document>
```

To solve the attribute problem, we just needed to change the included apostrophe into its escaped equivalent. (We could have also changed the apostrophes surrounding the string into double quotes like this: abrev="this isn't as long"). By alternating between using single and double quotes, you can see which solution suits your data and project best.

To correct the data between the tags, we needed only escape the reserved characters to make the XML a valid document. This is a simple solution for small occurrences of invalid characters, but what happens when you have many characters that need to be escaped? This is where CDATA comes in. CDATA is a way to make sure everything in a node is escaped. And I do mean *everything*—if you use CDATA properly, you can have one XML document contain another document in its entirety, and the parser sees it all only as text. That's pretty strong stuff! Below is the previous example again, this time using CDATA (the changes are in bold):

```
<Document>
 <Message abrev="this isn't as long"><![CDATA[This is my
 → <b>test</b> string & I hope you like it!]]></Message>
</Document>
```

In this short example, it may feel like CDATA is just too much work. But as you start escaping more and more characters, you'll quickly see its value. CDATA sections begin like this <![CDATA[and end like this]]>. You put CDATA sections inside of another tag. The XML parser automatically skips anything inside of a CDATA section for you. You can even place other tags inside of CDATA sections and they will be skipped automatically.

Need a little more convincing on the CDATA issue? Here's a real-world example. Say you have a new shopping cart on your Web site. It's built in Flash and uses XML to communicate with the server. The product listing is stored in an online database, and the products are loaded into the system using a Web interface. You're pretty happy with how it works, but you want some of the words in the product descriptions to stand out. Since Flash can use HTML tags in text fields (I love that ability) you decide to just bold and italicize some words. You change some product descriptions—and instantly, your site stops working. After scratching your head for a bit, you realize it's because the XML parser is interpreting your newly added HTML tags and failing to parse properly. You start the painstaking task of replacing all your '<' and '>' signs with the appropriate escape codes to learn, much to your dismay, that Flash does not convert them back as you expected. You realize that once escaped, Flash doesn't use the HTML tags, it just shows them as

'<' and '>' in the display. So now your nice product listing looks like this before you try to display it:

```
Buy this &lt;i&gt;one-of-a-kind&lt;/i&gt; item
→ &lt;b&gt;CHEAP&lt;/b&gt;!
```

And like this after you put it in an HTML-enabled text field:

```
Buy this <i>one-of-a-kind</i> item <b>CHEAP</b>!
```

Not quite what you were hoping for. Right about now you'd be cursing your decision to use XML in the first place. Take a deep breath. There's a solution: Use CDATA. By wrapping each product description in a CDATA section, you'll have the functionality you want without any fuss.

Single Root Element

Each XML document can have only one root element. This may seem confusing at first, but it's quite simple. Below is an invalid XML document:

```
<FirstName>John</FirstName>
<LastName>Smith</LastName>
```

At first glance, this document would appear valid, but it breaks the "one root element" rule: At the highest level of an XML document, only one tag can exist. This means you need to ensure that your entire XML document has only one root tag. Once you're into the document proper, you needn't worry about this. A simple solution is to design the data in a nice format and wrap it with a "container" tag like "<Document>" or something that describes the data like "<Order>" or "<Address>". After being corrected, the previous example looks like this:

```
<Name>
 <First>John</First>
 </Last>Smith</Last>
</Name>
```

This is a simple rule to follow, and it's also an excellent guideline for designing XML documents. Typically, it's always good to segment your data with new tags. We'll discuss this in more depth later when we create a series of real-world XML documents.

Sum It All Up

That's a lot of rules to remember, but most are quite simple and they'll become second nature before long.

To illustrate all of these rules, let's make an invalid XML document and correct it. Below is the incorrect XML document containing at least one of each of the errors. Warning: If you ever write XML this badly, your fellow programmers will kill you.

```
<XML>
 <Message ID=332>
  <From>Me</From>
  <To>You</To>
  <Body sent='10/10/99">
    This is the body of the message.
 </Message>
 </body>
</xml>
```

The corrected version of the previous snippet:

```
<Messages>
 <Message ID="332">
  <From>Me</From>
  <To>You</To>
  <Body Sent="10/10/99">
    This is the body of the message.
  </Body>
 </Message>
</Messages>
```

As you can see, there were lots of errors in there. Rather than going through them all, just glance at the list of rules; the changes should be clear. The largest single problem was a mismatched root tag and the reversed </Message> and </Body>. This would cause the Flash XML parser to behave erratically and return odd results (if any at all).

XML Etiquette

While we've covered all of the specific rules that an XML document must follow, we left out some fundamental XML quirks that you need to know. These quirks can be broken down into this list:

- XML declarations

- Case sensitive, but what case?

- Segmenting your data

- Attributes vs. elements

- White space

XML Declarations

This topic is not under "XML Rules," since declarations are not strictly required, but they're good to use anyway. An XML declaration is a line that comes at the beginning of an XML file, before anything else (including carriage returns and spaces). The declaration tells the parser what type of data to expect in the document. Let's take the name snippet we talked about before and add the declaration to it.

```
<?xml version="1.0" encoding="UTF-8" standalone="yes"?>
<Name>
 <First>John</First>
 </Last>Smith</Last>
</Name>
```

The declaration of an XML document must always start with <?xml and end with ?>. There are three possible attributes in a declaration, but only the version attribute is required. The attributes must be in this order, regardless of which ones you have.

The "encoding" attribute relates to how the XML text is represented. For example, if you are on a Windows 9x machine using Notepad to create your XML documents, your encoding is "windows-1252" by default. Many parsers ignore or override this attribute based on how the data was received or loaded. Often this attribute is not included.

The "standalone" attribute is used to link XML documents and can be a rather advanced XML topic. Flash doesn't support it, so we won't discuss it.

You should have at least a minimal XML declaration on your XML documents. To keep the code brief, we won't include them in the chapter examples, but we will use them in the showcase project.

Case Sensitive—But What Case?

As we discussed, XML is case sensitive, but we didn't say which case you should use. There's no official recommendation for this: It's up to you. I use title case for my XML tags and will use it from now on in all my examples. Just remember, whatever you use, the closing tag must be the same and you can't break any of the XML naming rules. Below is a list of possible case suggestions:

```
<FullName>John Smith</FullName>
<full_name>John Smith</full_name>
<fullName>John Smith</fullName>
<full-name>John Smith</full-name>
```

As you can see, there are lots of options for you to choose from.

Segmenting Your Data

Segmenting your data is not a rule of XML, nor is it something you must do to get Flash to parse your document. It isn't required for your document to be well formed. Some XML developers will never do it and still develop effective XML applications. Yet it's a very useful, powerful thing. Segmenting your data is the process of breaking your data into bite-sized pieces that are easy to read and process. This makes it possible to reuse pieces of your parsing code as well as the XML format itself. Reuse in programming is always a good thing. Let's look at a simple XML document encompassing multiple names/emails:

```
<UserList>
 <Name1>James Hanson</Name1>
 <Email1>james_hanson @anydomain.com</Email1>
 <Name2>Michael Hanson</Name2>
 <Email2>michael_hanson @anydomain.com</Email2>
```

```
    <Name3>Jobe Hanson</Name3>
    <Email3>jobe_hanson@anydomain.com</Email3>
    <Name4>Amy Hanson</Name4>
    <Email4>amy_hanson @anydomain.com</Email4>
  </UserList>
```

For those of us used to the LoadVariable days of Flash 4, this may seem like
a logical step. You have merely used XML rather than URL-encoding the data.
In reality, this is a *bad* thing. This data should be segmented into something
much more readable. You should have a root element for all the name/email
pairs. Below is the same data, represented in a better format:

```
  <Users>
   <User>
    <Name>James Hanson</Name>
    <Email>james_hanson @anydomain.com</Email>
   </User>
   <User>
    <Name>Michael Hanson</Name2>
    <Email>michael_hanson @anydomain.com</Email>
   </User>
   <User>
    <Name>Jobe Hanson</Name3>
    <Email>jobe_hanson@anydomain.com</Email>
   </User>
   <User>
    <Name>Amy Hanson</Name4>
    <Email>amy_hanson @anydomain.com</Email>
   </User>
  </Users>
```

There are two major changes here. The most important change is that all
the name and email elements are now contained in a new element called
User and renamed to just Name and Email. The second change is from
UserList to Users. This is a personal preference, but if you plan on having
a list of something, it makes sense to enclose the entire list in the plural
of a single element of the list. Therefore, a list of User elements is enclosed
in a Users element; a list of Address elements is enclosed in an Addresses
element. This makes for a clear and logical separation. There are code
reasons for segmenting your data as well, but we'll get to those in a bit.

As with so many good things, it's possible to have too much. How much is too much? This is harder to quantify. To some extent, you have to go by instinct, but we'll also talk a bit about what to look out for. Let's look at a heavily segmented XML document:

```
<User>
 <Name>
  <First>John</First>
  <Middle>C</Middle>
  <Last>Adams</Last>
 </Name>
 <Phone>
  <Numbers>
   <Number>5</Number>
   <Number>5</Number>
   <Number>5</Number>
   <Number>1</Number>
   <Number>2</Number>
   <Number>1</Number>
   <Number>3</Number>
  </Numbers>
 </Phone>
</User>
```

As you can see, that's one heavy XML document. The phone number has been broken down too far. In some instances, the name might even be broken down too much. It's entirely possible to build and use XML documents like this, but it's cumbersome and, for distributed applications, quite bandwidth expensive.

The easiest way to determine if you have segmented your data too far is to think about how you are going to use it. In the case of the name, are you going to use the first name all by itself? For instance, will you address the customer by first name in your Flash application? If the answer is yes, then this is probably a good way to keep the data. If the answer is no, then you could probably condense the data into a single element of just <Name>John C. Adams</Name>. Remember, XML is designed to be flexible; you change it to suit your needs and as your application dictates.

In the case of the phone number, having every digit as its own element is probably a really bad idea in general, but it was a good way to illustrate the flexibility of XML. Here's a more condensed, reworked form of the previous example:

```
<User>
 <Name>John C. Adams</Name>
 <Phone>5551213</Phone>
</User>
```

Attributes vs. Elements

If attributes and elements can contain the same data, why would you use one over the other? This is a loaded question that's often debated. Let's explore the possibilities.

```
<Name>
 <First>John</First>
 <Last>Smith</Last>
</Name>
```

This is the name example we like to use so much. Made into attributes, it would look like this:

```
<Name First="John" Last="Smith" />
```

What are the advantages and disadvantages of each? Some people think attributes are easier to read, but others think tags are, so that's a blind alley of personal preference. From a size standpoint, attributes typically save you a fair amount. As you can see, the second example contains the same data in much less code. From a programming standpoint, attributes are a little easier to work with. When I first started learning XML, I read an article that made a good suggestion concerning this issue. It said that if the data is going to be presented to the user, place it in a tag. Indexes, non-user information, and so on should be placed in attributes. This suggestion is a nice compromise between the two options. I use this method to determine how to design my own XML documents (it's also the method used in the showcase project).

White Space

White space is defined as characters such as carriage return, line feed, and space. XML treats these characters differently than HTML does, and it's important to know this, as it can affect your display. There are two places where white space occurs in XML: between a start and end tag, and between elements.

Let's first discuss white space between start and end tags. Below is a simple HTML code snippet illustrating this:

```
<P>There is a lot of                white space here</P>
```

If you were to run this in a browser, it would look like this:

```
There is a lot of white space here
```

A Web browser ignores all consecutive white space characters beyond the first occurrence. An XML parser treats white space as it does any other character.

The second occurrence of white space causes an amazing number of problems for newbie XML developers. In between the end tag of one element and the start tag of another, you'll often use spaces, tabs, and carriage returns to make your XML document more readable (all of the examples in this chapter are created this way). This text is actually considered a special type of node called a *text node*. When you try to read a list of all elements, you'll see that these nodes will have been inserted between all your "real" nodes, causing a lot of confusion.

There are three solutions for this problem. The first is to remove all white space between elements before you parse it in Flash. To illustrate this, look at this example:

```
<Name><First>John</First><Last>Smith</Last></Name>
```

The second solution is to use the ignoreWhiteSpace attribute of the XML parser in Flash. The third solution is to use a function that will strip the white space for you. We'll cover these options, and more, in detail when we discuss how a parser lets you read an XML document. For now, it's enough just to note it.

Some XML Examples

We've talked a great deal about the rules you must follow to design and build an XML document. We've shown some small snippets of XML as examples, but so far we haven't covered any real XML documents. In this section, we'll discuss some various real-world XML examples that should give you a better understanding of XML in general.

As with all software design, you must understand the business data and processes involved in your project before you can begin. Therefore, we'll begin each example with an in-depth look at the data we need to model before we build it. We're going to work through an email message, a news article, a guest book, and the shopping cart. We'll start small and work into more complicated documents. None of these are going to be mind-blowing, but they should get you going in the right direction.

Email

What's in an email message? We have a sender, a receiver, a date, the title, and a message, of course. Those are the obvious things, but there's a lot more going on under the cover, as well. Some of the more important pieces of hidden information are message ID and content type. Message ID is a unique identifier assigned by the mail server. It's a *really* big string. Content type is a string that says whether the email is HTML-formatted or plain text. (For all you Unix junkies using Pine or some other text editor, you're probably familiar with this one.) Now that we know all the data, let's make an XML document out of it.

```
<Message ID="12345689123456789@server" Date="12/27/1999">
 <To>
  <Name>John Q. Adams</Name>
  <Email>j_adams@whitehouse.gov</Email>
 </To>
 <From>
  <Name>Eric Robinson</Name>
  <Email>Eric@ericsdomain.com</Email>
 </From>
 <Subject>Hey man, just dropping you a line!</Subject>
 <Body>
  Hey man!
  I'm just dropping you a line to see how you are doing!
  Want to catch the game this weekend? Talk to ya later!
   Eric
 </Body>
</Message>
```

An email document is fairly simple to model. There are two things to note in this document. The first is that the date is an attribute of the Message tag. I thought it fit better there than as another separate tag under Message. (Either solution will work fine; this is a personal preference.) The second thing is that both the To and From elements contain a Name and Email element. I chose this because it's more elegant than using FromName,

FromEmail, and so on. Repeating elements often lets you better segment your data, as well as reuse the parsing code more often. Another thing this separation gives us is flexibility: If, at a later date, we wanted to add Nickname to the From element, that would simply require a new tag and minor parsing changes under the current scheme. Using the other solution, it would require a new tag and significant parsing changes.

News Articles

Modeling news articles should be a similar exercise to modeling an email message. The biggest change is that we're going to support multiple articles, where we only handled one email message. Let's say you're building a news section to a major site, providing international news feeds to your users. Aside from the basic data like headline, tagline, body, and date, you also need to support categories, article ID, and related articles. Article ID should be simple, but categories and related articles require thought. Right now there may be only one or two categories, but it's conceivable that more will be added or needed. There might also be many related articles. This means we need to use a format that can grow with variable data. Below is an example of a single article:

```
<Article ID="23443" Date="12/27/1999">
<Title>Flash 5 Super Samurai Released!</Title>
<TagLine>An amazing new Flash 5 book has been released.
→ Read more!</TagLine>
<Body>This is where the body of the article would
→ go....</Body>
<Categories>
 <Category ID="17">Computers</Category>
 <Category ID="234">Flash</Category>
</Categories>
<RelatedArticles>
 <RelatedArticle ID="1232">Flash is Great!</RelatedArticle>
 <RelatedArticle ID="3456">Flash is Wonderful!</
 → RelatedArticle>
 <RelatedArticle ID="8972">Everyone Likes Flash!</
 → RelatedArticle>
</RelatedArticles>
</Article>
```

This seems to be an effective enough solution for a single article. As you can see, Date is an attribute on Article (using the same rationale as the email message example). Also, note the relationship of Categories to Category, and RelatedArticles to RelatedArticle. This is something we discussed in the data segmentation section. We knew there would be several possible categories and related articles. An easy way to represent this was use Categories as an element that contained individual Category elements. There are many situations where this is a useful and easy way to represent relationships.

But part of our task here was to represent multiple news articles, not just a single instance. Fortunately, this is simple to accomplish. Below is a solution:

```
<Articles>
 <Article ID="23443" Date="12/27/1999">
  ..... Elements and Data ......
 </Article>
 <Article ID="12233" Date="12/27/1999">
  ..... Elements and Data ......
 </Article>
 <Article ID="9876" Date="12/27/1999">
  ..... Elements and Data ......
 </Article>
 <Article ID="56443" Date="12/27/1999">
  ..... Elements and Data ......
 </Article>
</Articles>
```

See? Not too hard at all. Once you've created a few XML documents for various projects you'll get a feel for what works and what doesn't. At that point, designing XML documents will become second nature.

Guest Book

Guest books are a place where people can post their thoughts and feelings on your Web site. A single entry in a guest book typically contains an author's name and email, an ID from the database, the date it was posted, the topic, and the message itself. If you think this seems a lot like an email message, you're correct. The biggest difference is that a guest book needs multiple XML documents. So far we've only modeled data coming from the server. How does data get to the server? We know that at some point Flash must send it. In this example, we'll model all points of interaction between

Flash and the server. Let's first model the document that contains the existing entries.

```
<Entries>
 <Entry ID="12" Date="12/27/1998" Time="13:24:25">
  <Author>
   <Name>John Smith</Name>
   <Email>john@smith.com</Email>
  </Author>
  <Subject>Great Site!</Subject>
  <Body>Great site! I love it!</Body>
 </Entry>
 <Entry ID="16" Date="12/29/1999" Time="08:56:42">
  <Author>
   <Name>Edgar Poe</Name>
   <Email>edgar@allenpoe.com</Email>
  </Author>
  <Subject>XML is cool ;)</Subject>
  <Body>You know we all love XML.</Body>
 </Entry>
 <Entry> ... more data here ... </Entry>
 <Entry> ... more data here ... </Entry>
</Entries>
```

This snippet illustrates a simple method for handling a series of guest book entries. It should look pretty familiar to you, as we didn't introduce anything new. The next snippet shows how to take the existing XML format, and, with some slight changes, use it to send a new entry back to the server.

```
<Entry>
 <Author>
  <Name>Edgar Poe</Name>
  <Email>edgar@allenpoe.com</Email>
 </Author>
 <Subject>XML is cool ;)</Subject>
  <Body>You know we all love XML.</Body>
</Entry>
```

The only change from this snippet and the previous one is that we've removed the Date/Time and ID attributes of the `<Entry>` tag. We removed the ID because we won't know it until the database inserts it. We removed the Date and Time for a more subtle reason. When you use Flash to get the time, you're getting the time from the user's machine. To avoid odd times in your guest book, it's best to use the server's time rather than the client's. If you use the client's time, when you return a list of all guest book entries, it will look like some have been made in the future. This isn't uncommon on the Internet, but it's easily solved and should be avoided whenever possible.

Now we're missing just one last piece. When you send your new entry to the server, the server needs to respond to tell you if it succeeded or not. Many server-side applications forget this, and leave the client to determine if the submission was successful. This is a terrible practice and should be avoided if possible.

Each piece of a distributed n-tier application needs to ensure that its own data is correct. If you don't do this, bad data can be sent from one tier into another and then sent right back out as if it were valid. This bad data could persist until it's used and suddenly, something breaks. At that point no one knows where it came from in the first place. This makes for a difficult problem to debug.

A simple example of this would be a Flash front end where a user enters some invalid data; Flash takes that data and sends it to the database. The database saves the invalid data and runs some processing against it. Three weeks later, when the data is used by another application, it will still be invalid and an error will be caught. At that point, it's likely that no one will know what, or who, entered the bad data in the first place. This could have been corrected with some simple data validation.

In the guest book example, we validate if our data was inserted properly. There are two possible states: success and failure. Both are illustrated below.

```
<Response>
 <Status>Success</Status>
 <Message>This data inserted successfully</Message>
</Response>

<Response>
 <Status>Failure</Status>
 <Message>This data failed to insert</Message>
</Response>
```

Your application would use the Status element to determine if it was successful. The Message element could be for internal debugging, or what the user sees. Your program would read these values and determine if the data was inserted as planned. It can often be useful to have two messages: One friendly message to the user and one containing the gritty details of what failed.

Shopping Cart

In this example, we'll go through all the XML documents used in the shopping cart project. This first snippet is the product listing that the client gets from the server.

```
<Products>
 <Product ID="10" SWF=" file10.swf">
  <Name>Product 1</Name>
  <Description>
   <Short>Short Description</Short>
   <Long>Long Description Long Description Long Description
    → Long Description Long Description Long Description
    → Long Description Long Description </Long>
  </Description>
  <Price>10.00</Price>
 </Product>
 <Product ID="20" SWF="file10.swf">
  <Name>Product 2</Name>
  <Description>
   <Short>Short Description</Short>
   <Long>Long Description Long Description Long Description
    → Long Description Long Description Long Description
    → Long Description Long Description </Long>
  </Description>
  <Price>20.00</Price>
 </Product>
</Products>
```

As you look through this document, you'll see it's pretty standard, and follows the same rules that were used in the previous examples.

The next XML snippet we need to use is one that represents a credit card number. It needs to contain only the card number, card expiration, card type, and the name on the card.

```
<CreditCard>
 <Type>Visa</Type>
 <Number>5555-5555-5555-5555</Number>
 <Expiration>09-2000</Expiration>
 <Name>Wilbur Smith</Name>
</CreditCard>
```

TIP Typically, I use a Name element containing First and Last elements to store a name. There's no need for it here: When dealing with the name on a credit card, you don't need to break it into first and last.

A shopping cart needs to represent two different addresses: one for shipping and another for billing. Below I have created an address XML document that could be used to represent either:

```
<Address>
 <Line1></Line1>
 <Line2></Line2>
 <City></City>
 <Province></ Province >
 <PostalCode></ PostalCode >
 <Country></Country>
</Address>
```

TIP Why didn't I break out the Line1 and Line2 nodes? It seems like too much abstraction, and the likelihood of adding a new line would be slim. It would be better to add something like an Apartment Number node if you needed to extend it.

The next item that needs to be represented would be a person. You have two people involved in a shopping cart, though they are often the same (the person you are shipping to and the person you are billing). If you think about it in database terms, a person really is a name, contact information, and an address. So the previous address fragment we talked about will fit right in.

```
<Person>
 <Name>
  <First></First>
  <Last></Last>
 </Name>
 <Email></Email>
```

```
<Phone></Phone>
<Address>
 … Address here …
</Address>
</Person>
```

There, that wasn't so difficult. The phone element is currently a single field, but at a later date, it's easy to envision the need for "children nodes" like cell phone, pager, work, and home.

The next step is to represent the various products and their quantity in the cart. We need to store only the product ID and the quantity ordered this time around. Line items are commonly used to do this. A line item is a single entry in a shopping cart with only one product ID and the total quantity selected.

```
<LineItems>
<LineItem ProductID="" Quantity="" />
… More Line Items…
</LineItems>
```

That's it! We have represented all the individual components of a shopping cart save one: the order itself. An order is simply a combination of line items: Bill To address, Ship To address, and credit card. I have represented all this below:

```
<Order>
<LineItems>
 ... Line Item ...
</LineItems>
<ShippingMethod ID="" />
<ShipTo>
 <Person>
  <Name>
   ... Name ...
  </Name>
  <Email></Email>
  <Phone>
   ... Phone ...
  </Phone>
  <Address>
   ... Address ...
  </Address>
```

```
    </Person>
   </ShipTo>
   <BillTo>
    <Person>
      ... Person ...
    </Person>
   </BillTo>
   <CreditCard>
      ... Credit Card ...
   </CreditCard>
  </Order>
```

The Order XML document didn't contain anything new except for a simplified ShippingMethod node, which is necessary to specify the order's shipping method. This document is just the combination of a series of smaller documents. As we've discussed, this is a useful practice to follow.

To finish our shopping cart, we need to create one last XML document. As with the guest book example, we need to create a document to represent the server's response when you place an order. Both possible answers are included below:

```
  <Response>
   <Status>Success</Status>
   <Message>The order was placed properly</Message>
  </Response>

  <Response>
   <Status>Failure</Status>
   <Message>The order failed for x reason</Message>
  </Response>
```

Give yourself a pat on the back—that was a lot of XML code to go through. With all these examples and your new foundation in XML, you should be able to design and create your own XML documents for various applications without any trouble. The next step is to learn how an application reads and understands an XML document.

Traversing an XML Document

Now that we've covered the basics of XML, it's time to bring Flash into the picture. In this section, we'll first discuss how Flash interprets and parses XML. From there, we'll discuss how to use Flash's XML object and its methods to get at the data in an XML document. From now on, we'll focus on the shopping cart XML documents that we created in the last section.

How Flash Understands XML

When you give Flash an XML document to parse, what exactly happens? Flash takes that document and places it in memory. At this point, Flash sees the data only as a string of text. Flash loops through this string and generates a series of objects within objects (**Figure 8.2**). The topmost object is the XML object; inside of it are various node objects called XMLNodes. The XMLNode object is undocumented, but you can extend it if you want to. This distinction is academic, though, from a functional standpoint it doesn't change how you develop your applications.

 The information in this section is generic enough to apply to any XML-based application, not just Flash.

Root Node
Parent To <Name> and <Email>

Name node
Child of <Person>
Parent of <First> and <Last>

```
<Person>
    <Name>
        <First></First>
        <Last></Last>
    </Name>
    <Email></Email>
```

First node
Child of <Name>
Parent to a #text node
Sibling of <Last>

Last node
Child of <Name>
Parent to a #text node
Sibling of <First>

Email node
Child of <Person>
Parent to a #text node
Sibling of <Name>

Figure 8.2 *This diagram illustrates the relationships between various nodes and elements.*

Meet the Family

XML is navigated with an "ancestry" model. This means that parent nodes have children and those children can have other children. Let's diagram this:

```
<Person>
 <Name>
  <First></First>
  <Last></Last>
 </Name>
 <Email></Email>
```

I just pasted in a snippet of the Person XML document we're using for the shopping cart. To use our terminology from earlier in the chapter, Person is considered our root element or node. (Remember an XML document can have only one root element.) The Name element is a child of the Person element. First is a child of Name, and a grandchild of Person. Email is also a child of Person and a sibling of Name. Pretty simple, huh?

Occasionally you'll hear someone talking about XML as a tree, equating pieces of it to branches and leaves. I don't recommend this metaphor because all of Flash's XML object methods are already based on the parents-and-children model that's built into the XML terminology already.

Attributes

How do attributes fit into this model? Below is a snippet from the Product XML document for the shopping cart:

```
<Product ID="" SWF="">
 <Name></Name>
```

Attributes are not considered child elements; they're a collection of name/value pairs. If you're not familiar with collections, think of your typical associative array in Flash. You can easily add and remove items from the collection, and the underlying XML document is changed. When you add or remove an attribute from the collection, the XML object you pulled the collection from is updated. If you were to view the document again, you'd see that the attributes had been updated.

White Space

When Flash parses an XML document, it translates all the text into nodes. For all intents and purposes Flash supports two node types: text nodes and element nodes. Earlier, we mentioned two types of white space. The first was space between a start and an end tag; the second was space between the various nodes. Here's where things get a little tricky. When the parser encounters space between the nodes, it doesn't throw it away—it makes the space into a new text node. The biggest difference between an element node and a text node is that the latter can't have children or attributes.

In our previous example, we have a Product and a Name element. Between them are a carriage return and a tab. These characters would get placed in a text node. Name would get placed in an element node. This may not seem like a big deal, but it can cause many problems. Let me illustrate:

```
<Name>
 <First></First>
 <Last></Last>
</Name>
```

Here's a simple name snippet. If you were to get all the nodes inside the name element, it would look something like this:

```
Text Node
Element Node
Text Node
Element Node
Text Node
```

As you can see, the white space is now doing a lot more then just setting off our code. Let's rewrite the snippet to this:

```
<Name><First></First><Last></Last></Name>
```

Now when we get the nodes, it looks like this:

```
Element Node
Element Node
```

That's exactly what we're looking for! And that solution wasn't very hard. Sometimes it's easiest to manually remove the white space from the XML document, before you attempt to parse it. I don't recommend this method, as it reduces the readability of the document unless it's being generated on the fly for Flash. But in that case, it's probably the best option.

If you know the XML data you're about to receive contains white space, you have two options. The first is to use some programming logic to clean the white space either before or after the parse. This can be a rather time-intensive operation, as Flash is notoriously slow at parsing strings. There are a lot of free routines on the Web to handle this, so I won't add another to the list.

The other option is to use the `ignoreWhite` property of the XML object. By setting this property to "true" before you parse your XML, the Flash parser will automatically ignore white space. Seems like the perfect solution, right? Wrong. This capability was introduced in the R41 version of the Flash player, but Flash 5 uses an older player version, so you won't be able to use this functionality when you're developing. For me, that's a real showstopper. The other downside is the huge number of pre-R41 players on the Internet. Both of these issues make `ignoreWhite` a bad choice.

Before you consider yourself doomed and start searching for the string routines, there's a silver lining to this problem. As knowledge of Flash 5 spread, some low-level routines were discovered that allowed certain processing to be sped up. Branden Hall of Fig Leaf Software (a super nice guy and brilliant Internet developer) has created a replacement for the `parseXML()` method of the XML object. This replacement, called XMLNitro, does two things: It speeds parsing, and it enables the `ignoreWhite` property in all versions of the Flash player.

To use XMLNitro, you need only include the .as file in your Flash application before you attempt to parse. I recommend you use it for every XML project, as it has few downsides and lots of benefits. To put value to my words, the showcase project for this chapter uses XMLNitro extensively.

 An .as file is an ActionScript that has been saved into a text file. Flash will pull this file in automatically when you make it a SWF. By saving your code outside of Flash, you can to reuse it more easily. For more information, refer to the #include command in the Flash documentation.

 XMLNitro is saved on the CD-ROM as XMLNitro.as. You can find it in the Source_Code sub-folder of the Chapter 8 examples folder.

Mixed Nodes

All this talk of text nodes and element nodes probably makes you wonder if it's possible to use real data rather than just white space in between these elements. The short answer is yes. Nodes that contain both text and other elements are commonly called mixed nodes. Here's an example:

```
<Tag>
  Some Text in here
  <AnotherTag>Some more Text</AnotherTag>
</Tag>
```

Although XML is fully capable of using the data in this way, writing XML in this style makes it more difficult to read. The style doesn't break any XML rules, but it does break some of the fundamental concepts of XML. If you do this, the data is not as self-describing as it could be.

Text Node vs. Element Node

What happens when you're inside an element and there are no more child elements? In this case, all the text inside the last element is a new text node. Simple, huh?

Parsing Performance

This is a sticky subject. People who frequently use Flash with XML often complain of how poorly Flash performs when parsing an XML document. This problem can be mitigated with various design techniques and by modifying some of the underlying XML parsing routines with more efficient code. One of the best examples of this is XMLNitro, which greatly speeds the Flash parsing process.

One of the main reasons for slow XML performance in Flash is the sheer size of the data you're parsing. If it's thousands of lines, Flash won't handle it well. How much is too much? It all depends on the system you're using. I recommend you send only the data you need to send. Prune unnecessary information from your XML document. Keeping the data minimal will save you precious CPU cycles, as well as simplify your code.

In Flash, the more nodes you have, the more node objects are created. This is costly in terms of memory and processor time. Just as you should segment your data for good design, you can reverse that process and strip out nodes that are not essential. Attributes are generally faster than nodes. Converting some nodes into attributes will improve performance as well.

As with all performance tuning, do it last! Develop the system with a good design, and then identify potential bottlenecks. When you test and run the system, you can determine if these bottlenecks are indeed the problem. Choose and tune the problem with the most overall performance impact. With XML, it's almost always the initial parse. It's important to design your XML document properly up front and performance-tune it when it's all working to ensure the least number of system changes and to keep the cleanest design possible. Too often we start tuning as we develop the system and end up with a mess to maintain due to improper design.

Accessing XML Data

Whew! It's been a long trip to get this far. You know how to build and design XML documents, you understand how Flash parses XML, and you're familiar with some of the Flash XML pitfalls. Now it's time to put this to work and get some data.

Data from Nodes

We'll continue to focus on the XML documents used in our shopping cart. Below is the Name snippet:

```
<Name>
 <First>Abe</First>
 <Last>Lincoln</Last>
</Name>
```

Let's make this into an XML document that Flash understands. To do this, we only need this code:

```
xmlString =
"<Name><First>Abe</First><Last>Lincoln</Last></Name>";
myXMLDoc = new XML(xmlString);
```

That's it! That bit of code made an XML document in Flash. By simply passing in a string, the XML object will parse it automatically, and you'll be able to access it directly with the various XML methods.

OK, so maybe that in itself isn't so exciting, but getting the data is. Let's say we want to get the child nodes of the <Name> element (that is, we want to see the first and last names of the customer). Simple: We just add this line.

```
nameNodes = myXMLDoc.childNodes;
```

childNodes is a property of the XML object that points to a read-only collection of nodes. (Remember that a collection is handled like an array.) To see what we have so far, let's trace it.

```
Trace(nameNodes);
```

This is what will be returned in the output window:

```
<Name><First>Abe</First><Last>Lincoln</Last></Name>
```

Wait a minute?! That's not what we expected. We didn't see the First and Last name nodes, we just saw the entire XML document as the only item in the collection. This is a subtle and often confusing point for new XML developers. An XML document has only one root element, remember? That root element has a parent element as well. When you pass in:

```
<Name>
 <First>Abe</First>
 <Last>Lincoln</Last>
</Name>
```

XML sees it as this:

```
<ROOT>
 <Name>
  <First>Abe</First>
  <Last>Lincoln</Last>
 </Name>
</ROOT>
```

At first this might seem daunting, but it's simple to overcome. We need only get the first child element inside the document before we begin our real parsing. We need to get the Name node first. Fortunately, XML has a simple way to do this:

```
rootLevel = myXMLDoc.firstChild;
```

firstChild is a property of an XML node that can be used, not surprisingly, to return the first child of that node. It's an incredibly useful property and one you'll use a great deal. Below is all the code so far:

```
xmlString = "<Name><First>Abe</First><Last>Lincoln</Last>
→ </Name>";
myXMLDoc = new XML(xmlString);
rootLevel = myXMLDoc.firstChild;
nameNodes = rootLevel.childNodes
trace(nameNodes);
```

Now our trace will return something friendly like this:

```
<First>Abe</First>,<Last>Lincoln</Last>
```

This is exactly what we wanted to see. Let's break it down farther using what we've already discussed to get the data. By adding these lines, we get the individual nodes:

```
firstNameNode = nameNodes[0];
lastNameNode = nameNodes[1];
```

And a trace on firstNameNode will give us:

```
<First>Abe</First>
```

To get the value out of the nodes, you have to remember that text inside of an element is a node as well. It's just a text node. So there's still one more level to dive into.

```
firstNameNodeText = firstNameNode.firstChild;
lastNameNodeText = lastNameNode.firstChild;
```

Finally! That's the lowest level we can go, node-wise. Now, this is a little confusing: If you were to run a trace(firstNameNodeText), you'd get this:

```
Abe
```

This is the result we want, but not the way we should get it. Whenever you use an XML object as a string, it will return the contents of the object. In this case, we used our text node as a string and its only contents are the data we want. It's possible to avoid getting the data directly with this technique but I recommend against it: It's bad practice to hack your way through programming.

All that's left now is to get the data the right way. This last bit of code should do the trick:

```
firstNameValue = firstNameNodeText.nodeValue;
lastNameValue = lastNameNodeText.nodeValue;
```

Running a trace on firstNameValue, we'll see:

```
Abe
```

This is the data we were looking for. All of the code is listed below, in case you got lost along the way:

```
xmlString =
"<Name><First>Abe</First><Last>Lincoln</Last></Name>";
myXMLDoc = new XML(xmlString);
rootLevel = myXMLDoc.firstChild;
nameNodes = rootLevel.childNodes;
firstNameNode = nameNodes[0];
lastNameNode = nameNodes[1];
firstNameNodeText = firstNameNode.firstChild;
lastNameNodeText = lastNameNode.firstChild;
firstNameValue = firstNameNodeText.nodeValue;
lastNameValue = lastNameNodeText.nodeValue;
trace(firstNameValue);
```

Before you lynch me for giving you so much code to do something that should have been simple, let me explain. I went through this grueling process to illustrate every step along the way. When you do your own XML parsing, you'll understand the process that much better. I know you'll thank me later.

This file is saved on the CD-ROM as Data_From_Nodes_1.fla. It's in the Source_Code sub-folder.

It's simple to condense this code into something a bit more real world. The odds of ever needing direct access to every node in the document is pretty slim and this new iteration of the previous code uses that knowledge to good effect:

```
xmlString = "<Name><First>Abe</First><Last>Lincoln
→ </Last></Name>";
myXMLDoc = new XML(xmlString);
nameNodes = myXMLDoc.firstChild.childNodes;
```

```
firstNameValue = nameNodes[0].firstChild.nodeValue;
lastNameValue = nameNodes[1].firstChild.nodeValue;
trace(firstNameValue);
```

See? Less code, and it still works great. You notice we're using the child nodes collection even though there are only two items in it.

 This file is saved on the CD-ROM as Data_From_Nodes_2.fla.

It's also possible to get at this data in a slightly different way, as illustrated below:

```
nameNodes = myXMLDoc.firstChild;
firstNameValue = nameNodes.firstChild.firstChild.nodeValue;
lastNameValue = nameNodes.lastChild.firstChild.nodeValue;
```

I only needed to change nameNodes from a collection into an object representing the Name node itself, and then use firstChild for the First element and lastChild for the last element to get the same data. Obviously, firstChild and lastChild complement each other nicely here. While this may seem a convenient way to handle nodes, in most cases I find myself just getting the collection to always be consistent.

Data from Attributes

We've seen some basic techniques for getting data from nodes, but we haven't addressed attributes yet. Getting data from attributes is simple and quick. Below is the XML document for a single product:

```
<Product ID="10" SWF="http://www.blah.com/file.swf">
 <Name>Product 1</Name>
 <Description>
  <Short>Short Description</Short>
  <Long>Long Description </Long>
 </Description>
 <Price>10.00</Price>
</Product>
```

In this case, we'll focus on getting the attributes from the first element; we won't go over how to parse the rest of the nodes. We start by drilling down to the appropriate node using the techniques we covered previously. Once we're there, we use the attributes property of the object. This property returns a collection of nodes available for reading and writing. (Yes, that

means you could add attributes the same way, but we'll get to that later.)
The code to this point is:

```
myXMLObj = new XML(xmlString);
productNode = myXMLObj.firstChild;
productAttributes = productNode.attributes;
```

If you attempt to run trace(productAttributes), you'll get a message that says something like [type Object]. To get at the real data, you need to dig a little deeper and designate the specific attribute you're interested in.

```
IDAttribute = productAttributes.ID;
SWFAttribute = productAttributes.SWF;
```

Running a trace on IDAttribute will return "10", which is the correct value.

 This file is saved on the CD-ROM as Data_From_Attributes_1.fla.

While this method is simple and effective, it's not the only way you can get at the attributes. You can also use this:

```
IDAttribute = productAttributes["ID"];
SWFAttribute = productAttributes["SWF"];
```

I prefer this method, as it easily lets you use a variable for the name of the attribute if necessary.

 This file is saved on the CD-ROM as Data_From_Attributes_2.fla.

Traversing Nodes

We've talked about getting data from nodes and drilling down into the XML document, but what about traveling from one node to the next? You can use various techniques to do this. Let's look at the Line Item XML document:

```
<LineItems>
 <LineItem ProductID="1" Quantity="1" />
 <LineItem ProductID="2" Quantity="1" />
 <LineItem ProductID="3" Quantity="1" />
 </LineItems>
```

We could use the `childNodes` property we used before or we could do something a little trickier. I'll first show the code and then explain it.

```
myXMLObj = new XML(xmlString);
lineItemNode = myXMLObj.firstChild;
currentNode = LineItemNode.firstChild;
while(true) {
 trace(currentNode);
 currentNode = currentNode.nextSibling;
 if(currentNode == null) { break; }
}
```

The first two lines should look familiar. We're just building the object and burrowing down to the appropriate level. The next line of code gets us the first line item element. We don't do anything with it yet, though. At line 4, we enter an infinite While loop. This is used to keep us iterating until further notice. We immediately trace the `currentNode` just to see if it worked. At this point, you'd have your real application logic to handle processing the data. The next line shows us setting the `currentNode` to the `currentNodes.nextSibling`. This does what it sounds like it does. You just advanced down one node. The last line is used to get us out of the loop when we've gone as far as possible.

Before you ask: Yes, there is a `previousSibling` property that does the exact opposite for you.

 This file is saved on the CD-ROM as Next_Sibling.fla.

If you think about it, this example might seem quite frivolous. These same nodes could have been pulled using the `childNodes` collection—and probably with less hassle. This example was merely to illustrate a way to use the `nextSibling` property (and, by inference, the `previousSibling` property as well).

We keep talking about going down and deeper into an XML document, but there are ways to climb back up the document as well. The `parentNode` property is designed to let you do just that. This is illustrated with the code below:

```
xmlString = "<LineItems ID='100'><LineItem ProductID='1'
 → Quantity='1' /></LineItems>";
myXMLObj = new XML(xmlString);
deepChildNode = myXMLObj.firstChild.firstChild;
parentID = deepChildNode.parentNode.attributes["ID"];
```

This code uses a subset of XML from the last snippet. It illustrates how you could drill all the way to a deep child node in one line of code and still access information from above.

 This file is saved on the CD-ROM as Parent_Node.fla.

Getting Information About the Current Node

It's time for us to cover some of the other properties you can use on an XML node. One of the more useful is hasChildNodes. This method, surprisingly enough, tells you if the current node has any child nodes. Below is a simple example:

```
xmlString = "<Name><First>Abe</First><Last>Lincoln</Last>
→ </Name>";
myXMLDoc = new XML(xmlString);
nameNode = myXMLDoc.firstChild;
trace(nameNode.hasChildNodes());
```

Our trace line will return "true" as we expect. If we run this line:

```
trace(nameNode.firstChild.hasChildNodes());
```

You would expect the results to be "false", right? Not so! Remember that text nodes are still children. So the "First" element still has a single child node. Here is a tweaked version of the same thing that will return "false:"

```
trace(nameNode.firstChild.firstChild.hasChildNodes());
```

 While you can stack properties and methods together forever, it's quite hard to read. I wouldn't recommend using it in your production applications.

 You can find the file hasChildNodes.fla on the CD-ROM.

Next on our list is nodeName:

```
xmlString =
"<Name><First>Abe</First><Last>Lincoln</Last></Name>";
myXMLDoc = new XML(xmlString);
nameNode = myXMLDoc.firstChild;
trace(nameNode.nodeName);
```

The trace action returns "Name" as it should. The nodeName property is useful if you don't know the order of nodes in your XML document, or if you want to set up an event-driven model.

There are two important things to remember about `nodeName`. First, if you use it against the topmost XML node, it will return null. To illustrate this, just add the following line to the last example:

```
trace(myXMLDoc.nodeName);
```

Second, if you run it against a text node, you'll get null. Add this line to the example to see this:

```
trace(nameNode.firstChild.firstChild.nodeName);
```

This is contrary to the XML specs put out by the W3C. According to them, `nodeName` should return "#text".

 This file is saved on the CD-ROM as nodeName.fla.

The last method to discuss is `nodeType`. This returns a number that represents what type of node it is. While the official W3C spec calls for 12 node types in XML, Flash really only understands two. I say "really" because while Flash can access the data in some of the other types, by using `nodeType` you'll never see anything but two numbers. Element nodes will return the number 1 and text nodes will return 3. Below is an example of this:

```
xmlString = "<Name><First>Abe</First><Last>Lincoln
→ </Last></Name>";
myXMLDoc = new XML(xmlString);
nameNode = myXMLDoc.firstChild;
firstNameNode = nameNode.firstChild;
trace(firstNameNode.nodeType);
trace(firstNameNode.firstChild.nodeType);
```

The first trace returns 1, and the second, 3. The `nodeType` property is useful if you want to iterate over a series of nodes and see what type they are before you use them. A good example of this would be a program that needs to count the number of text nodes in an XML document. You would have a function that takes an XML document, gets the child node list, and loops over it. If it's a text node, it will increment the counter; else, the function calls itself passing in the new node. This powerful capability is good to have in your toolbox, but in your day-to-day development, you probably won't use it.

 This file is saved on the CD-ROM as nodeType.fla.

Getting Information About the XML Document

A few pieces of information returned at the document level are quite useful. One of the most overlooked is the status property of the XML object. After an XML document is parsed, the status property is set with a status code. Below is the list of codes and possible values. These values and codes are pulled directly from the Flash 5 documentation.

STATUS	STATUS MEANING
0	No error; parse completed successfully.
-2	A CDATA section was not properly terminated.
-3	The XML declaration was not properly terminated.
-4	The DOCTYPE declaration was not properly terminated.
-5	A comment was not properly terminated.
-6	An XML element was malformed.
-7	Out of memory.
-8	An attribute value was not properly terminated.
-9	A start-tag was not matched with an end-tag.
-10	An end-tag was encountered without a matching start-tag.

To illustrate this point, I've created a simple example. This code parses three XML snippets and checks their status:

```
xmlStringOne = "<Name><First>Abe</First><Last>Lincoln
→ </Last></Name>";
xmlStringTwo = "<Name><First>Abe</First><Last>Lincoln
→ </Last></Name";
xmlStringThree = "<Name><First>Abe</First><Last>Lincoln
→ </Name>";
myXMLDoc = new XML(xmlStringOne);
testOne = myXMLDoc.status
myXMLDoc = new XML(xmlStringTwo);
testTwo = myXMLDoc.status
myXMLDoc = new XML(xmlStringThree);
testThree = myXMLDoc.status
```

Tracing the output of testOne, testTwo, and testThree will return various numerical codes that you can use to determine the error. Particularly if you're getting the XML document from an unknown or untrusted source, it may be useful to check the XML status to determine if there was a processing error. This allows you to present a friendly message rather than the usual behavior of letting the user just crash out.

This file is saved on the CD-ROM as status.fla.

Of course, it's possible to add a new method to the XML object that returns some more useful information to begin with. To that end, I've created an .as file that you can include in your Flash applications. It will return the status message rather than the status code. Its text is below:

```
XML.prototype.getStatusMsg = function() {
 statusCode = this.status;
 if(statusCode == 0) {
  message = "No error; parse completed successfully.";
 } else if(statusCode == -2)  {
  message = "A CDATA section was not properly terminated.";
 } else if(statusCode == -3)  {
  message = "The XML declaration was not properly
   → terminated.";
 } else if(statusCode == -4)  {
  message = "The DOCTYPE declaration was not properly
   → terminated.";
 } else if(statusCode == -5)  {
  message = "A comment was not properly terminated.";
 } else if(statusCode == -6)  {
  message = "An XML element was malformed.";
 } else if(statusCode == -7)  {
  message = "Out of memory.";
 } else if(statusCode == -8)  {
  message = "An attribute value was not properly
   → terminated.";
 } else if(statusCode == -9)  {
  message = "A start-tag was not matched with an end-tag.";
 } else if(statusCode == -10)  {
  message = "An end-tag was encountered without a matching
   → start-tag.";
 }
 return message;
}
```

Not terribly powerful, but still effective. To call it, you need only include it and execute the getStatusMsg() method off the XML object.

 The getStatusMsg.as file is included on the CD-ROM, along with an example of its use, called statusMsg.fla.

Previously, we had talked about XML declarations. Flash provides a property to get and set this data. The property is called xmlDecl and it's quite simple to use. To read a declaration, you do this:

```
trace(myXMLObj.xmlDecl);
```

The trace method would display nothing if the declaration has not been set, or it would return a string representation of the data. Setting a declaration is equally simple:

```
MyXMLObj = new XML();
myXMLObj.xmlDecl = "<?xml version=\"1.0\" ?>";
```

Other XML Object Methods

I'd like to discuss two more XML methods before we move on to using Flash to make your XML documents. The first is the toString() method. You should be quite familiar with this method already, as we have used it extensively. Every time you run a trace() on an object, it will search for a toString() method. If the object has one, it will execute that and return a string representation of the object. This is fairly standard among languages; for example, Java and JavaScript both support this capability.

The second method is parseXML(). This takes a string containing XML and applies it to the specified XML object. To illustrate:

```
myXMLObj = new XML();
myXMLObj.parseXML("<test>This is a test</test>");
```

In this example, parseXML() took the text string and replaced the contents of myXMLObj with the newly formed XML document. As you recall, a string can also be passed into the constructor of an XML object and it gets parsed as well. The constructor internally calls parseXML() and passes in the string.

Building XML Documents

Now it's time to learn how to build an XML document in Flash. So far we've passed strings into the constructor or used the parseXML() method. From now on, we'll use Flash XML methods to generate a new XML document.

Creating Nodes and Attributes

Building an XML document in Flash starts with the XML object. First, you need to instantiate a copy of the XML object like this:

```
myXMLObj = new XML();
```

This generates a generic XML object, ready to do your bidding. To illustrate generating nodes, let's use our trusty Name XML document again:

```
<Name>
 <First>Abe</First>
 <Last>Lincoln</Last>
</Name>
```

To make an element, you need only use the createElement() method. The name of the new node is passed in as a parameter. Note that this method returns an XMLnode object; it doesn't automatically bind the new node to the object that generated it.

```
nameNode = myXMLObj.createElement("Name");
```

Running a trace on nameNode will return "<Name />" to the console. Let's make the rest of our nodes now.

```
firstNode = myXMLObj.createElement("First");
lastNode = myXMLObj.createElement("Last");
```

You might wonder why I'm not using the nameNode object as the source object for the new nodes. Honestly, I don't have a good answer, but using the same object for all node and attribute creation seems simpler to follow in general.

To create the text nodes, we need to use a different method: createTextNode(). This method is passed a single string as a parameter. The string contains the contents of the text node.

```
firstNodeValue = myXMLObj.createTextNode("Abe");
lastNodeValue = myXMLObj.createTextNode("Lincoln");
```

To put this all together, we need to introduce a new method: appendChild(). This method takes another XML object as a parameter. To illustrate:

```
firstNode.appendChild(firstNodeValue);
lastNode.appendChild(lastNodeValue);
nameNode.appendChild(firstNode);
nameNode.appendChild(lastNode);
```

We just built the Name XML document from scratch. If you step back, you can see some patterns to our code that could be exploited to make it simpler. Below is the complete code, reorganized slightly to improve readability:

```
myXMLObj = new XML();
// name node
nameNode = myXMLObj.createElement("Name");
// First name
firstNode = myXMLObj.createElement("First");
firstNodeValue = myXMLObj.createTextNode("Abe");
firstNode.appendChild(firstNodeValue);
nameNode.appendChild(firstNode);
// Last name
lastNode = myXMLObj.createElement("Last");
lastNodeValue = myXMLObj.createTextNode("Lincoln");
lastNode.appendChild(lastNodeValue);
nameNode.appendChild(lastNode);
```

 This code is saved on the CD-ROM as Create_Elements.fla.

Attributes are even simpler than elements. In fact, creating attributes uses a property we've already discussed: XML.attributes. To explain attributes previously, we used the Product XML document. We'll use this snippet again for reference:

```
<Product ID="10" SWF="file.swf " />
```

To get started, we build the product node like usual.

```
myXMLObj = new XML();
productNode = myXMLObj.createElement("Product");
```

From here, we get the attributes collection.

```
productAttributes = productNode.attributes;
```

To add attributes, you need only do this:

```
productAttributes.ID = 10;
productAttributes.SWF = "http://www.blah.com/file.swf";
```

When you run a trace against productNode, you'll get the results we're looking for. It's also possible to use the collection like an associative array. The code to do that would look like this:

```
productAttributes["ID"] = 10;
productAttributes["SWF"] = "http://www.blah.com/file.swf";
```

The second method lets you easily use variables as the name of the attribute. This is useful for dynamically creating XML documents with unknown data.

 This code is saved on the CD-ROM as Create_Attributes.fla.

Removing Nodes and Attributes

We've talked about adding elements and attributes, but now let's try to remove them. If you received an XML document that contained more information than you needed to pass on, removing that information would be the perfect solution.

Removing a node involves drilling down to the appropriate node and then using the removeNode() method. This automatically removes a node and all of its children from the XML document.

Going back to our trusty Name XML document, let's remove the first name element. Below is a possible solution:

```
xmlString =
"<Name><First>Abe</First><Last>Lincoln</Last></Name>";
myXMLDoc = new XML(xmlString);
nameNodes = myXMLDoc.firstChild.childNodes;
nameNodes[0].removeNode();
trace(myXMLDoc);
```

The output window will return "<Name><Last>Lincoln</Last></Name>", which is what we want. Remember that this delete is recursive and will remove everything from this level down.

 This file is saved on the CD-ROM as Remove_Node.fla.

Removing attributes requires you to use the delete keyword. Using the Product XML snippet from before, it would look like this:

```
myXMLObj = new XML(xmlString);
productAttributes = myXMLObj.firstChild.attributes;
delete productAttributes.ID;
```

 This file is on saved the CD-ROM as Remove_Attributes.fla.

Cloning Nodes

Cloning nodes is often useful. Just like when you clone a sheep, the new clone (the child) has all the attributes and elements of the original. The cloneNode() method takes one parameter—a Boolean value—and returns a new XML object. This parameter defines whether all of the children of the node should be copied. If the Boolean is true, then all of the child elements of the node will be duplicated. If the Boolean is false, only the current level is returned. Let's use the LineItem XML document to show this:

```
<LineItems>
 <LineItem ProductID="1" Quantity="1" />
 <LineItem ProductID="2" Quantity="1" />
 <LineItem ProductID="3" Quantity="1" />
</LineItems>
```

You could create each of the LineItem elements individually, or you could create one and clone it as needed. Cloning is often useful for building an XML document from an array or collection of data. Let's see it in action:

```
myXMLObj = new XML();
lineItemsNode = myXMLObj.createElement("LineItems");
lineItemSeed = myXMLObj.createElement("LineItem");
for(i=1; i < 5; i++) {
 tempItem = lineItemSeed.cloneNode(true);
 lineItemAttributes = tempItem.attributes;
 lineItemAttributes.ProductID = i;
 lineItemAttributes.Quantity = 1;
 lineItemsNode.appendChild(tempItem);
}
```

This code starts off similarly to the other snippets. We create a base XML object from which to generate new elements. We make the lineItemsNode object, then we make a seed object for handling the specific line items. At this point we go into a `for` loop to generate new nodes. In a real project, you would most likely be looping over an array of data, rather than just incrementing numbers.

The next line of the code is the one we want to look at:

```
tempItem = lineItemSeed.cloneNode(true);
```

This line takes the lineItemSeed object and clones it and its children. As it has no children in this case, the Boolean could have been set to "false" without any changes to the results. From here, we get the attributes collection, and add the attributes we want. The last step (not shown here) is to add this node back into the main XML document.

 This file is saved on the CD-ROM as Clone_Elements.fla.

Getting XML Documents Into and Out of Flash

Getting XML documents into and out of Flash is a key point to any application. Usually, XML is used to communicate between applications, but occasionally it's also helpful to use an XML document inside of Flash. Once Flash has loaded in an XML document, you can pass it between movie clips that internally parse and display only the data they need. This simplifies pulling the data from the XML document and passing it around as variables.

Loading XML Documents

The `load()` method of the XML object is used to load data from a remote location. It works much like the `loadVariables()` method. It will pull in an XML document and automatically parse it. To see this in action, let's use a file called Products.xml and put it in the same directory as the SWF file containing this code.

```
productsObj = new XML();
productsObj.load("products.xml");
```

Yes, that's it. It doesn't take a lot of work to load data into Flash from a file.

 This file is saved on the CD-ROM as Load.fla. The Products.xml file is also on the CD-ROM.

We need to remember one thing, though. Like the `loadVariables()` method, `load()` doesn't stop the movie from executing. This means we can't immediately attempt to access the data in our new XML object. We need to wait for it to finish loading first. Fortunately, unlike `loadVariables()`, `load()` has several effective ways to determine if the document has finished. The easiest and often most useful way is the `loaded` property. This property returns a Boolean "true" if the document has finished loading. Here's a convenient routine to handle this is included below:

```
current = _root.currentFrame;
goto = (myXMLObj.loaded) ? current + 1 : current – 1;
_root.gotoAndPlay(goto);
```

I'm sure anyone who has used `LoadVariables()` will be quite familiar with the concept. This code would need to be placed at least two frames after your attempt to load the XML document.

 This file is saved on the CD-ROM as Loaded.fla.

A better way to catch when data has been loaded would be to use the provided callback method: XML.onLoad(). A callback is a method that's called when some event occurs. With `XML.load()`, the event is when the data has finished loading and parsing. When this occurs, Flash will automatically call the `onLoad()` method. You need to set `onLoad` equal to a function you create to ensure that it's called when the XML document is finished loading and parsing. This means that when the XML document has finished, your function will be called, and it can then move the playhead, throw an error, and so on. Whatever function you designate will be passed a Boolean. This parameter will tell you if the data loaded successfully. Here's a snippet that illustrates the concept:

```
productsObj = new XML();
productsObj.onLoad = dataLoaded;
productsObj.load("products.xml");
function dataLoaded(success) {
 if(success) {
  _root.gotoAndStop("Success");
 } else {
  _root.gotoAndStop("Failure");
 }
}
stop();
```

This file is saved on the CD-ROM as onLoad.fla.

In this example, we create an XML container object, set the callback, and tell it to load the data. Once it's done, it will call the function `dataLoaded()` and automatically pass in the Boolean. At this point we only move the play head to a new frame, but in a real-world example, we would often place parsing code here as well.

Sending XML Documents to the Server

You've seen how to get XML documents from the server, but now it's time to get them back to the server. To do this, you need to use the `sendAndLoad()` method on the XML object. This method takes two parameters: the URL to send the data to, and the receiving XML object. To call it, you need only do this:

```
outgoingXML = new XML("<testDoc>test data</testDoc>");
incomingXML = new XML();
incomingXML.onLoad = dataLoaded;
outgoingXML.sendAndLoad("SendAndLoad.asp", incomingXML);
function dataLoaded(success) {
 if(success) {
  _root.gotoAndStop("Success");
 } else {
  _root.gotoAndStop("Failure");
 }
}
stop();
```

This is similar to a previous example, except we now have two XML objects floating around. One of them is the object to send to the server; the second is the container for the data coming from the server. Note that the `incomingXML` object is the one that will throw an onLoad event, not the other way around.

On the server side, things are much more complicated. Flash posts the data to the specified URL, but it doesn't specify a variable name for it. I don't understand Macromedia's reasoning behind this, but I do know that it makes the process of loading data much harder than it should be.

Some languages don't handle this lack of a variable name well at all. The most obvious example of this is ColdFusion. ColdFusion doesn't directly provide access to the request information; thus, there is no clean and simple way to get the XML data. There are various hacks out there, but most seem intermittent at best. Because of this, we won't cover them in this chapter.

Languages that do provide access to the necessary information in one way or another are PERL (or CGI in general), ASP, PHP, and Java. The shopping cart project uses ASP, so I will show how ASP handles this data. In the previous code snippet, we referenced a file called SendAndLoad.asp. The contents of this file are listed below.

```
<%@ LANGUAGE="VBSCRIPT" %>
<%
Option Explicit ' Always use this
' Declare the used variables
Dim parser, rootElement, testDocNode
' Get the XML parser
Set parser = Server.CreateObject("Microsoft.XMLDOM")
' Pull in the data from Flash
parser.loadXML("<Document>" & Request.Form & "</Document>")
' Get the root element
Set rootElement = parser.documentElement
' Get the testDoc node
Set testDocNode = rootElement.selectSingleNode("testDoc")
' Set the response type
Response.ContentType = "text/xml"
' Write it out to the screen
Response.write("<Response>" & testDocNode.Text &
→ "</Response>")
%>
```

 The SendAndLoad.asp file is included on the CD-ROM, as is the companion file SendAndLoad.fla.

I've left all the comments in the code to make it easier to follow, but this book is not about ASP programming, so I won't describe the code in detail. The most important thing to note is what happens in these three lines:

```
Set parser = Server.CreateObject("Microsoft.XMLDOM")
parser.loadXML("<Document>" & Request.Form & "</Document>")
Set rootElement = parser.documentElement
```

These lines get the Microsoft XML parser, take the data sent from Flash, and parse it. The rest of the code is standard ASP code. To learn more about ASP, search for ASP tutorials online or read Chapter 6, Creating Dynamic Flash Pages.

Lastly, you can only use `load()` and `sendAndLoad()` *on the root*. You cannot use them inside another movie clip. This appears to be a bug in Flash and (as bugs tend to do) has caused no end of headaches.

Speaking of the limitations of movie clips, here's another: You can't have a movie clip bind the functions to the root in its `onLoad()` event and attempt to run them from the root. It will not work in all browsers.

The Shopping Cart

Now it's time for the payoff section of this chapter—the showcase project.

The showcase project is a Flash 5 shopping cart using XML and ASP. While we won't get into micro detail on the ASP side of things, we'll talk about how the project was designed, and demonstrate how the code we've explained so far all comes together.

Design

The shopping cart was designed in three distinct phases: the object model, the server-side scripting, and the Flash front end. Because this chapter is on Flash and XML, we'll cover the object model more than anything else, as that's where XML and Flash interact.

Object Model

The shopping cart was designed from the ground up using object-oriented programming (OOP) practices. For the uninitiated, OOP is a popular and effective style of programming that allows you to separate business and presentation logic into discrete pieces. This makes applications more robust in general and more able to adjust to changing requirements.

The shopping cart is not a perfect OOP example. It uses many of the practices, but I kept it simple, as this chapter focuses on XML, not OOP techniques. I used OOP because it allowed for a clean and elegant method of handling and generating the XML data without tying the display into it. The pure abstraction makes it easier to understand how the data is created and used than if I were constantly juggling movie clips with XML snippets in them.

As we discussed, XML is not the most performance-centric method for handling data. Always looking up the values you need in the XML document makes it slow and memory-intensive. Because of this, it's often useful to translate the XML data into some other variable storage, and build it again when needed. In the shopping cart, I decided to use various objects to store and maintain the data. These same objects can also to rebuild their XML document again when needed. This provides more flexibility in the design, as we don't need to be careful with the original XML document once its data has been parsed.

When we discussed the XML documents for the shopping cart, I broke them down into various segments. For the most part, each segment represented the data contained within an Actionscript object. Here's the list of objects in the shopping cart:

- Address

- CreditCard

- LineItem

- Order

- Person

- Product

- ShippingMethod

In OOP, it's typically good practice to create objects that correlate to the business issues you're trying to solve. It's also easier to follow the model if you use real-world objects whenever possible. If you were to develop a car in OO code, you wouldn't want to call the engine an "InternalPropulsionUnit" without a good reason. If you don't use names that make sense to the layperson, the layperson will have trouble understanding your object model. To this end, I've attempted to create objects that make sense in both the physical world and in code.

Most of these objects contain other objects and can't stand alone. While an address is an independent piece of data, it always belongs to a given person. In the object model, this is expressed by the fact that the Person object contains an Address object. The LineItem object contains a Product object and a quantity. An Order object, for instance, contains two Person objects (one for Bill To and one for Ship To), multiple LineItem objects, a ShippingMethod object, and a CreditCard object.

All of these objects have a few base concepts in common; they all use *getter* and *setter* methods, they all have a toXML() method of some sort, and they are all included externally as .as files.

The concept of a getter or setter method is simple. To avoid someone calling a variable in your object directly, you provide a single point of interaction with it. Let's say you have an object called DriversLicence. It has a member variable or property called Name. You could access the variable like this:

```
DriversLicence.Name
```

This would work fine, but no one could ever change the Name variable without breaking all code that references it. What happens when you need to change Name into firstName and lastName? You can prevent this problem by using a getter method to act as a liaison to the variable. The method would look something like this:

```
DriversLicense.prototype.getName = function() {
  return this.Name;
}
```

Any code that needed to access the Name variable would call it like this:

```
DriversLicence.getName();
```

If you had to add support for firstName and lastName, you would change the getter to this:

```
DriversLicense.prototype.getName = function() {
  return this.firstName + this.lastName;
}
```

Setter methods are the same as getter methods, but reversed. You use them only to set member variables.

In the shopping cart object model, I've used getter and setter methods religiously. Overall it may seem odd to some, but getter and setter methods protect your code and objects from change. They let you make business logic changes without having to retrofit your entire application. If you need to use these same objects in a lot of different applications, this can be a lifesaver.

The second commonality mentioned above was how all objects contain a toXML() method of some sort. As each object encapsulates XML data, the toXML() method is used to pull that data back out. When you need to access an XML object from one of the objects in the system, you call the `toXML()` method on that object. It will go through all of its member variables to build and return the XML to you. If it's an object that contains other objects, like Order, the object will call the `toXML()` method of its child objects automatically. In other words, calling `Order.toXML()` will return a single XML document containing Person objects XML along with `CreditCard` and all the rest. This makes for a clean and elegant method to quickly generate a lot of data.

Lastly, all of the objects are .as files that are included when you export the movie. By leaving them in external .as files, you can easily reuse them in other projects and maintain only one code source for them. This is a real benefit of object-oriented programming.

Some of the objects implement helpful methods that simplify programming the cart. The `LineItem` object has a method called `calculateTotal()` that will tell you what the total cost of that `line item` is worth. The `Order` object also has a `calculateTotal` method that will tell you what the total order will cost.

The most useful helper method in the object mode is the `isValid()` method on the Credit Card object. This method will check to see if the expiration date is in the future, if the card number matches the card type specified, if the card number length is valid for the card type, and finally, if the card number is valid. The last step is performed using Mod10 validation of the number itself.

 The Mod10 algorithm is an equation used to ensure that the digits making up a credit card number are valid. You don't need to understand the details of how it works in order to use it. For the Credit Card object, I ran a search for the algorithm on the Internet and found several free examples in various languages. I re-wrote it in ActionScript and made it an object for your use.

All of this logic will ensure the card number is as valid as it can be determined without actually running it through an authorizer.

That's the extent of the object model, for the most part. As we walk through the various aspects of the application, you'll see how it all ties together and works with the underlying business logic. On to the server-side portion of the application!

Server Side

I tried to make the server-side portion of the application as simple as possible while still providing the functionality needed to support the shopping cart. If you were to use this shopping cart in production, you would need to overhaul pieces of it to ensure that it was secure and scalable.

I include the database as a server-side component as it's only accessed from the server. I used Microsoft Access to create the database because it's readily available to most developers and it's easy to use—with ASP, and in general. (And anyway, it would be difficult to include an Oracle database on the CD.) The data model is very similar to the object model. This is intentional—it keeps the entire project easier to understand and develop. Below is a diagram of the data tables and their relationships (**Figure 8.3**).

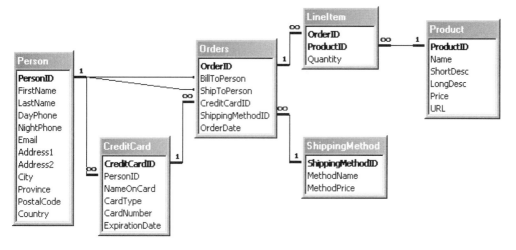

Figure 8.3 Diagram of the shopping cart database.

Note that the credit card information is bound to a person, but not on the same table. This is because it's possible that a single person would have multiple credit cards. While the shopping cart doesn't support it currently, it wouldn't be difficult to add in the ability for returning customers. They wouldn't need to retype their information, as it's all stored for them. The database is built with this flexibility in mind.

There are several points of interaction between Flash and the server. The first is GetProducts.asp. This file is used to get all the products in the database, generate the populated products XML document, and return it to Flash. The contents of this file are included below:

```
<%@ LANGUAGE="VBSCRIPT" %>
<%
Option Explicit ' Use it and LOVE IT!
' Declare some vars
Dim connection, connectionString, recordSet, xmlDoc
' Create the database connection
Set connection = Server.CreateObject("ADODB.Connection")
' Create the connection string
connectionString = "DBQ=" &
→ Server.MapPath("ShoppingCart.mdb") & ";DRIVER={Microsoft
→ Access Driver (*.mdb)}"
connection.ConnectionString = connectionString
' Open the connection
connection.Open()
' Create the record set to use
Set recordSet = Server.CreateObject("ADODB.Recordset")
' Get the data
recordSet.Open "Select ProductID, Name, ShortDesc, LongDesc,
→ Price, URL from Product Order by Name desc", connection
' Start the XML document
xmlDoc = "<Products>"
' Iterate over the records
Do Until recordSet.EOF = true
 ' Build the XML doc
 xmlDoc = xmlDoc & "<Product ID=""" &
 → recordSet("ProductID") & """ SWF=""" & recordSet("URL")
 → & """>"
  xmlDoc = xmlDoc & "<Name>" & recordSet("Name") &
  → "</name>"
   xmlDoc = xmlDoc & "<Description>"
    xmlDoc = xmlDoc & "<Short>" & recordSet("ShortDesc") &
    → "</Short>"
    xmlDoc = xmlDoc & "<Long>" & recordSet("LongDesc") &
    → "</Long>"
   xmlDoc = xmlDoc & "</Description>"
```

```
    xmlDoc = xmlDoc & "<Price>" & recordSet("Price") &
 → "</Price>"
  xmlDoc = xmlDoc & "</Product>"
  ' Move to the next record
  recordSet.MoveNext
Loop
' Finish up the document
xmlDoc = xmlDoc & "</Products>"
'Close and delete the recordSet object
recordSet.Close
Set recordSet = Nothing
'Close and delete the connection object
connection.Close
Set connection = Nothing
' Set the response type
Response.ContentType = "text/xml"
' Write it out to the screen
Response.write(xmlDoc)
%>
```

I've included the entire file here, as it shows you the format used for all
ASP pages in the shopping cart admin pages. As you can see, this is a pretty
straightforward ASP page. We create a connection to the database, run the
query, and manually build the XML document. This ASP file doesn't use the
Microsoft XMLDOM parser object to generate the product XML document
for two reasons: First, it isn't necessary, and second, we want to keep the
application as simple as possible. After we've built the XML string, we close
all open connections, set the output mime type to "text/xml," and write out
the XML.

TIP The XMLDOM is the Microsoft XML parser. You can call it from VBScript
in your browser as well as from the server in ASP pages and COM objects.
While it's too off-topic for this book, the Microsoft Developer Network
(http://msdn.microsoft.com) as well as various ASP pages on the Internet
offer a great deal of information about it.

Flash first calls GetProducts.asp with the load() method and doesn't pass in
any parameters. As this data is needed to load the shopping cart, the entire
shopping cart file pauses until it's done loading and parsing.

The second point of interaction is GetShippingMethods.asp. This page is
called when the user has chosen some products and is looking at shipping
costs. It hits the ShippingMethod table in the database, creates the

ShippingMethod XML document, and passes it back to Flash. This file is similar to the GetProducts.asp page, so we won't examine the ASP code used.

The last point of interaction between Flash and ASP is the PlaceOrder.asp page. This file is designed to take in an XML document from Flash, parse through it, and enter the data into the database. This page creates an instance of the XMLDOM parser and uses it to retrieve data from the XML document. Since the XMLDOM parser is similar to the Flash parser, the commands used should be familiar and fairly self-explanatory. To learn more about how it works, visit the Microsoft Developer Network Web site.

To avoid replication in the Person table, I've used the email address to determine if a person already exists—no email address can be entered in the system twice. A lookup is also provided against the credit card number to ensure no duplicates exist. If the user doesn't already exist in the system, then an entry will be created for them. If they already exist, we'll just add this order in their name. This lets us track multiple orders from a single person (**Figures 8.4** and **8.5**).

Figure 8.4
The Shopping Cart Administrator. From here, you can administer the various aspects of the cart from handling orders to modifying the product and shipping method listings.

Several ASP pages included with the shopping cart are not used from Flash, because they're related to the cart administration and not the user experience. Sometimes it's useful to use Flash for the entire system, but to keep this cart simple, the admin pieces are straight HTML and ASP. Most of these pages are related to entering content like shipping methods and products into the database. A few pages are used for viewing and deleting orders in the system.

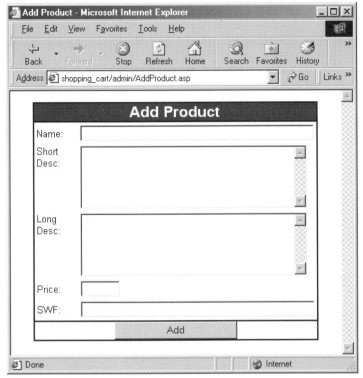

Figure 8.5 *The Add Product interface is accessible from the Shopping Cart Administrator.*

 You can find all of the administration pages in the Shopping_Cart\Admin folder on the CD-ROM.

Flash Front End

The Flash front-end portion of the application is quite simple. The object model handles the majority of our business logic for us, so the front end is used only to enter and retrieve data. Rather than a step-by-step walkthrough of the front end, we'll cover the major sections and what they do.

The shopping cart was designed to illustrate how you build Flash applications using XML. To this end, the Flash application doesn't validate the data you enter in the shopping cart (except on the credit card fields). If you enter blanks or other inappropriate characters, the program will pass that information to the database and it could return errors or stop running properly.

The entire movie is broken into major sections. I chose to divide the movie into discrete pieces to simplify explaining it and make it easier to follow the flow of logic.

The first frame of the movie contains many #include statements to pull in all the necessary external files. I built them externally, as it's simpler to reuse and maintain them this way. The first frame also defines most of the functions used throughout the rest of the shopping cart. The functions are primarily related to displaying various data, but several are related to other tasks. The most notable of these are addToCart, removeFromCart, and changeQuantity. Note that the Order object contains these methods already. These functions gather the necessary information and pass it through to the Order object, which does the work.

The next frame of importance is labeled *Load*. This is where we pull in the necessary data. To proceed with the cart, you need to get a product list and a shipping method list from the server. (The shipping method information could be postponed until later, but ganging the two together simplifies the application.) When this frame is reached, the movie starts loading two XML documents in the background: shippingMethodsDoc and productsDoc. The playhead is stopped while we wait for these documents to finish loading. Once the appropriate callback methods have been triggered, we parse and build the product list (**Figure 8.6**).

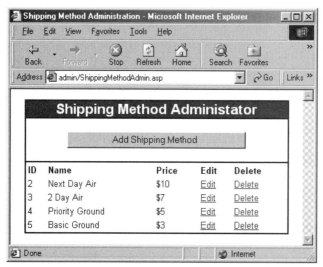

Figure 8.6 *This image shows the Shipping Method Administration page populated with data. You can get here through the Shopping Cart Administrator.*

To build the product list and avoid coupling the object model with the display logic, we use two objects. One is a movie clip called productClip and the other is the Product object included in the first frame. The Product object interacts with the data and XML, and the productClip takes these values and displays them on the screen. We pass the Product object into a duplicated instance of the productClip. When the onClipEvent(Load) handler is fired, it will use the data from the Product object to populate its fields. This style is used for the shippingMethodClip movie clip as well (**Figure 8.7**).

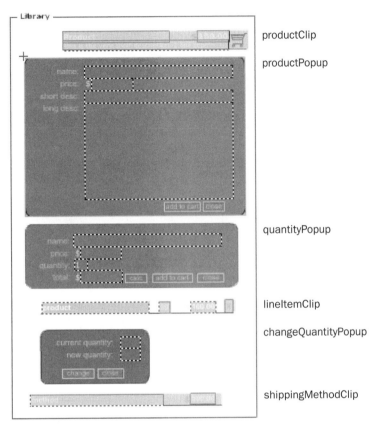

Library

productClip

productPopup

quantityPopup

lineItemClip

changeQuantityPopup

shippingMethodClip

Figure 8.7 *I prefer to keep movie clips like this on the Stage rather than in the Library, as you can include code on the clip itself. You can't if it's pulled from the Library.*

When you add a product to the shopping cart, a window pops up that lets you specify the quantity. Each popup window is responsible for cleaning up after itself. The windows all decrement the depth counter and unload themselves from memory when they are closed. All movie clips employ this method, with one exception. When we show or hide the product listing, we don't delete and rebuild its movie clips. This is because in a single user's session in the shopping cart, the product listing will never change—so there's no reason to rebuild it every time. When we hide the product list, it's really just slid 1,000 pixels off the screen. To display it, we slide the list back. This is not the case with the cart contents: As the data in this list can and will change often, it's simpler to rebuild the list with each subsequent visit.

Moving forward in the FLA file, you'll see a "ChooseShipping" label. At this point, the user is provided the list of shipping methods that we parsed earlier. Like the cart contents list, we create the necessary movie clips on the fly and destroy them when the user chooses one. Unlike the cart contents list, we create and destroy the shipping methods on the fly even though the data is static, as it's very unlikely a user will come to this page two times in one session.

After choosing a shipping method, you are presented with the first of several forms. Each form lets you enter various pieces of information. The "BillingAddress" and "ShippingAddress" labels could be condensed into a single frame if you wish. I left them apart for simplicity. When you press the Continue button on either form, an Address object and a Person object are built from the rest of the data on the form. Once the Person object is built, it's added to the Order object as either the BillTo or ShipTo property.

The CreditCard label is similar to the other forms, but it also performs validation. When the Finish button is pressed, the credit card object is created, and the isValid() method is executed. As mentioned earlier, this method will validate a credit card for everything except enough money in the account.

At this point, the Order object has all the necessary data populated and we can send it to the server. We call the toXML() method on the Order object, and in turn, it calls all of its children objects' toXML() methods. This makes for a clean and elegant way to generate XML documents.

Once we have the XML document, we use XML.sendAndLoad() to send the data back to the server and get the response. We get the response message and display it back to the user.

Congratulations—you've completed the shopping experience. Now that we've covered the entire cart in detail, with a little investigation you should have no trouble understanding how it works. There are many features that could be added to the cart without too much trouble. The easier ones include a confirmation screen, product images, a more sophisticated interface (hey—I never said I was a graphic artist!), and product categories. I intentionally left the cart as a skeleton form for you to work with. Many portions of it could be redesigned to reduce the amount of code and frames involved.

Wrap Up

By now, you should have a good understanding of the basics of XML and how Flash can interact with it. We've discussed when XML is useful and how you can use it to its full potential in your own applications.

Flash and XML are both young in the computer industry. Your knowledge of these technologies will suit you well for some time to come, allowing you to start developing your own applications that cross the boundaries of operating systems and microprocessors.

One last comment—have fun! Whether you program for a living or do it as a hobby, it shouldn't be drudgery. Take a break from the day-to-day grind and learn something new.

9: JavaScript-Flash Interactions

Klaus L. Hougesen is a designer and art director currently living in Tokyo and working for Furifuri.com. When he's not working, he is enjoying life, photographing the world around him, painting, practicing kendo, doing freelance work, and trying to keep his personal site (www.alphalounge.org) up to date. Klaus takes inspiration from the people around him and B movies from the '50s.

A lot can be done when JavaScript and Flash work together. The combination of these two technologies can create very complex applications. In this chapter, we'll explore various issues pertaining to client-side integration via JavaScript.

JavaScript, a scripting language that is interpreted by a client's browser, can be used to open Flash and add to its features. Like any other programming language, JavaScript has benefits and shortcomings; if used correctly, it can be an invaluable tool for any Web developer.

This chapter assumes you're familiar with JavaScript and are some-what comfortable with dynamic HTML. JavaScript is a big subject, and this chapter will teach you only the basics. To truly harness the power of client-side scripting in conjunction with Flash, you should learn the more complex aspects of JavaScript programming via alternate resources.

The Basics of Integration

Flash is a very stable platform for programming. ActionScripts run com-piled inside the Flash player and are executed outside the normal client-side architecture. This means that once you'60ve created and compiled your pro-gram, it will run on nearly every operating system that supports Flash.

Sadly, this is not the case with JavaScript, which is implemented differently in various browsers and operating systems. Simple things such as opening a new window or calculating sizes and positions can sometimes become so convoluted that you may feel as if you are trudging alongside Sisyphus.

There are two methods for creating JavaScript-Flash integrations. One approach is to directly influence the Flash plug-in by sending various com-mands to and from an in-page embedded player. This method is executed through the FSCommand function, which communicates with a Flash movie's host application (in our case, a JavaScript-supporting browser) and the built-in methods of embedded movie objects accessible by the JavaScript object model.

The other method is a more low-level approach in which communication between the player and JavaScript is one-way only. An example of this is to use document.write() to write out an entire embed block based on some prior information.

We will discuss both methods in this chapter.

Support for Scripted Interaction

At the time of this writing, only Internet Explorer and Netscape Navigator support any sort of communication with the Flash plug-in. In Internet Explorer, this is accomplished via ActiveX. Though stable and fast, ActiveX is not supported on the Macintosh. Netscape handles things in an entirely different way. It uses a Java resource handler called LiveConnect, which creates a connection between HTML elements, Java, JavaScript, and plug-ins. Because Java is supported on Mac, so are integrations between JavaScript and Flash.

 Because LiveConnect is Java, it adds approximately 15 seconds to load time while Netscape's Java engine is initialized and started.

If you intend to develop scripted Flash movies, you need to know which environments your application will run in. Currently, scripted Flash is supported in the following browsers:

- Netscape 3.x and 4.x on Win95/98/NT/2000/XP and Mac PPC

- Internet Explorer 3 and up on Win95/98/NT/2000/XP

These browser do not support FSCommand:

- Anything running on Windows 3.1 to 95

- Anything running on 68k-based Macs

- Internet Explorer browsers on any Mac

- Netscape 6.x

 LiveConnect doesn't work with the new Mozilla engine because Mozilla requires all plug-in vendors to update their plug-ins to the new plug-in API. For more information, go to http://www.mozilla.org/docs/plugin.html.

Browsers that don't support FSCommand simply lack the support for ActiveX (Internet Explorer) or LiveConnect (Netscape 4 and up).

There's no significant difference between accessing JavaScript via FSCommands or the getUrl("javascript:") method; however, the latter is more widely supported (**Figure 9.1**), so I strongly recommend you use it exclusively.

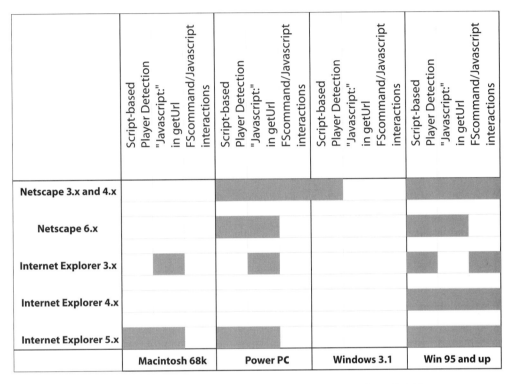

Figure 9.1 *Matrix showing various plug-in methods support on a number of platforms.*

Except for Internet Explorer 3.x on Windows 95 and up, where FSCommand is the only way to connect with a client script, most Web sites don't require a version created for Internet Explorer 3.x browsers. It's your choice whether you want to spend the extra time supporting Internet Explorer 3.x browsers. In this chapter I've chosen not to.

Controlling Flash Plug-ins with JavaScript

Controlling the Flash plug-in via a scripting language is easy and offers an array of benefits to developers and users. With these methods, outside sources can control the plug-in and make the playing movie aware of—and respond to—previously inaccessible information. This section gives a brief overview of how basic JavaScript-to-Flash interaction works. I'll also provide an example of a possible use for this methodology.

JavaScript-to-Flash Interaction

JavaScript can access the properties of an embedded movie via the window.document object of the page, but it's important that the embedded movie has a number of properties correctly set.

For Internet Explorer, the <OBJECT></OBJECT> tag has to have an ID set. For Netscape, the <EMBED></EMBED> tag has to have swLiveConnect set to TRUE and a NAME defined.

An example embedded movie looks like this:

```
<OBJECT classid="clsid:D27CDB6E-AE6D-11cf-96B8-444553540000"
codebase="http://download.macromedia.com/pub/shockwave/
cabs/flash/swflash.cab#version=5,0,0,0"
WIDTH=400 HEIGHT=300 id="Mymovie">
    <PARAM NAME=movie VALUE="moviesourcefile">
    <PARAM NAME=quality VALUE=high>
    <PARAM NAME=bgcolor VALUE=#000000>
    <EMBED src="moviesourcefile" quality=high
    → bgcolor=#000000 WIDTH=400
HEIGHT=300 NAME=Mymovie swLiveConnect=true
TYPE="application/x-shockwave-flash"
    → PLUGINSPAGE="http://www.macromedia.com/shockwave/download/
index.cgi?P1_Prod_Version=ShockwaveFlash">
    </EMBED>
</OBJECT>
```

Note that both the ID and the NAME properties have the same name. This is necessary for us to access the movie by using the same name handle.

An example of accessing this embedded player via its name is `window.document.Mymovie.[method]`, where `method` is one of the movie's methods accessible by JavaScript.

When Flash calls a JavaScript in a page, we have the option of using FSCommand or `getUrl()`.

The `getUrl()` option is fairly simple: Imagine we have a JavaScript function called `popup()` on the same page as the Flash movie. Calling this function via the `getUrl()` option would be as simple as this:

```
getUrl("JavaScript:popup()");
```

If we choose the other option of using FSCommand, we have a bit more work on our hands. Since FSCommand runs through the browser's ActiveX layer on Internet Explorer, we have to add a bit of VBScript to catch the FSCommand and send it to JavaScript, as follows:

```
<SCRIPT LANGUAGE="VBScript">
<!--
Sub Mymovie_FSCommand(ByVal command, ByVal args)
    call Mymovie_DoFSCommand(command, args)
end sub
// -->
</SCRIPT>
```

Netscape will completely ignore this part, but the essence of the previous code is very simple: When executing an FSCommand in Flash, Internet Explorer will automatically fire a VB event under ActiveX. We use this fact to re-map the event and its arguments to JavaScript instead.

If we use an FSCommand like `fscommand ("changePage", "./index.html")`, the corresponding JavaScript code will look like this:

```
<SCRIPT LANGUAGE="JavaScript">
<!--
function Mymovie_DoFSCommand(command, args) {
  if (command == "changePage") {
    document.location.href=args;
  }
}
//-->
</SCRIPT>
```

Making the Back Button Work Inside Flash

Usability advocates have a bone to pick with Flash: The browser's Back button does not work as intended when a Flash movie is playing. Instead of returning to a previous section or page of a site, as it does in standard HTML pages, the Back button unloads the Flash movie and returns to the last page you visited.

 The following example will remedy the Back button problem by using simple JavaScript and ActionScript. You can find this example in the back-button folder in this chapter's example folder on the CD-ROM. To follow along, open flash.html, index.html, and page1.html.

First, load index.html in a suitable browser. Click around a bit, and then click the back button on the browser. Notice how it influences the embedded movie.

The Flash movie itself is pretty straightforward: In each visited section of the Flash movie, it loads one of the numbered page[X].html files in a hidden frame to generate a history object we can use. Each of these numbered pages, in turn, initializes the JavaScript function setPage() in the main frame, which updates the _root.page variable in the Flash movie. For example, "page4.html" sets _root.page = "page4".

The important part of our example is this small JavaScript in the flash.html file:

```
<script language="JavaScript">
function setPage(nPage) {
 if (window.document.backmovie) {
  window.document.backmovie.SetVariable("page", nPage);
 }
}
</script>
```

Notice the SetVariable() function, which makes the setting of variables possible via JavaScript; it is one of the methods available via Flash.

See Appendix B for more information about the various methods available. You should familiarize yourself with the Flash methods, and which properties you can read and write.

Storing and Retrieving Information

Storing and retrieving information via JavaScript is one of the most useful things to know. It's the hidden ace that enables you to perform feats impossible or burdensome without it. It provides the data you need to create things such as cookie-based user customization, global scope variables that can be easily read and written to by other technologies, and much more.

There are numerous ways to store information on a page via JavaScript. The three most common practices are as follows:

Cookies. Where a small amount of data is stored on the host system. This is the most reliable way of storing data client-side; cookies can retain information even after a client closes. For better or worse, people are wary of cookies, often setting their browser options to warn them if a site attempts to write a cookie. They can then decide whether to allow the site to write the cookie or not. If they choose not to accept the cookie, it might break your page.

Query strings. Where data is directly accessible in the URL of the page. This is supported universally, but it has a number of reliability issues; for instance, a user could retype the URL and, in so doing, lose all data.

Hidden forms. Where a hidden form field stores information on the page. A hidden frame or layers can easily be used as a substitute for a form field (as show in the previous example).

 These methods of storing data client-side make sense only for temporary data or data that can be "lost" without major consequences. Data that needs a more permanent storage solution should always be stored on a server. (Databases are good for this.)

Passing Cookie Data through a Query String

The following example uses JavaScript to store a cookie and send that data to Flash via a query string. This method can be used wherever settings should be retained between sessions. In the Back button example, we used the `setVariable()` method to pass data to Flash. This method can be used in the following example, but it isn't really necessary and isn't as widely supported as the query string technique. As a bonus, the example is fully supported in all browsers in which the "javascript:" in getUrl() method is supported.

 This example (**Figure 9.2**) can be found in the cookies folder. To follow along, open the cookies.html and cookie.js files.

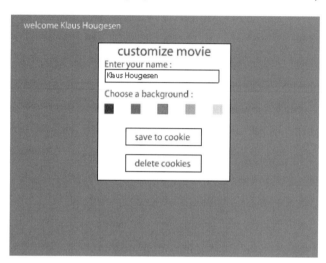

Figure 9.2
The customization example interface.

The example is based on two specific features of browsers and the Flash plug-in.

- You can use document.write-type calls to dynamically create the HTML content of a page on the client side. Doing so lets you change the embed section of our page depending on information stored client-side (in this case, cookies).

- You can pass name-value pairs (in a URL-encoded string) to the Flash movie by adding a query string to the movie's path. This is done within the Object-Embed section of the HTML code of the host page, like this:

```
<OBJECT classid="clsid:D27CDB6E-AE6D-11cf-96B8-444553540000"
codebase="http://download.macromedia.com/pub/shockwave/
cabs/flash/swflash.cab#version=5,0,0,0"
WIDTH=400 HEIGHT=300 id="myMovie">
    <PARAM NAME=movie
    → VALUE="myMovie.swf?var1=value1&var2=value2">
    <PARAM NAME=quality VALUE=high>
    <PARAM NAME=bgcolor VALUE=#000000>
    <EMBED src="myMovie.swf?var1=value1&var2=value2"
    → quality=high
```

```
    bgcolor=#000000 WIDTH=400 HEIGHT=300 NAME= myMovie
    TYPE="application/x-shockwave-flash"
  → PLUGINSPAGE="http://www.macromedia.com/shockwave/download/
    index.cgi?P1_Prod_Version=ShockwaveFlash">
        </EMBED>
      </OBJECT>
```

Notice how the two movie sources in the embedded object have
`?var1=value1&var2=value2` added to the end. The Flash plug-in will
catch these variables and values and make them available for use in the
root of the movie.

To access these variables, a simple `_root.var1` and `_root.var2` is sufficient.

To pass a cookie to a movie, we have to follow these steps:

1. Create some JavaScript routines that handle the creation and retrieval
of the cookies, some of which we'll call later in our Flash movie using
`getUrl("javascript:")`.

2. Dynamically write out the object and embed tags using
`document.write()`, and then add our cookie information to the
src of the movie using basic name-value query string formatting.

3. Create some routines in our Flash file that use this passed information,
and some routines that will call our JavaScript routines.

Cookies are stored in the document.cookie object of the page, which
returns a semicolon-delimited list of name-value pairs in the format
`name=value` with all the cookies associated with the domain of the document. This means that the string returned by document.cookie may contain
other cookie values that have nothing to do with the data we're seeking;
therefore, we'll also have to create some JavaScript routines that search
for our specific cookies and return the data they contain.

All the data written to a cookie is automatically stored in the browser's
memory until the browser quits. If an expiration date is part of the cookie
data, and the specified time has not yet expired, the cookie data is saved to
the cookie data file; otherwise, the cookie is deleted.

As many as 20 pairs can be stored in the cookie property for a given domain
with no more than 4,000 characters in the cookie. A standard cookie object
takes the following parameters, of which only name and value are obliga-
tory: *name*, *value*, *expiration date*, *path*, *domain*, and *secure*. In the following
example, however, we'll only concern ourselves with the name, value and
expiration date parameters.

Our example will do two things: Remember the user's name and recall which background color the user chose.

We use the following JavaScript code to store the cookie information that we want:

```
function setCookie(name, value, expires, path, domain,
→ secure) {
  var today = new Date()
  var expires = new Date(today.getTime() + expires);
  value = escape(value);
  expires = (expires) ? ';expires=' + expires.toGMTString()
  → :'';
  path = (path) ? ';path=' + path :'';
  domain  = (domain) ? ';domain=' + domain :'';
  secure  = (secure) ? ';secure' :'';
document.cookie =
  name + '=' + value + expires + path + domain + secure;
}
```

Some quick notes about this code:

- The `var = (var) ? ';var=' + value:';` syntax is an abbreviated form of an if...else statement.

- We use JavaScript to get information about the current time. We could also do this in Flash, but for the sake of compatibility, we'll skip that option.

- The Date object in JavaScript returns a number that corresponds to milliseconds relative to zero hours on January 1, 1970. Because the expiration date has to be in GMT format, we use the `toGMTString()` function of the *Date* object to convert the string to a standardized format. Normally, I'd recommend using the newer `toUTCString()`, but it's not supported by Netscape 3.x browsers.

To store our gathered data, we need to call the above function with a `getUrl("javascript:setCookie('CookieName','CookieValue', 'Expiration date');")` call in the Flash movie.

We have to make two calls to this function—one for the background color and one for the user name. Unfortunately, you can set cookies only one at a time, so two getUrl setCookie calls after another will not work. Therefore we will call the `setCookie()` function twice in the same `getUrl ()`, like this:

```
getUrl("javascript:setCookie(values);setCookie(values)");
```

To retrieve our cookies, we use the following JavaScript code:

```
function getCookie(name) {
    var cookies = document.cookie;
    var start = cookies.indexOf(name + '=');
    if (start == -1) return null;
    var len = start + name.length + 1;
    var end = cookies.indexOf(';',len);
    if (end == -1) end = cookies.length;
    return unescape(cookies.substring(len,end));
}
```

As you can see, the function above needs to be passed only the name of the cookie in order to find the value of it. Because we know the name and each cookie is separated by a semicolon, we can use these two pieces of information to extract a substring of the document.cookie string.

To pass our cookie values to Flash, we use document.write to dynamically create our object and embed blocks. But first we have to figure out if this is the first time the user has accessed the page. This happens in the following JavaScript block in cookie.html:

```
if(getCookie('Ccolor')){
Ccolor= getCookie('Ccolor');
Cname= getCookie('Cname');
str="cookieName="+Cname+"&";
str+="cookieColor="+Ccolor+"&";
}else{
str="";
}
```

I have called my two cookies Ccolor and Cname, and I use the `getCookie('Ccolor')` function to check for the presence of my cookies. If they are found, I construct a name-value query string from the values of the two cookies. If they aren't found, I reset my query string as a precaution.

After that, all I need to do is `document.write()` my object, embed the tags in the page, and add to the output the query string I just created. Once I do this, my two variables will be available for use in the Flash movie.

The Flash movie itself is basic; examine it and notice how the expiration date is set based on UTC in the first frame of the as:basic layer.

```
day = 86400000;
week = day * 7;
month = day * 31;
year = day * 365;
expires=1*day;"
```

The previous code sets the expiration date to 24 hours later.

To delete a cookie, I call the delCookie("cookieName") JavaScript function, which sets the expiration date of the named cookie to January 1, 1970 (which, as you might recall, is the zero hour of the UTC standard time format).

As you see, it is not always necessary to use LiveConnect or the Internet Explorer equivalent to create usable integrations between JavaScript and Flash; sometimes it will be a hindrance, instead.

Flash and Third-Party Plug-ins

In this section we'll look at some methods of communicating with a third-party plug-in, RealPlayer, and we'll use what we learn to create a mini API to control it. The general theory behind the example in this section can be applied to nearly every plug-in that can be called with JavaScript methods.

The RealPlayer Plug-in

The RealPlayer plug-in is much better suited for streaming audio than Flash because it was designed with sound in mind. I encourage you to take advantage of its powers in your Flash movies, which is exactly what we'll do in this section.

 Open player.html and player.rpm from the flashreal player folder. First, take a look at player.html (**Figure 9.3**).

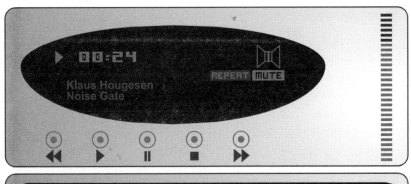

Figure 9.3
The customization example interface.

When you load player.html in a browser, you should be able to see the player (make sure you have Real Player G2 or newer installed).

 RealNetworks made some confusing version jumps a while back, changing its player from Version 5.0 to Version G2. Shortly after, when Apple Computer launched the G3, the player reverted to Version 6.0. The current version is 8.5 or above. Also note that RealPlayer Basic is Real's free player, while RealPlayer Plus can only be bought. The Basic version, however, will suffice for our example.

The RealPlayer format is engineered for streaming. This means RealPlayer can detect a user's bandwidth and send the appropriate-quality audio stream. Luckily for us, RealPlayer uses the same architecture as Flash for communicating with JavaScript. We'll use this to make a small JavaScript API for the interactions between the two plug-ins.

The RealPlayer uses a special file format called RPM to store a list of clips to play. The format is pretty simple—it's a collection of URLs that references Real files and/or MP3 files.

It could look like one of these:

```
http://www.foobar.com/real/01.rm
http://www.foobar.com/real/02.rm
http://www.foobar.com/real/01.mp3
```

When you create your own RPM file, be sure to use strict HTTP URL format in the links (no spaces, and so on).

 You can easily test your own RPM file by renaming its file extension to RAM and double-clicking it. The RealPlayer should open and start playing your list of files.

To embed RealPlayer on the page, use the following code:

```
<OBJECT ID="player" NAME="player"
CLASSID="clsid:CFCDAA03-8BE4-11cf-B84B-0020AFBBCCFA" HEIGHT="1"
  WIDTH="1">
<PARAM NAME="controls" VALUE="imagewindow">
<PARAM NAME="console" VALUE="player">
<PARAM NAME="autostart" VALUE="false">
<PARAM NAME="prefetch" VALUE="false">
<PARAM NAME="src" VALUE="playlist.rpm">
<PARAM NAME="nologo" VALUE="true">
<param name="backgroundCOLOR" value="#ffffff">
<EMBED SRC="playlist.rpm" nologo="true"
→ backgroundCOLOR="#ffffff"
type="audio/x-pn-realaudio-plugin" CONSOLE="player"
→ NAME="player"
CONTROLS="imagewindow" HEIGHT="0" WIDTH="0" PREFETCH="false"
AUTOSTART="false">
</OBJECT>
```

As you can see, this code resembles the way we embed Flash files on a page, the sole difference being its parameters. Like the Flash plug-in, RealPlayer uses Java to enable LiveConnect in Netscape. This feature is, however, always enabled by default; only if you include NOJAVA = TRUE will it be disabled.

The Mini API

To let our plug-ins chat with each other, we need to create two things: JavaScript routines that handle the communication between JavaScript and Flash, and a wrapper for the RealPlayer API that will let us query and set various data in the embedded RealPlayer plug-in.

For the JavaScript-to-Flash interactions, we use the same function as before:

```
function flashSetVariable(movieName,variableName,value){
  window.document[movieName].SetVariable(variableName,value);
}
```

We use the SetVariable() function of the JavaScript Flash methods to send data directly to Flash's root level.

Load the player.html file and look at the JavaScript block in the header. All information about clip length, clip title, author, length, and so on, are handled by the `checkstate()` JavaScript function.

```
function checkstate(){
state=window.document[RealPlayer].GetPlayState();
if(state==0){
 state="stopped";
 }else if(state==1){
 state="contacting";
 }else if(state==2){
 state="buffering";
 }else if(state==3){
 state="playing";
 }else if(state==4){
 state="paused";
 }else if(state==5){
    state="seeking";
    }
flashSetVariable(movieName,"stream_status",state);
flashSetVariable(movieName,"stereo",vl_stereo());
flashSetVariable(movieName,"currenttime",ci_getpos());

total=ci_gettotal();
flashSetVariable(movieName,"playlist_total",total);

current=ci_getcurrent();
flashSetVariable(movieName,"title",ci_gettitle(current));
flashSetVariable(movieName,"author",ci_getauthor(current));
}
```

`GetPlayState()` is part of the JavaScript RealPlayer methods. It returns a number from 0–5 depending on what state RealPlayer is currently in. We send this information to Flash by using our `flashSetVariable()` function. The information sent will trigger two movie clips in the Flash movie that monitor _root.stream_status, namely the player state and stream state clips. They perform no other action than visual confirmation of RealPlayer's current state.

TIP Read more about the parameters used in the embed section in the dev zone at realnetworks.com (http://service.real.com/help/library/guides/extend/embed.htm).

flashSetVariable(movieName,"stereo",v1_stereo()); is a bit different here. We set the root.stereo variable in the Flash movie by calling v1_stereo() inside of flashSetVariable().

Let's examine the v1_stereo() function

```
function v1_stereo(){
    stereo=window.document[Realplayer].GetStereoState();
    if(stereo){stereo="stereo";}else{stereo="mono";}
    return stereo;
}
```

All it does is query RealPlayer as to whether the clip currently playing is mono or stereo. It then returns the stereo variable, which is used in the Flash movie by the speaker clip to give visual confirmation of the current clip's stereo state.

All the other functions called within checkstate() work in much the same way except for the ci_getpos() function, which uses another function called convertMsec() to convert the returned milliseconds to the more readable Hour:Min:Seconds format.

To call this data, we could use a getUrl("javascript:") in our Flash movie, but we'd run into a problem we wouldn't encounter if we had used FSCommand. The JavaScript in getUrl() method triggers a browser-level event that's slower than the route through the ActiveX component. It also produces an audible event "click" in some versions of Internet Explorer.

To avoid this, we could use FSCommands in Internet Explorer. Instead, we use a feature of JavaScript called setInterval, a method of calling functions by a timed interval. To be sure that all the scripts have been loaded, we place a call to checkstate() via setInterval at the bottom of our page.

```
<SCRIPT LANGUAGE="JavaScript" TYPE="text/JavaScript">
<!--
//setIntervall calls the checkstate() function every second
timer= setInterval("checkstate()",1000);
//-->
</SCRIPT>
```

Adding Basic Features to the API

We still need to add some basic features such as play and stop to the mini API. Here, you can see the script that starts playing the clips:

```
function pl_play(){
if (window.document[Realplayer].CanPlay()==true){
    window.document[Realplayer].DoPlay();
    flashSetVariable(movieName,"state","playing");
    }
}
```

If you've examined the RealPlayer methods, you may realize that all the play-related methods have an added query function that returns TRUE if a call to the main function will accomplish anything. We check this function in the code above, and if it returns TRUE, we send off the DoPlay() function to start playing. The same goes for all the other play-related functions.

The last thing we have to add is toggle functions such as repeat and mute.

```
function vl_mute(){
if (window.document[Realplayer].GetMute()==true){
    window.document[Realplayer].SetMute(false);
    flashSetVariable(movieName,"mute","normal");
}else{
    window.document[Realplayer].SetMute(true);
    flashSetVariable(movieName,"mute","mute");
    }
}
```

There's really not much to it other than noting that the _root.mute variable is monitored by the mute clip in the Flash movie, which changes its current frame to reflect changes to _root.mute.

The repeat function repeats the whole playlist defined in the RPM file instead of replaying just a single clip.

An application like this could be used in many ways. For instance, record companies could add streaming music to their Flashed Web sites without breaking the sense of wholeness by loading a RealPlayer, and the stream would still be protected from download. Other places where you can use the same methods are in 3D plug-ins, text-to-voice plug-ins, and a multitude of other readily available solutions.

Extending the Flash Toolbox

Many of Flash's functions and methods ease application programming, but because Macromedia has prioritized plug-in size over effectiveness, some of its more advanced methods are ineffective or simply not present when compared with JavaScript—among them, *regular expressions*. Regular expressions assist in locating text that matches a predefined pattern of characters or characteristics. For example, a regular expression can be used to find out quickly if an email form field is formatted correctly.

Defining a pattern requires knowledge of a special notation syntax that's beyond the scope of this chapter. A list of syntax can be found in Appendix C.

The next example shows how you can extend Flash's functionality by hooking into various JavaScript functions. The regular expression object is only a small part of this, but I chose this example because of its usefulness.

 This example can be found in the toolbox folder. To follow along, open regularExpressions.html.

We'll start by simply replacing characters with a string (you could use this, for example, to remove all numeric characters from an address). This may sound like a small thing, but when you combine it with the power of regular expressions, you may well be astounded by the possibilities.

The JavaScript code is a basic wrapper for the regular expression object. We'll use this script in our example to quickly enable regular expressions.

```
function replaceCharacters( strValue, strMatchPattern,
→ strReplace ) {
 var objRegExp =  new RegExp( strMatchPattern, 'gi' );
 //replace passed pattern matches with strReplace
  result =  strValue.replace(objRegExp,strReplace);
}
```

To access this function from Flash and use it, we have to do two things:

- Send the data we want to verify—a match pattern and a replacement string—to the JavaScript function.

- Return the result to Flash in a usable way.

We'll use the JavaScript in getUrl() method to send the data from Flash to JavaScript. To send the data back again, we'll create a wrapper for the setVariable() function, which is as simple as the following:

```
function flashSetVariable(movieName,variableName,value)
{
window.document[movieName].SetVariable(variableName,value);
}
```

We'll then call the above function from replaceCharacters() to send the data back again. The final piece of code looks like this:

```
var movieName="regexpress";
function flashSetVariable(movieName,variableName,value)
{
window.document[movieName].SetVariable(variableName,value);
}
function replaceCharacters( strValue, strMatchPattern,
→ strReplace ) {
 var objRegExp =  new RegExp( strMatchPattern, 'gi' );
 //replace passed pattern matches with strReplace
  result =  strValue.replace(objRegExp,strReplace);
  flashSetVariable(movieName,"result",result);
}
```

Notice how I define the movieName variable in the start of the script and use it to minimize the maintenance requirements if I suddenly decide to change the name of my embedded movie.

Try entering different text and search patterns in the fields. Consult Appendix C for various patterns and then search the Web for more information about regular expressions. You may want to try creating your own Flash movie using regular expressions.

 To see some predefined functions, open the regExp.js file from the toolbox folder; it contains a number of examples for you to use.

The benefits of this method of extending Flash should be obvious: No longer are you confined to Flash Player's painfully slow handling of array functions and string manipulation functions. This method is worth using in mathematics-intensive applications, especially those that deal with sorting data. String manipulations also gain a significant speed increase. It does take a tiny amount of time to go from the Flash plug-in to JavaScript and back again, but the speed increase makes any hassle worthwhile.

Opening New Windows

Opening a new window is a marvelous way to maximize screen estate, and lets you show pages in an alternative way.

Pop-up windows, however, can annoy users if they're executed without proper consideration. All pop-up windows break with normal functionality; thus, most users find them slightly irritating. The question is whether the benefits of presenting information in a pop-up outweigh the disadvantages. These are issues you'll have to consider on a project-by-project basis.

To open a new window, we use the `window.open()` function of the window object. Calling `window.open()` by itself is sufficient to open a new window. The function does, however, take a number of variables to customize how the popup will look.

```
window.open(URL, WindowName [, Window features]);
```

You can specify an URL to load into that window or set that parameter to an empty string to allow scripts to `document.write()` to the window. The WindowName parameter lets you give the new window a name that can be referenced later and used by scripts.

A often overlooked problem is that a new window can get buried under the main window; therefore, all scripts that open new windows should include at least a `WindowName.focus()`, which will bring the named window back to the front in case it's already opened. Additional calls to the `window.open()` function with the same WindowName as the previous call will automatically address the previously opened window.

The optional third parameter lets you control different physical parameters of the opened window. It's a single string consisting of a comma-delimited list of attribute/value pairs. For instance, a browser window with only a status bar, menu bar, and a height and width of 400 could be opened like this:

```
popwin = window.open("blank.html",
"popwin","statusbar,menubar,HEIGHT=400,width=400");
popwin.focus();
```

 You can find plenty of lists of possible attributes and their values via a simple Web search.

Controlling a Pop-up Window from Flash

Now we'll open a window and have Flash interact with it. I've chosen to have a Flash movie "push" a window around the screen (**Figure 9.4**).

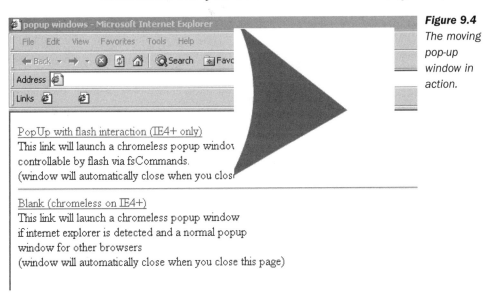

Figure 9.4
The moving pop-up window in action.

 This example can be found in the popup windows folder. To follow along, open popup.html and launcher.html.

To move the window, I use the `window.moveTo(x,y)` method, which takes two parameters: the *x* and *y* value of the window's new position. All I need to do is call this function continually from a Flash movie, with the new *x* and *y* parameters, but here I run into trouble. Using the `getUrl("javascript:")` method triggers a browser-level event, which is slow when called continually and, as you may recall from our RealPlayer example, triggers an audible event "click" in some versions of Internet Explorer. To overcome this, I use FSCommands: They're faster when called continually and they traverse the browser object through ActiveX, with no audible click.

 To enable FSCommands for Internet Explorer, remember to include a small VBScript to catch the FSCommands and relay them to JavaScript.

It's not a good idea to make the movable window move outside the user's screen area; therefore, I include a small code snippet to detects the user's current screen height and width and send that information to Flash via the document.write() method:

```
//create our init string with the width and height of
→ the page
str="w="+screen.width+"&h="+screen.height;
//create our embed code and assign it to the embed variable
embed="<OBJECT classid='clsid:D27CDB6E-AE6D-11cf-96B8-
→ 444553540000'";
embed+=" codebase='http://download.macromedia.com/
→ pub/shockwave/cabs/flash/swflash.cab#version=5,0,0,0'";
embed+=" WIDTH=100% HEIGHT=100% id=popper>";
embed+="    <PARAM NAME=movie VALUE='popper.swf?"+str+"'>";
embed+="    <PARAM NAME=quality VALUE=high>";
embed+="    <PARAM NAME=bgcolor VALUE=#ffffff>";
embed+="    <EMBED src='popper.swf?"+str+"'";
embed+="  quality=high bgcolor=#ffffff WIDTH=100%
HEIGHT=100% swLiveConnect=true NAME=popper";
embed+=" TYPE='application/x-shockwave-flash'
→ PLUGINSPAGE='http://www.macromedia.com/shockwave/download/
→ index.cgi?P1_Prod_Version=ShockwaveFlash'>";
embed+="    </EMBED>";
embed+="  </OBJECT>";
//output the embed variable
document.write(embed);
```

Inside Flash, the engine clip uses this information to stop the movement of the pop-up window when the maximum values are reached. Just remember to subtract the size of the opened window from the actual values.

```
if (startX>_root.w-200) {
  startX = _root.w-200;
}
if (startY>_root.h-200) {
  startY = _root.h-200;
}
```

Now all I have to do is open the new window. If you look at launcher.html, you'll see a JavaScript block containing some pop-up code. It's invoked by calling:

```
popUp(url,name,w,h,extra,left,top);
```

This wrapper for the `window.open()` method has some added features: The width(w) and height(h) have been separated from the attributes string, and two additional parameters (`left` and `top`) have been added.

When set, `left` and `top` will place the pop-up window at those two coordinate points. If they're not defined, the function will automatically center the pop-up at the middle of the screen.

Furthermore, two triggers have been added inside the function:

```
autoclose=true;
chromeless=true;
```

When set to TRUE automatically, `autoclose` will try to close the pop-up window if the origin window changes to a different URL (for example, if the user clicks the Back button).

`Chromeless` is a special variable that, when set to TRUE, lets you launch a browser window stripped of all interface, even borders and title bar. It only works, however, in Internet Explorer version 4.x and up. If Internet Explorer isn't detected, the function will try to launch a normal browser window.

When launching a chromeless pop-up, the function first launches a full-screen Internet Explorer in kiosk mode and then resizes it to the given height and width.

 For your convenience, I've included this function as the popup.js file in the popup windows folder. Feel free to use it for other projects.

Conclusion

In this chapter, we've discussed the basics of using JavaScript with Flash, as well as how to extend Flash's functionality by calling our own custom JavaScript functions or using third party plug-ins. JavaScript is an effective tool for opening Flash and adding to its features. Like all tools, though, it comes with some restrictions. You should consider whether narrowing the scope of the supported browsers on your project is worth the added functionality.

I hope you've gained some new insights into Flash and where it can be extended to cover new areas of functionality. The power of JavaScript is definitely worth the effort of using it.

Appendices

Appendix A: Reserved Words

ASP

And	Else	Implements	On	Single
As	ElseIf	In	Option	Static
Boolean	Empty	Integer	Optional	Stop
ByRef	End	Is	Or	Sub
Byte	EndIf	Let	ParamArray	Then
ByVal	Enum	Like	Preserve	To
Call	Eqv	Long	Private	True
Case	Event	Loop	Public	Type
Class	Exit	Lset	RaiseEvent	TypeOf
Const	False	Me	ReDim	Until
Currency	For	Mod	Rem	Variant
Debug	Function	New	Resume	Wend
Dim	Get	Next	Rset	While
Do	GoTo	Not	Select	With
Double	If	Nothing	Set	Xor
Each	Imp	Null	Shared	

ColdFusion

Application	Client	Form	Session	Variables
Caller	Cookie	Request	ThisTag	
CGI	File	Server	URL	

Microsoft Access

ADD	CreateTableDef	FUNCTION	Macro
ALL	CreateUser	GENERAL	Match
Alphanumeric	CreateWorkspace	GetObject	Max, Min, Mod
ALTER	CURRENCY	GetOption	MEMO
AND	CurrentUser	GotoPage	Module
ANY	DATABASE	GROUP	MONEY
Application	DATE	GROUP BY	Move
AS	DATETIME	GUID	NAME
ASC	DELETE	HAVING	NewPassword
Assistant	DESC	Idle	NO
AUTOINCREMENT	Description	IEEEDOUBLE, IEEESINGLE	Not
Avg	DISALLOW	If	NULL
BETWEEN	DISTINCT	IGNORE	NUMBER, NUMERIC
BINARY	DISTINCTROW	Imp	Object
BIT	Document	IN, In	OFF
BOOLEAN	DOUBLE	INDEX	OLEOBJECT
BY	DROP	Index, Indexes	ON
BYTE	Echo	INNER	OpenRecordset
CHAR, CHARACTER	Else	INSERT	OPTION
COLUMN	End	InsertText	OR, Or
CompactDatabase	Eqv	INT, INTEGER, INTEGER1	ORDER
CONSTRAINT	Error	INTO	Outer
Container	EXISTS	IS, Is	OWNERACCESS
Count	Exit	JOIN	Parameter
COUNTER	FALSE	KEY	PARAMETERS
CREATE	Field, Fields	LEFT	Partial
CreateDatabase	FillCache	Level	PERCENT
CreateField	FLOAT, FLOAT4, FLOAT8	Like	PIVOT
CreateGroup	FOREIGN	LOGICAL, LOGICAL1	PRIMARY
CreateIndex	Form, Forms	LONG, LONGBINARY, LONGTEXT	PROCEDURE
CreateObject	FROM		Property
CreateProperty	Full		
CreateRelation			

384

Microsoft Access (continued)

Queries

Query

Quit

REAL

Recalc

Recordset

REFERENCES

Refresh

RefreshLink

RegisterDatabase

Relation

Repaint

RepairDatabase

Report

Reports

Requery

RIGHT

SCREEN

SECTION

SELECT

SET

SetFocus

SetOption

SHORT

SINGLE

SMALLINT

SOME

SQL

StDev, StDevP

STRING

Sum

TABLE

TableDef, TableDefs

TableID

TEXT

TIME, TIMESTAMP

TOP

TRANSFORM

TRUE

Type

UNION

UNIQUE

UPDATE

VALUE

VALUES

Var, VarP

VARBINARY, VARCHAR

WHERE

WITH

Workspace

Xor

Year

YES

YESNO

PHP

$argc	else	list()
$argv	elseif	new
$HTTP_COOKIE_VARS	empty()	not
$HTTP_GET_VARS	endfor	NULL
$HTTP_POST_VARS	endforeach	or
$HTTP_ENV_VARS	endif	parent
$HTTP_SERVER_VARS	endswitch	PHP_OS
$PHP_SELF	endwhile	PHP_VERSION
$$HTTP_POST_FILES	E_ALL	print()
__FILE__	E_ERROR	require()
__LINE__	E_PARSE	require_once()
__sleep	E_WARNING	return
__wakeup	exit()	static
and	extends	stdClass
break	FALSE	switch
case	for	$this
class	foreach	TRUE
continue	function	var
default	global	virtual()
die()	if	while
do	include()	xor
echo()	include_once()	

SQL

ADD	CONVERT	EXISTS
ALL	COUNT	EXIT
ALTER	CREATE	FETCH
AND	CROSS	FILE
ANY	CURRENT	FILLFACTOR
AS	CURRENT_DATE	FLOPPY
ASC	CURRENT_TIME	FOR
AUTHORIZATION	CURRENT_TIMESTAMP	FOREIGN
AVG	CURRENT_USER	FREETEXT
BACKUP	CURSOR	FREETEXTTABLE
BEGIN	DATABASE	FROM
BETWEEN	DBCC	FULL
BREAK	DEALLOCATE	GOTO
BROWSE	DECLARE	GRANT
BULK	DEFAULT	GROUP
BY	DELETE	HAVING
CASCADE	DENY	HOLDLOCK
CASE	DESC	IDENTITY
CHECK	DISK	IDENTITYCOL
CHECKPOINT	DISTINCT	IDENTITY_INSERT
CLOSE	DISTRIBUTED	IF
CLUSTERED	DOUBLE	IN
COALESCE	DROP	INDEX
COLUMN	DUMMY	INNER
COMMIT	DUMP	INSERT
COMMITTED	ELSE	INTERSECT
COMPUTE	END	INTO
CONFIRM	ERRLVL	IS
CONSTRAINT	ERROREXIT	ISOLATION
CONTAINS	ESCAPE	JOIN
CONTAINSTABLE	EXCEPT	KEY
CONTINUE	EXEC	KILL
CONTROLROW	EXECUTE	LEFT

SQL (continued)

LEVEL	PREPARE	SUM
LIKE	PRIMARY	SYSTEM_USER
LINENO	PRINT	TABLE
LOAD	PRIVILEGES	TAPE
MAX	PROC	TEMP
MIN	PROCEDURE	TEMPORARY
MIRROREXIT	PROCESSEXIT	TEXTSIZE
NATIONAL	PUBLIC	THEN
NOCHECK	RAISERROR	TO
NONCLUSTERED	READ	TOP
NOT	READTEXT	TRAN
NULL	RECONFIGURE	TRANSACTION
NULLIF	REFERENCES	TRIGGER
OF	REPEATABLE	TRUNCATE
OFF	REPLICATION	TSEQUAL
OFFSETS	RESTORE	UNCOMMITTED
ON	RESTRICT	UNION
ONCE	RETURN	UNIQUE
ONLY	REVOKE	UPDATE
OPEN	RIGHT	UPDATETEXT
OPENDATASOURCE	ROLLBACK	USE
OPENQUERY	ROWCOUNT	USER
OPENROWSET	ROWGUIDCOL	VALUES
OPTION	RULE	VARYING
OR	SAVE	VIEW
ORDER	SCHEMA	WAITFOR
OUTER	SELECT	WHEN
OVER	SERIALIZABLE	WHERE
PERCENT	SESSION_USER	WHILE
PERM	SET	WITH
PERMANENT	SETUSER	WORK
PIPE	SHUTDOWN	WRITETEXT
PLAN	SOME	
PRECISION	STATISTICS	

Appendix B: Standard Methods

GETVARIABLE

Syntax	GetVariable(varName)
Description	Returns the value of the Flash variable specified by varName. Returns null if the variable does not exist. The argument type is string.

Example	var firstName = movie.GetVariable("FirstName");
	
	var radioButtonValue =
	movie.GetVariable("/Form/RadioButton:Value");

Plug-in Version	4, 5
ActiveX Version	4, 5

GOTOFRAME

Syntax	GotoFrame(frameNumber)
Description	Activates the frame number specified by frameNumber in the current movie. If the data for a requested frame is not yet available, the player goes to the last frame available and stops, causing unexpected results during playback. Use the PercentLoaded method to determine if enough of the movie is available to execute the GotoFrame method. The argument frameNumber is zero-based; that is, frameNumber is 0 in the first frame of the movie, 1 for the second frame, and so on. This differs from the Goto action within Flash, which begins at 1. The argument type is integer.
Example	movie.GotoFrame(24);
Plug-in Version	2, 3, 4, 5
ActiveX Version	2, 3, 4, 5

ISPLAYING

Syntax	IsPlaying()
Description	Returns true if the movie is currently playing.
Example	if (movie.IsPlaying()) { alert("movie is playing"); }
Plug-in Version	2, 3, 4, 5
ActiveX Version	2

Syntax	IsPlaying()
Description	Returns true if the movie is currently playing.
Example	if (movie.IsPlaying()) { alert("movie is playing"); }
Plug-in Version	NA
ActiveX Version	3, 4, 5

Syntax	LoadMovie(layerNumber, url)
Description	Loads the movie identified by URL to the layer specified by layerNumber. The argument type is integer for layerNumber and string for URL.
Example	movie.LoadMovie(0, "mymovie.swf");
Plug-in Version	3, 4, 5
ActiveX Version	3, 4, 5

Syntax	Pan (x, y, mode)
Description	Pans a zoomed-in movie to the coordinates specified by x and y. Use mode to specify whether the values for x and y are pixels or a percent of the window. When mode is 0, the coordinates are pixels; when mode is 1, the coordinates are percent of the window. Pan does not pan beyond the boundaries of the zoomed-in movie. The argument type for all arguments is integer.
Example	This example pans 50% right and 50% down: movie.Pan(50, 50, 1) This example pans –25 pixels left and –25 pixels up: movie.Pan(-25, -25, 0)
Plug-in Version	2, 3, 4, 5
ActiveX Version	2, 3, 4, 5

Syntax	PercentLoaded()
Description	Returns the percent of the Flash Player movie that has streamed into the browser so far; possible values are from 0 to 100.
Example	if (movie.PercentLoaded() == 100) { loaded = true; }
Plug-in Version	2, 3, 4, 5
ActiveX Version	2, 3, 4, 5

PLAY

Syntax	`Play()`
Description	Starts playing the movie.
Example	`movie.Play();`
Plug-in Version	2, 3, 4, 5
ActiveX Version	2, 3, 4, 5

REWIND

Syntax	`Rewind()`
Description	Goes to the first frame.
Example	`movie.Rewind();`
Plug-in Version	2, 3, 4, 5
ActiveX Version	2, 3, 4, 5

SETVARIABLE

Syntax	`SetVariable(variableName, value)`
Description	Sets the value of the Flash variable specified by variableName to the value specified by value. The argument type for both arguments is string.
Example	`movie.SetVariable("/Form:UserName", "John Smith");`
Plug-in Version	4, 5
ActiveX Version	4, 5

SETZOOMRECT

Syntax	`SetZoomRect (left, top, right, bottom)`
Description	Zooms in on a rectangular area of the movie. The units of the coordinates are in twips (1,440 units per inch). To calculate a rectangle in Flash, set the ruler units to points and multiply the coordinates by 20 to get twips. (There are 72 points per inch.) The argument type for all arguments is integer.

Example	This example zooms in on a 200-x-200-pixel rectangle in the upper left corner of the movie:
	
	`var pointsToTwips = 20;`
	`movie.SetZoomRect(0, 0, 200 * pointsToTwips, 200 * pointsToTwips);`

Plug-in Version	2, 3, 4, 5
ActiveX Version	2, 3, 4, 5

STOPPLAY

Syntax	StopPlay()
Description	Stops playing the movie.
Example	movie.StopPlay()
Plug-in Version	2, 3, 4, 5
ActiveX Version	2, 3, 4, 5

TOTALFRAMES

Syntax	TotalFrames()
Description	Returns the total number of frames in the movie.
Example	var totalFrames = movie.TotalFrames();
Plug-in Version	2, 3, 4, 5
ActiveX Version	2, 3, 4, 5

ZOOM

Syntax	Zoom(percent)
Description	Zooms the view by a relative scale factor specified by percent. Zoom(50) doubles the size of the objects in the view. Zoom(200) reduces the size of objects in the view by one half. Zoom(0) resets the view to 100%. You cannot reduce the size of objects in the view when the current view is already 100%. The argument type is integer.
Example	movie.Zoom(50);
Plug-in Version	2, 3, 4, 5
ActiveX Version	2, 3, 4, 5

TellTarget Methods

Syntax	`TCallFrame(target, frameNumber)`
Description	In the timeline specified by target, executes the action in the frame specified by frameNumber.
Example	This example runs the actions in the fifth frame of the main timeline: `movie.TCallFrame("/", 4);`
Plug-in Version	4, 5
ActiveX Version	4, 5

Syntax	`TCallLabel(target, label)`
Description	In the timeline indicated by target, executes the action in the frame specified by the label frame label. The argument type for both arguments is string.
Example	This example runs the actions in the frame labeled HandleScriptNotify in the main timeline: `movie.TCallLabel("/", "HandleScriptNotify");`
Plug-in Version	4, 5
ActiveX Version	4, 5

Syntax	`TCurrentFrame(target)`
Description	Returns the number of the current frame for the timeline specified by target. The frame number returned is zero-based, meaning frame 1 of the Flash movie would be 0, frame 2 would be 1, and so on. The argument type is string.
Example	`var currentFrame = movie.TCurrentFrame("/MovieClip");`
Plug-in Version	3, 4, 5
ActiveX Version	3, 4, 5

Syntax	TCurrentLabel(target)
Description	Returns the label of the current frame of the timeline specified by target. If there is no current frame label, an empty string is returned. The argument type is string.
Example	var currentLabel = movie.TCurrentLabel("/MovieClip");
Plug-in Version	3, 4, 5
ActiveX Version	3, 4, 5

TGETPROPERTY

Syntax	TGetProperty(target, property)
Description	For the timeline indicated by target, returns a string indicating the value of the property specified by property. For property, enter the integer corresponding to the desired property.
Example	var nameIndex = 13; var name = movie.TGetProperty("/", nameIndex);
Plug-in Version	4, 5
ActiveX Version	4, 5

TGETPROPERTYASNUMBER

Syntax	TGetPropertyAsNumber (target, property)
Description	For the timeline indicated by target, returns a number indicating the value of the property specified by property. For property, enter the integer corresponding to the desired property.
Example	var framesLoadedIndex = 12; var framesLoaded = movie.TGetProperty("/", framesLoadedIndex);
Plug-in Version	–
ActiveX Version	–

TGOTOFRAME

Syntax	TGotoFrame(target, frameNumber)
Description	For the timeline indicated by target, goes to the frame number specified by frameNumber. The argument type for target is string. The argument type for frameNumber is integer.
Example	movie.TGotoFrame("/MovieClip", 2);
Plug-in Version	3, 4, 5
ActiveX Version	3, 4, 5

TGOTOLABEL

Syntax	TGotoLabel(target, label)
Description	For the timeline indicated by target, goes to the frame label specified by label. The argument type for both arguments is string.
Example	movie.TGotoLabel("/MovieClip", "MyLabel");
Plug-in Version	3, 4, 5
ActiveX Version	3, 4, 5

TPLAY

Syntax	TPlay(target)
Description	Plays the timeline specified by target. The argument type is string.
Example	movie.TPlay("/MovieClip");
Plug-in Version	3, 4, 5
ActiveX Version	3, 4, 5

TSETPROPERTY

Syntax	TSetProperty(target, property, value)
Description	For the timeline indicated by target, sets the value of the property specified by property to the value specified by value, which can be a string or a number. For property, enter the integer corresponding to the desired property.

Example	var visibilityIndex = 7;var nameIndex = 13;
	movie.TSetProperty("/MovieClip", visibilityIndex, 1);
	movie.TSetProperty("/MovieClip", nameIndex, "NewName");

Plug-in Version	4, 5
ActiveX Version	4, 5

TSTOPPLAY

Syntax	TStopPlay(target)
Description	Stops the timeline specified by target. The argument type is string.
Example	movie.TStopPlay("/MovieClipToStop");
Plug-in Version	3, 4, 5
ActiveX Version	3, 4, 5

Standard Events

Syntax	FSCommand(command, args)
Description	Generated when an FSCommand action is performed in the movie with an URL and the URL starts with FSCommand. Use this to create a response to a frame or button action in the Flash movie. The argument type is string.
Plug-in Version	2, 3, 4, 5
ActiveX Version	2, 3, 4, 5

ONPROGRESS

Syntax	OnProgress(percent)
Description	Generated as the Flash movie is downloading. The argument type is integer.
Plug-in Version	2, 3, 4, 5
ActiveX Version	2, 3, 4, 5

ONREADYSTATECHANGE

Syntax	OnReadyStateChange(state)
Description	Generated when the ready state of the control changes. The possible states are: 0=Loading, 1=Uninitialized, 2=Loaded, 3=Interactive, 4=Complete. The argument type is integer.
Plug-in Version	2, 3, 4, 5
ActiveX Version	2, 3, 4, 5

Appendix C: Regular Expressions

CHARACTER	MEANING
\	Indicates next character should not be interpreted literally if it normally is, and should be interpreted literally if it normally isn't.
^	Matches beginning of input or line.
$	Matches end of input or line.
*	Matches 0 or more instances of preceding character.
+	Matches 1 or more instances of preceding character.
?	Matches 0 or 1 instances of preceding character.
.	Matches any single character other than the new line character.
(x)	Matches x and remembers the match.
x|y	Matches either x or y.
{n}	Matches exactly n instances of preceding character (where n is an integer).
{n,}	Matches at least n instances of preceding character (where n is an integer).
{n,m}	Matches at least n and at most m instances of preceding character (where n and m are integers).
[xyz]	Matches any one of enclosed characters (specify range using hyphen, such as [0-9].
[^xyz]	Matches any character not enclosed (specify range using hyphen, such as [^0-9].
[\b]	Matches a backspace.
\b	Matches a word boundary, such as a space.
\B	Matches a non-word boundary.
\cX	Matches a control character, X.
\d	Matches a digit character (same as [0-9]).
\D	Matches a non-digit character (same as [^0-9]).
\f	Matches a form feed.
\n	Matches a line feed.
\r	Matches a carriage return.
\s	Matches a single white space character, including space, tab, form feed, and line feed (same as [\f\n\r\t\v]).
\S	Matches a single non-white-space character (same as [^\f\n\r\t\v]).
\t	Matches a tab.

\v	Matches a vertical tab.
\w	Matches any alphanumeric character, including the underscore (same as [A-Za-z0-9_]).
\W	Matches any non-word character (same as [^A-Za-z0-9_]).
\n	Refers to the last substring matching the nth parenthetical (where n is a positive integer).
\ooctal	Matches an octal escape value (for embedding ASCII codes).
\xhex	Matches a hexadecimal escape value (for embedding ASCII codes).

Index

audio *(continued)*
adding to animations, 88–89
adjusting volume, 152–153
amplitude, 147–148
asynchronous, 154–155
attached, 158, 168–169
attaching sounds, 150–151, 171–173
audio control component, 204–208
bit resolution, 148–149
compression, 178
controlling multiple sounds, 156–161
controlling single sound, 150–155
described, 147
digital audio concepts, 148–149
event, 161
frequency, 147–148
global volume control, 177–178
master controls for, 160
maximum number of, 159–160
mixers, 157–160
MP3 compression, 149, 178, 179
number of sounds, 179
panning, 153
pitch, 147
preloading, 168–169
quality of, 178
recorded, 148
recording sound coordinates, 166–167
sample rate, 148–149
starting playback, 151–152
stopping playback, 152, 160, 179
streaming, 370–371
synchronization, 161
third-party software for, 179
tips for, 178–179
turning off, 205–206, 207
visual sound mixer, 170–178

volume. *See* volume
volume/pan sliders, 152–154
audio clips, 207
audio tracks, 204–205
autoclose variable, 381
axes. *See also specific access*
2D Cartesian coordinate system, 20
3D coordinate system, 20, 21
collisions along, 139–140
rotation around, 42–52, 58–59

B

Back button, 287, 364
Bias Peak software, 179
bit rates, 149, 178
bit resolution, 148–149
bitmaps, 273–277
Booch, Grady, 292
bounding boxes, 126
bounds, object, 127
button markers, 208
buttons
actions assigned to, 58
controlling rotations with, 58–60
navigation, 198–200
rollover, 199, 208–211

C

calculateTotal() method, 348
Cartesian coordinate system, 20, 102
CDATA (Character Data), 301–303
CFM-Resources Web site, 260
CFML (ColdFusion Markup Language), 218
CGI scripts, 344
Character Data (CDATA), 301–303
chat rooms, 255–260
checkstate() function, 374
childNodes property, 326, 331
chromeless variable, 381
ci_getpos() function, 374

circle collision detection, 133–134
circles, 42, 129–130
circumfrence, 42
client-server programming, 294
clip events, 5, 6, 7, 58–60
clips
acceleration of, 114–115
actions assigned to, 58–60
adding gravity to, 117–118
alpha value, 27–28
attaching Sound objects to, 171–173
attaching sounds to, 150–151, 171–173
attaching symbols to, 171–173
container movie clips, 185–187
containing ActionScript, 263
deceleration of, 121
duplicating, 244
empty, 185–187
looping, 241
moving with arrow keys, 33–37
pop-up windows and, 355
product lists and, 354–355
removing unwanted, 56
setting depth of, 29
sizing, 26
velocity of, 113–115
widgets. *See* widgets
z-ordering, 29–30
cloneNode() method, 340–341
ColdFusion
described, 218–219
message board project, 222–237
reserved words, 383
resources, 260
server-side scripting, 218–219
XML and, 343–344
ColdFusion Markup Language (CFML), 218
ColdFusion scripts, 224–237
ColdFusion Studio, 219

points *(continued)*
    locating in 3D space, 21
    ordered triplets, 21, 22–25, 37
    overlapping, 126
    positioning on stage, 25–26
    random placement of, 28–31
    rendered, 28, 68–69
    rotating field of, 55–62
    rotating in space, 42–52, 68
    size of, 26
    translating, 30–38, 63, 66
    viewer position and, 37–38, 69
    z-sorted random points, 30
pop-up windows, 355, 378–381
popup() function, 363
POST method, 222
preloading, 194–198
previousSibling property, 331
primary key, 223
programmatic event syncs, 161
programs
    3D, 80–82
    3ds max, 80, 81, 85
    audio software, 179
    Bias Peak, 179
    enterprise applications, 292–293, 294
    HomeSite, 295
    LightWave 3D, 80
    Sonic Forge, 179
    SoundEdit 16, 179
    Swift 3D, 80, 81, 84–86, 93
    Swift-MP3, 179
    third-party, 80–82, 179
    Vecta3D, 80, 82
    Vegas Audio LE Multitrack Editor, 179
    XML and, 292–293
projection, 105–107, 110
projects
    3D menu system, 71–79
    3D world, 62–70
    chat room, 255–260
    component-based Flash site, 189–215
    components in, 187–189
    counter, 251–254
    interactive spider, 3–8
    message board, 222–251

photo albums, 264–277
rotating field of points, 55–62
shopping cart. *See* shopping cart project
spaceship animation, 82–92
Stargate Interface, 93–99
tool palettes, 277–286
visual sound mixer, 170–178
walking insect, 9–17
XML. *See* XML projects
properties
    childNodes, 326, 331
    currentNode, 331
    firstChild, 326–327
    firstNameNode, 326–329
    lastNameNode, 326–329
    loaded, 342
    parentNode, 331–332
    previousSibling, 331
    _rotation, 103
    status, 334
    _visible, 53
    _x, 162
    XML.attributes, 338–339
    _xscale, 166, 171
    _y, 162
    _yscale, 166, 171, 277
push() method, 167
Pythagorean theorem, 104–105

Q

query strings, 365–370
quoting attributes, 300

R

radians, 103, 175
RAM, 178
random actions, 16
RandomMove() method, 281, 282
reaction() function, 139
RealPlayer plug-in, 370–372
Record button, 166
rectangle collision detection, 129–133
regExp.js file, 377
regular expressions, 376–377, 397–398

relative paths, 184
removeNode() method, 339
rendered 3D, 22–29, 80–99
rendering
    animation, 83
    frames, 83
    hidden objects and, 53
    points, 28, 68–69
rendering engine, 37–38
replaceCharacters() function, 377
reply scene, 250–251
reserved words, 222, 383–388
resolving, 109, 110
Rew, Richard S., 260
rewind() method, 391
right triangles, 104–105
rollovers
    buttons, 199, 208–211
    hyperlinks, 265
    icons, 284–285
root elements, 303
root movies, 185, 193
rotation, 39–52
    3D world, 66
    around x-axis, 49–52
    around y-axis, 42, 49–52
    around z-axis, 42, 43, 45–49, 52
    basic concepts, 39–42
    controlling with buttons, 58–60
    controlling with keys, 60–62, 66
    drag actions and, 176–177
    Flash coordinate system, 102
    points, 42–52
    rotating field of points, 55–62
    sound mixing and, 170
    speed of, 170
    trigonometry for, 39–42, 44–45
    variables, 56
rotation angles, 43, 54, 56, 58, 67
_rotation property, 103
rotational values, 176–177
RPM files, 371

S

_xscale property, 166, 171
XYPNO Interactive, 216

Y

y-axis. *See also* axes
    3D coordinate system, 21
    3D world movement, 63, 66
    described, 102
    projection and, 106, 107
    rotation around, 42, 49–52
y-component vector, 109–111
y-coordinates, 162, 166, 167
y-position
    described, 20
    perspective and, 22–29
    translating points, 30–38
_y property, 162
_yscale property, 166, 171, 277

Z

z-axis. *See also* axes
    3D coordinate system, 21, 22
    3D world movement, 63, 66
    rotation around, 42, 43, 45–49, 52
z-ordering, 29–30
z-position
    perspective and, 22–29
    setting clip depth based on, 29
    translating points, 30–38
z-sorted random points, 30
Zap Designs, 260
zoom() method, 391